Coming to stay

A COLUMBIA RIVER JOURNEY

For Jane and Helene Mezer
You, too, have a
journey I would love to
read about!
    Mary Dodds Schlick

Mary Dodds Schlick

Coming to stay

A COLUMBIA RIVER JOURNEY

Oregon Historical Society
in association with
University of Washington Press

Oregon Historical Society Press
1200 SW Park Avenue, Portland, Oregon 97205, USA
www.ohs.org

in association with
University of Washington Press
P.O. Box 50096, Seattle, Washington 98145, USA
www.washington.edu/uwpress

The paper used in this publication is acid-free. It meets the minimum requirements of American National Standard for Information Sciences — Permanence of Paper for Printed Library Materials, ANSI Z39.48—1984. ∞

Design: Corinna Campbell-Sack

Unless otherwise noted, all photographs are courtesy of the author. All of those photographs were taken by the author, except those by Bill Pyle, p. 5; by W.T. Schlick, pp. 9, 14, 23, 31, 33, 40, 46, 62, 71, 86, 109, 139, and 143; by Richard Mittauer, p. 49; by Harold Weaver, p. 78; by James Rayner, p. 104; by J.W. Thompson, p. 127; by Joseph Schlick, pp. 155 and 172; by Katherine Schlick Noe, pp. 147 and 157; and by Allan Galbraith, p. 181.

Library of Congress Cataloging-in-Publication Data

Schlick, Mary Dodds.
  Coming to stay : a Columbia River journey / by Mary Dodds Schlick.
    p. cm.
  "In association with University of Washington Press, Seattle."
  Includes bibliographical references.
  ISBN-13: 978-0-295-98670-8 (alk. paper)
  ISBN-10: 0-295-98670-0 (alk. paper)
1. Schlick, Mary Dodds. 2. Indian agents' spouses—Columbia River Valley—Biography. 3. Indians of North America—Columbia River Valley—Social conditions. 4. Indian reservations--Columbia River Valley. I. Title.
  E78.C64S353 2006
  305.897'097954—dc22
                        2006026095

To
Josephine Hungerford Dodds
who saved the letters

Contents

Preface

Full-turn twining: An ancient technique in which the
*weaver works images from her life into her baskets.**

At a writing workshop in 1993, a young tribal policeman from the Colville Indian Reservation read a piece about tribal leader Lucy Covington. As we left the room, I told Bill Joseph how good it was to hear his story.

"The Covingtons were one reason my husband stayed in the Indian Service," I said, and told him of the time Lucy and Johnny Covington rescued my husband Bud from a stranded pickup on a cold night on the reservation. Returning home after a long day scaling logs fifty miles away in the San Poil Valley, Bud had slipped off the icy Cache Creek Road in a snowstorm.

Wintertime. It was always dark when we heard his rig turn into the alley behind our house at the agency south of Nespelem. His stomp on the back porch was the signal for our three toddlers to race to the door. No matter how tired he was, he listened to their chatter as he ate his supper, bathed them, read a book, and put them to bed. "How else will I know them?" he asked.

But that night when the Covingtons dropped him off, the children were long asleep. Distraught by visions of what could have happened, I had given them baths, read stories, and tucked them into bed. In my mind I had packed up the four of us and fled the hundred miles to Spokane to catch a plane for Iowa and home.

"Home" was not a word Bud would use for that quiet midwestern place where we had grown up. He insisted that home is where we *are.* In those days, most American men thought the jobs they found would be like their marriages, for life. As a bride of the 1950s, I expected and welcomed the same future. As far as Bud was concerned, we had come to this place to stay. Or, if not here, at least at another Indian reservation in the Northwest where a good forester was needed to help manage a valuable timber resource. As a result, our neighbors at the Colville Agency and our other new friends on the reservation were people we expected to know forever.

We moved around after those early years on the Colville Reservation but always among related people of the Columbia Plateau—to Warm Springs in Oregon and Toppenish on the Yakama Reservation. During alternating stays in Washington,

---

*Paraphrased from Schlick, *Columbia River Basketry,* p. 219.

D.C., reservation friends came to town and to dinner. Today, at my door up here in the woods above the Hood River Valley or at celebrations and other visits, I continue to see people Bud and I knew before our children were born. More often now, I see the children and grandchildren of those friends. For us, our expectation proved to be true. We stayed.

I told Bill Joseph that I wanted to write about this life—stories of gifts, of mysteries and joy, of anguish and heart's ease. I had come as a bride to the Colville Reservation; our children were born there. They went to grade school at Warm Springs and swam in Shitike Creek, bicycled over the red hills to Kah-Nee-Ta. They grew toward adulthood on the Yakama Reservation. One is buried there. Although there were intermittent stays in Washington, D.C., we always returned to this land we call home. Why did it work for us? How did we change? These were the questions I hoped to answer.

"I have lived my entire adult life in touch with Native people of the Columbia Plateau," I told Bill. "Can I write about this?" I asked. "Are these stories mine to tell?"

The young man thought a minute. "Are there children here who call you 'Auntie?'"

I pictured Crissy and Ocha, Renea, Tess, and others. "Yes," I said.

"Then write about that."

And so I begin.

Mary Dodds Schlick
Mount Hood, Oregon

Acknowledgments

My warmest thanks go to the Colville, Warm Springs, and Yakama people who opened their homes and hearts to us, and to their relatives across the Plateau whom we have come to know. Special acknowledgement goes to Bill Joseph for giving me permission to begin this story, to the Confederated Tribes of the Umatilla Reservation's Convocation 2000 for moving me forward, and to Gloria Krantz for quoting Goethe: "Whatever you can do, or dream you can, begin it."

I thank readers Katherine Schlick Noe for wise suggestions at every step, Joseph Dodds Schlick for steady support and encouragement, and Jonathan Cobb for the generous gift of his sharp editor's eye. For guidance and inspiration, I thank Mary Clearman Blew, Robin Cody, Debra Magpie Earling, Teresa Jordan, Craig Lesley, Kathleen Dean Moore, Joanne Mulcahy, Sandra Osawa, Robert Michael Pyle, Kim Stafford, and Luis Alberto Urrea. I am deeply grateful to Naomi Pascal for believing in my vision, to Jarold Ramsey for validating my efforts, and to Marianne Keddington-Lang, Eliza Jones, Corinna Campbell-Sack, and Dean Shapiro for bringing it to life.

Contributing in various ways were Diane Allen, Eugenia and Jack Condon, Barbara Dills, John Parry Dodds, Donald Ellegood, Robert Fletcher, Allan Galbraith, Ann George, Nettie Jackson, Connie Johnson, Bonnie Kahn, Cheryl Mack, John Marker, Rick McClure, Mary Ann Meanus, Thomas Morning Owl, Charlie Moses, Olney Patt Jr., Josiah Pinkham, Lillian Pitt, Donna Mae Rickard, Bruce Rigsby, Amelia Sohappy, Viola Sohappy, Marilyn Trueblood, David Wright, the Mount Hood Basketmakers, and the authors listed in the bibliography. To each of them and to all others who helped me relive this journey, my sincere gratitude.

Prologue—The Garden

I hold to my heart when the geese are flying
A waving wedge on the high, bright blue—
— Grace Noll Crowell*

It's late May. As we drive through the gate and make our way slowly around the gravel road that circles Satus Point, the Jim family pauses over their hoes to nod hello. Across the way, Tom Eli is raking the dried remnants of last year's growth. Wherever we turn we see friends.

The sun is high over Cherry Hill across the valley to the east. That gravel face where a bulldozer once found dinosaur bones is a dusty contrast to the mass of green along the Yakima River below. Between our high spot and that hill, the flat patchwork of irrigated fields stretches alive with new growth—asparagus, mint, corn, early shoots of squash to be canned for pumpkin pie. Just below us is a soft disorder—horses along a meandering creek, a brush-edged pasture, a small house with a clutch of ragged outbuildings. Each time we come, we bless those who, long ago, let us join them in this place and share this view.

Getting out our rake and hoe, we start to work. We leave the orange globe mallow and balsamroot but chop out the barbed greenery that turns into tumbleweed. The lizard is here hugging the warm stone, and the centipede. None of us stirs up the ants this time, but a snake unwinds from the shade of last year's flowers. Rattlesnake? The grandchildren look closer, maybe a Western racer. Lazy, it slips back into cool shelter. We work in another spot and let it sleep.

This view, these plants, this gravely soil, these creatures so familiar were new to us when we first came to this place many years ago. It was winter, cold on Satus Point, barren. But even that day it was not lonely; a soaring Wáashat song sustained us in the ancient ritual of burial. The song brought comfort as we circled the open grave, each lifting a handful of earth from the proffered shovel, each handful tossed in three offerings onto the box below to join the sacred soil of Smohalla's resting place.

---

*From "Wild Geese," published in c. 1931 by Carl Fischer.

As we few stood together on this rocky ridge that day, the Wáashat song faded into the wind and a dissonant chorus arose over our heads. A great wedge of wild geese flew noisily toward the Yakima River as if voicing a welcome to our young son's spirit from those beloved who already rested here.

Coming to stay

A COLUMBIA RIVER JOURNEY

Corinna Campbell-Sack

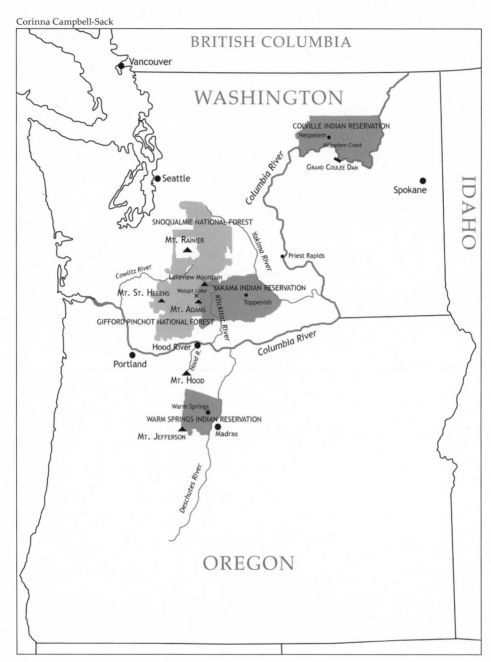

BRITISH COLUMBIA

Vancouver

WASHINGTON

COLVILLE INDIAN RESERVATION
Nespelem
Nespelem Creek

Columbia River

GRAND COULEE DAM

Seattle

Spokane

IDAHO

SNOQUALMIE NATIONAL FOREST
MT. RAINIER

Yakima River

Priest Rapids

Cowlitz River
Lakeview Mountain
MT. ST. HELENS
Walupt Lake
✕
MT. ADAMS
GIFFORD PINCHOT NATIONAL FOREST

YAKAMA INDIAN RESERVATION

Toppenish

Klickitat River

Columbia River

Hood River

Portland

Hood R.

MT. HOOD

Warm Springs

WARM SPRINGS INDIAN RESERVATION

MT. JEFFERSON

Madras

Deschutes River

OREGON

The Columbia River Journey

1. FINDING WILD GOOSE BILL

*Twining: An ancient weaving method in which two strands are twisted together around each warp to build a strong fabric.**

September 1972

I can't do this, I thought, as I pulled on my moccasins in the parking lot beside Wapato Longhouse. I wrapped the hightops tight around my ankles, tied them with their long deer hide strings, and, picking up my shawl, stepped from the car. I could hear the drums.

Bud touched my elbow. "Okay," he murmured. "We'll be okay." I knew he was trying to convince himself.

"I know." Eyes on the ground, trying to miss the stones that dug into the thin soles of our moccasins, we made our way toward the longhouse.

This was the funeral for Stanley Smartlowit, a well-known Yakama tribal leader. We needed to be here, out of both friendship and respect, even though our son's memorial service had been just two weeks before.

I followed Bud through the longhouse door, and, moving away from the entrance as was the custom, we stood with others who had just arrived to wait for the song to end. So many people, I thought. I longed to be at home. When the drumming stopped, I knew, we all would walk around the longhouse and receive each person's gentle handshake before we sat down. Could I do that? Could I face all these dear friends without weeping?

The song ended. The leader began to ring his small handbell softly in a steady cadence. It was time to be greeted. I followed my husband, as I knew to do, and we moved down the line, touching each offered hand. I found myself carried along, hand by hand. When I came to Josephine George, Levi's wife, she grasped my hand in both of hers and, holding my glance, said softly, "I'm so sorry." Instead of tears, a warmth spread through me. I realized that she was not the only one who knew how hard it had been for us to come here today.

---

*Paraphrased from Schlick, *Columbia River Basketry*, p. 219.

When we finished the formal round of welcome, Bud joined the men sitting on benches on the north side of the longhouse. As the Wáashat service resumed, someone made room for me on a bench along the south wall with the women. I put on my shawl, leaving one arm free to shake the hands of those who came in after us or, later, to raise my hand in prayer. As the service progressed, I absorbed the comforting sound of the big wafer-shaped drums held high as the seven men sang. The soaring music, the songs that had seemed strange to me when we came here three years ago were now so familiar that I hummed them in my head.

As more people arrived and each song ended, the ceremony was repeated and we became part of the greeters. Between songs, those who were moved to speak came to the front to talk about Stanley Smartlowit, the man we were honoring. There were stories and praise and tears. It was a long service—a final time to speak his name, to remember his works, and to cry for the loss.

I looked across at Bud among the Yakama men he had come to know so well; there were familiar faces from Colville and Warm Springs, too.* We'll be all right, I thought. This day, spent in intense companionship with the dead and those who mourned the dead, was strangely strengthening. How we came to this place so far in distance and custom from our own beginnings is a long story. It had begun on the day of the summer solstice twenty-three years before. Those years had seemed like a lifetime then, but as I write this now they are clearer than yesterday.

Crossing the Columbia

We walked into Ma's Cafe in Wilbur, Washington, a couple of Iowans with no idea that we were stepping into the future. It was just another restaurant in a small prairie town along U.S. Highway 2, a place to stop for lunch.

We had been married a week and thought the plains had ended in eastern Montana, but after Spokane the landscape had turned as flat and dull as any we had driven through. The mountains ahead, where we were to spend the summer, were only pale shadows on the horizon. The wheat fields, at least, were green, and the town looked shady with giant box elder trees just coming into full leaf.

Grain elevators lined the railroad track along the south side of the dusty street, wide enough for cars to park in the middle. There was a block or so of stores, and on a corner we spotted the restaurant's sign. "That looks okay," Bud said and pulled the old blue Ford to the curb.

---

*The Yakama Nation has restored the spelling of the tribe to that used on the Treaty of 1855.

By now I knew enough to get myself out of the car, but he held the restaurant door for me. Not the chair, though. We had known each other since the seventh grade, and such chivalry would be a bit much even for a honeymoon.

Farmers, foreheads pale above sun-stained faces, sat bareheaded, their hats hung by the door. I could see plates of pork with mashed potatoes on bread in gravy. It looked terrible to me, but the place smelled good, like my mother's kitchen. Bud point-ed at the menu.

"I'll have that," he told the waitress, "Hot Roast Pork Sandwich, 75 cents. Drink included." I ordered a tuna fish sandwich and asked if I could keep the menu for a bit. Drawn by the foggy photo of an old-timer on the back, I began to read the town's history.

"Listen to this," I said. "'A story of the Old West is the story of Samuel Wilbur Condit, better known as Wild Goose Bill.'"

Bud leaned over to look at the menu. "Condit?" It was his grandmother's name,

Mary D. and William T. Schlick begin their life together at the First Congregational Church in Ames, Iowa, on June 13, 1949.

not very common. The town was named for him. Wilbur. Funny name for a town, I thought. Too bad they didn't use the Condit.

Samuel Wilbur Condit had come from New Jersey in about 1859, according to the menu. Thought to be the first white settler in the Columbia River's entire Big Bend Country, he ran a pack train of cayuses between Walla Walla and the "un-settled regions to the north."

"What's a cayuse?" I asked Bud. He'd spent more time in the West than I had. "I guess it's some kind of a range horse," he replied. "Maybe a wild horse."

The waitress brought our plates. Bud picked up his fork and stirred the gravy into the potatoes. I picked up the sandwich and read on: "It says his log cabin still stands at the western edge of town." We looked at the bearded man in the picture. Bud's grandmother's family had come from New Jersey. Could this be a relative?

"I hope not," I told him and read the last line: "'Eyewitness accounts tell of a pistol duel that ended in death for Wild Goose Bill'"—I paused a bit, not sure I wanted to go on—"'as well as the jealous husband.'"

"Wow," Bud said. "Now *there's* a way to go!"

When Bud paid the bill, I asked if we could take the menu, explaining our interest. "Oh, that old guy?" the waitress said. "Must have been a character! They still celebrate Wild Goose Days here every year. You'll have to come back."

On the road again, we headed toward those hazy western peaks in the distance. Brown grass and lava outcroppings soon filled the landscape, and to the north the high steep walls of basalt rose on either side of a dry riverbed. The Grand Coulee, the map said. I had no interest in heading off that way to see the famous dam. Twice in the 1930s, my civil engineer father had dragged our family into that dusty sagebrush land to see the Grand Coulee Dam under construction.

Bud and I had covered some barren country on the long drive from Iowa, but this treeless stretch from Wilbur to Ellensburg was the most forlorn. Wheat fields soon gave way to miles of rough lava scabland and sparse brush. In later years, we learned that repeated floods from melting glaciers had scoured off the once-lush vegetation of this region. But on this warm day we had no interest in what had created such a drab moonscape. The land was something to get through on our way to the snow-covered Cascade Mountains on whose far slope we would spend our first summer together.

By mid afternoon we descended through steep basalt cliffs toward the bridge across the Columbia River at Vantage. Bud had looked forward to this crossing since the summer he had spent on a Montana fire lookout—a prairie-dweller's dream. He was seventeen then and waiting to enlist in the air corps during World War II. He had come west for a summer job grubbing out wild gooseberry, the alternate host for the devastating western white pine blister rust. Because of the wartime shortage of older summer employees, he was sent instead to man the lookout atop Cougar Peak in the Bitterroot Mountains near Thompson Falls, Montana. From that spot he had watched the shiny ribbon of the Clark's Fork of the Columbia flow toward the west and yearned to follow it to the Great River and on to the sea. Today, he would see the Columbia at last.

As we crossed the bridge at the bottom of the grade, we noticed a sign for Ginkgo Petrified Forest and turned off the highway to find some cool shade. The road led away from the trees beside the bridge and up around a stony knob to a barren slope that overlooked the river. "What?" I stared at the dry landscape. "No trees?"

"Right," he said, figuring out what had happened. "It's a *petrified* forest! The ginkgos were here long before the glaciers."

We laughed. In the twelve years of our on-again/off-again courtship, neither of us had known the other had a sense of humor. The trip had been full of such jokes, beginning with the unlikely sight of a giraffe's head peaking out above the trees from the city zoo as we entered Minot, North Dakota.

After another look at the Columbia, we left the park and headed west again. It was a hot anxious climb up the long hill toward Ellensburg, and we stopped frequently along the dusty highway to let the car cool down. We hardly spoke. But when we turned south at last to follow the Yakima River through its cool canyon, Bud began to sing "Oh, the lemonade springs where the bluebird sings." I was as surprised to hear the song as I had been at his jokes. He didn't even sing in church.

When we reached the outskirts of Yakima, we turned west on Highway 12, the road that would take us over the mountains in the morning, and spotted the Columbia Motor Court. We liked the name, the 1930s look, and the cool promise of its postage-stamp swimming pool. Settled at last in one of the red-roofed cabins, we looked out the screened door to see mountains silhouetted against a bright sunset. We were almost there.

We could not know that warm night in June that twenty years later almost to the day we would move into this motel again—not for overnight but for three months while building a house in nearby Toppenish. Except for air conditioning, the place would not change much in those years, but we, of course, did.

The next morning, we left the green and orderly orchards and entered the scrub oak and grasslands of the Cascade foothills. The car purred along in the morning's coolness as we drove over Chinook Pass to the Packwood Ranger District, headquarters for Bud's summer job. Soon, we were told, we could travel across the mountains on a shorter route through the new Tieton tunnel at White Pass.

The road was a thrill for a pair of flatlanders. Great plow-carved walls of snow on both sides blocked our view as we crossed the summit and came face-to-face with Mt. Rainier, the highest of the Cascade giants. We found a wide place in the road and stopped the car. Bud picked up a handful of snow and tossed it at me. This was where he wanted to be at last, in the mountains in the Far West.

I had seen Mt. Rainier for the first time when I was four, from Paradise Lodge on the west side. Too small to make the trek up and into the snow at Pinnacle Peak with the rest of my family, I had to wait at the lodge with Toodles, my mother's college roommate. My memory of that day is of a gift in a bright Wonder Bread wrapper. My twelve-year-old brother had used the paper that wrapped his sandwich to bring me a snowball—in August. To a child of the Midwest, it was a miracle.

Turning our backs on the mountain, Bud and I headed south. The highway dropped a winding ten miles through thick stands of timber and flattened out to become Packwood's main street. We found the ranger station as we entered town and met the other summer employees, most of them college forestry students. The ranger was Reuben Jacobsen, an Iowa State forestry graduate—possibly the reason Bud got the job. He told us we would be stationed at Walupt Lake Guard Station on the eastern edge of the district next to the Yakama Indian Reservation. Trips to town fifty-five miles away would be rare, he said, although station personnel would bring things up when they came to check on us.

A remote place sounded fine to me. I had returned to Ames from New York City only three months before. After a busy spring teaching Iowa State freshmen and preparing for our wedding, I was eager to start this new life. It would be a change, I knew, from an eleventh-floor view of Manhattan at night and a magazine job on Park Avenue by day, and I welcomed it.

But settling in had to wait. We were to spend the rest of the week at guard school at Cispus Camp, a former Civilian Conservation Corps camp thirty-seven miles into the forest east of Randle along the Cispus River. Crews from the Randle and St. Helens districts would be with us there to learn to detect and locate fires, read maps, and use the portable field radio. Except for one unmarried woman who would be working at a lookout, the rest of the women were employees' wives and not on the payroll. Still, we were encouraged to take the training and were expected to fill in as needed.

Before going to camp that afternoon, we had to come up with a list of supplies for the next several weeks. In a weak moment I had agreed to cook for the crew who was to work with Bud repairing the phone line near our guard station. I wouldn't be paid, but any unused canned goods and other food could stay with us when the week was over. Free food sounded like a good deal to me, a child of the Great Depression, but I had no idea what the Forest Service might send along. After much discussion, Bud and I pulled an order together, neither of us knowing much about the other's everyday food likes. Later, when I brought out the Lifesavers I had purchased for Bud and he did the same, we learned that peppermint was not one of them.

At Cispus Camp at last, we stowed our gear in separate barracks, Bud's with the men and mine with the women and one small boy. After supper, the entire camp, about forty of us, gathered around the campfire for general information about the Forest Service. Then Bud and I went for a drive. The white pines along that rich bottomland of the Cispus River were as tall as any I had seen. Looking for a private place to stop, we found cars parked all along the river road. We weren't the only newlyweds in camp.

The day finally came when we could head for the guard station. The maintenance boss, Elmer Hornquist, was an agile, no-nonsense man of indeterminate age who could hold

up his end of a conversation. Elmer introduced the phone crew,
Jim Martin, quiet and clean-
shaven, and dark-haired Ira
Blankenship Jr. probably still
in his teens. "Call him Juney,"
Elmer said of the younger man,
whose speech carried the faint
drawl of the Kentucky mountains. "This place is full of his
folk. I guess it makes 'em think
of where they come from."

None of the three was
as tall as Bud's six feet, but all
looked as if they could do a
day's work. They climbed into

*Lakeview Mountain on the Yakama Reservation boundary, reflected
in Walupt Lake, June 1949. According to tribal elders, Walupt Lake
was within the aboriginal territory of the Yakama peoples.*

the big stake truck that carried the crew's supplies, the grocery order, and our heavier
duffel, and we set off down the road behind them. There was no direct road to Walupt
Lake. To get to our cabin, we followed the truck south through Randle and then inland
on a gravel road across the Randle district to the guard station. We wondered if our
old blue Ford would survive the summer.

The view opened up as we left the Cowlitz Valley and followed the Cispus River.
Searching each new vista, we were disappointed not to find what we had come west
to be near—the snowy domes of Mt. Rainier and Mt. Adams. Close as it was, as the
summer went on we saw Rainier only when we drove out to Randle and Packwood,
but Adams came into view often and up close. Through the years of our marriage, the
mountain became a reassuring companion.

It was a long, jostling ride, and I was eager to find the turnoff to Walupt Lake. We
crossed a small creek and started up out of the open bottomland on an even rougher
road into the trees. The truck ahead stopped and backed up a bit to make a sharp turn
up a winding road. We saw the small sign for the guard station and followed the truck
toward the top of a rocky knob. Searching for the cabin, Bud saw the corner of a small
building. "There's the outhouse!" he cried. But as the road circled around to the front,
we saw a porch and realized that it was the guard station.

We stepped out of the car, boots sinking into the deep dust that lay wherever
there was no vegetation. Patches of snow lay on the ridge that rose behind the knob.
The garage, nearby and larger than the cabin, would be the bunkhouse for the phone
crew. Elmer climbed up on the small porch, took out the cabin key, and opened the

door. He stood aside to let us in, handing the keys to Bud.

Fourteen feet by twenty, freshly painted a soft green, the place appeared larger on the inside. On the table, two dismantled fire packs, left in the cabin for emergency, lay surrounded by shards of window glass. Someone had broken in. When Elmer discovered that the only contents missing were the standard emergency K rations, I felt better—the intruders had only needed food. The rest of the small cabin was clean and neat, and the broken window had cleared the air of the stuffiness of a place closed up over a long winter.

By the time the men drove down to the spring a half-mile away to fill the water cans, removed the old coffeepot from the chimney on the roof, and put up the stovepipe, I had rustled through the grocery boxes and pulled together a lunch. This was one thing I knew how to do. A lifetime of summers helping my mother feed a family

of six in a Minnesota border lake cabin was good preparation for a woodstove and no running water in this remote place. My father had established the summer camp that prepared Iowa State's civil engineers for primitive conditions they might face in future jobs. He couldn't have known that the experience would do the same for me.

At lunch, Elmer entertained us with stories of the mountains and the people on

Opening the Walupt Lake Guard Station for the season, Bud removes the coffeepot from the chimney.

the district, tossing in "Jeeter Moses!" when the story required an expletive. He told of Seattle writer Martha Hardy, who had written about her summers on lookout on the Packwood district. Later, when I checked out her book, *Tatoosh*, from the local library, we discovered that Elmer was a major character.

After lunch, the maintenance boss lined out the crew on their work for the week—hanging phone lines to connect us with the ranger station in Packwood. Until that was completed, we had only the radio. Bud had built a crystal set as a kid, but this would be his first real chance to use shortwave radio. After making an inventory of our needs, including the glass for the window, Elmer left for town. Jim and Juney went to make their nest in the garage.

Alone in our first home, Bud and I began to settle in. The bed was a challenge. It was a three-quarters size frame with two-by-four legs on one side, nailed to the wall on the other. Heavy ropes stretched across and lengthwise to hold the mattress, which was only as wide as a single bed. The last guard must have been alone. The more we looked at the ridiculous rigging, the funnier it seemed. This is our bridal bed, we laughed. We'll tell our children about it, if we ever have any.

The first question was how to cover the bristly ropes between the mattress and the wall. I knew this was *my* problem—it would be my side of the bed. Digging into the duffel bag, I pulled out the sleeping bag I had brought for an emergency. Tucking the bag into the empty spot between the mattress and the wall, we made up the bed, complete with bedspread. Wedding gifts all, these were among the few things we owned together.

Bud found a piece of cardboard to cover the broken window, and we spent the rest of the afternoon unpacking the crew food into a cabinet, leaving some of our own in the corner in the mercantile's wooden orange crates. Perishables went into a high, screened box just outside the door in the shade of the roof overhang. Bud dampened the burlap that hung across the front. Evaporating moisture would help keep the food cool, he explained. He had used such a cooler on lookout in Montana, and he assured me the box would work fine—if we could keep the squirrels out. We hung some clothes on hooks on the wall, leaving our good clothes in suitcases shoved under the bed. I probably wouldn't need my going-away outfit here, I thought, although I had brought it—hat, white gloves, and all.

When the boarders came in for supper, the cabin now seemed as small inside as it had looked on the outside when we arrived. We pulled the table away from the window, and Bud and Juney slipped in on the bench. Jim and I sat across, our backs to the bed. Bud climbed over Juney to get at the coffeepot on the little stove. The men ate as if they liked the food, and after supper they thanked me and retired to the shady garage.

The guard station faced directly into the Goat Rocks to the northwest. Bud and I stepped outside to study the long, jagged ridge that lay far across the Cispus drainage from our knob. Goat Ridge was snowy except where it was spotted with dark outcroppings of rough rock. I knew I would not trade this view for the lights of Manhattan.

The evening sun was hot, and we headed down to the main road to see the lake we had noticed on the map. If it had been dark, we would have walked into the water that began at the end of the road. I was glad to be wearing the calf-high boots Bud had given me as a wedding present. Ancient snags and downed logs shimmered around the lake's edge below dark firs, giving the place an abandoned look. We had been told that *walupt* meant bad or dangerous in the local Indian language. It simply seemed peaceful to me.

No whisper of wind marred the clear image of Lakeview Mountain, which loomed toward us across the water's glassy surface to the east. The mountain rose into the sky beyond the far end of the lake, shadows deepening in the failing light. Standing on the boundary of the national forest with the Yakama Reservation, the dark form held a certain mystery for us. Frogs took up a raspy chorus, and we could feel the dampness rise out of the bog at the edge of the lake. Dark shadows darted everywhere. I startled. "It's only the night hawks," Bud said, putting a warm hand on my shoulder. "They dive with their beaks open to catch insects that swarm at dusk." Something caught my eye in the darkening sky toward Lakeview. "Look!" I pointed toward the mountain. "Someone's climbing a lookout over there—with a lantern."

The sign of life was strangely unsettling. The joy of this place was that we would be alone up here. "I didn't see a lookout marked on that map," he said. As we stood watching, the light continued to rise. Up and up, it moved into the sky. We relaxed. It was only the earth rolling a star into view.

At Home on the Knob

The next morning came too early. I had pictured leisurely honeymoon days in the clear mountain air, time to read or pound out stories on my father's ancient L.C. Smith typewriter—lazy days with long naps and maybe practicing the whining concertina that Bud had hoped I would not bring along. Rising at dawn had not been in the picture, especially to pack lunches for a phone line crew and cook pancakes, bacon, and coffee on a wood-burning stove the size of a large footstool.

After washing the breakfast dishes in a battered kettle and rinsing them in the leaky dishpan that sizzled on the woodstove, I unpacked the linens I had brought. It seemed strange to care so much about making the place homelike when three months earlier all I had done to move out of my room in New York City was pack books and clothes. The strength of my nesting instinct surprised me.

The counter of the kitchen cabinet in the corner was shallow and dark. The table under the window would have to do for most food preparation, dining, washing up, deskwork, and even reading. A kerosene lamp, candles, and gas lantern—once we figured how to light it—provided light. I swept the floor and turned an orange crate on end for a washstand by the door. Cleaning supplies went inside the crate. Stringing wire for a towel rack, I pounded nails for the wash basin and dishpan and put a few more on the wall by the telephone for coats.

I had seen old telephones like this in the movies, a big wall-hung box with a mouthpiece like a black daffodil extending above a slanted shelf. The receiver hung in a cradle on the left, leaving the right hand free to crank the handle. It gave off a dull rattle when I tried it. When the line is connected, I guessed, turning the handle probably generated the electricity that made the bells ring in the district headquarters. Maybe the crew would get the line up today.

As long as I needed a fire to take the chill off the morning, I decided to learn how the oven worked by baking a cake. Our

Bud at the radio, our only contact with the outside world until the phone line was repaired.

Woman's Home Companion Home Service Center in New York, with its sparkling plastic and chrome, seemed far away, but the process of testing household appliances was the same the world over. I wished my colleagues at the magazine could see me now. The only hitch was trying to cook without a sink. Bud had set up the five-gallon can with the spigot for drinking water on one of the crates by the door, but all other water had to be tipped or dipped out of a larger can outside, carried in, used, toted out again, and dumped away from the cabin. I hadn't realized how much easier a sink makes life.

The day had not gone well for the men. Late coming home, they were cold and tired from trudging through snow to look for breaks in the phone line. The warm cabin and supper, with cake for dessert, sent all three off to bed in a better mood.

On Thursday, we all walked down to the lake together just to enjoy the evening. Friday was Jim and Juney's last day as boarders, and we had enjoyed their gentle company. As we scuffed through the deep silt of the road, something caught my eye and I stopped to pick it up. It was a man's ring set with a clear yellowish stone. Probably glass, a show-off piece, I thought. I dusted the ring off with my shirtsleeve, and we all examined it closely. "Wow," Jim said. "I'll give you ten bucks for it."

"Sold!" Bud said. It was a tempting offer, considering our finances, but I told Jim thanks and tucked the ring into my pocket. It seemed like a good omen. I'd keep it to remind us of this treasured place.

The Fourth of July weekend brought hordes of campers to Walupt Lake to fish. All along the edge of the road to the lake was a pile of wind-carried soil that the grader had pushed out of the way. With a full campground, many latecomers had pitched their tents in the brush behind this berm.

Wearing her new boots, Mary shares lunch on the trail with the Tokarczyk's dog Chief.

While Bud checked campers for the required shovel, ax, and bucket, I sat in our ancient Ford parked by the road, windows down to enjoy the smells of the forest. Suddenly, a small boy streaked out of a nearby tent, tripped on some brush, fell flat on his face, and howled. As his mother rushed out of the tent to dust him off, another child called to the boy to come and play. The mother yelled back, I could hear her clearly: "Willer ain't goin' nowhere, or I'll beat him to death!" With memories of child development classes fresh in my mind, I was astonished. Strangely, "Willer," so close to Bud's given name, William, became for us a term of endearment and, two years later, our firstborn's nickname.

Thus the summer began. Contrary to my expectations, this remote guard station in the Cascade Mountains was neither lonely nor quiet. The Korean War was on, and our cabin seemed to be directly under the flight pattern for McChord Air Base near Tacoma. We grew accustomed to the high hum of airplanes. One day, a heavy rumble like a loaded truck trying to climb our knob sent me outside, and I saw a huge airplane lumbering across the sky—the new B-36 on a test run out of Seattle's Boeing Field.

Our nearest neighbors and frequent companions were Shirley and Walt Tokarczyk at Midway Guard Station ten miles to the south. Midway was more like a real house than our cabin. I didn't envy them for that but rather for living so close to stolid snow-covered Mt. Adams. It was also on a direct route from the Yakama Reservation to the huckleberry fields and to destinations on the west side of the Cascades.

Bud was a practical man, and his wedding presents to me had been the L.L. Bean hiking boots, a portable radio, and a Kodak Tourist camera. The boots had hard use as we cleared trails and posted signs and, on days off, sought out places along the Cascade Crest Trail that looked interesting on the map. Years later, when we lived on the Yakama Reservation, we hiked in from the east side to revisit those spots on what was, by then, the Pacific Crest Trail.

My portable radio proved to be an inspired gift. Arthur Godfrey's morning show kept me company during my daily chores, and the radio brought in the world on evenings when we were not playing cards with other summer employees or entertaining visiting supervisors. Bud and I danced, boots and all, to "How High the Moon" by Les Paul and Mary Ford, who were also newlyweds that summer.

Friends from home and my cousins from Seattle showed up for overnight visits, and we bedded them down on the floor or outdoors on fir boughs. No one stayed a second night. We had been told at guard school to have coffee ready by noon in case a ranger station visitor dropped in, and, mastering the small cast-iron woodstove, I usually was prepared for company with something baked.

One day in August, we heard horses approaching. George Sellers, a sheepherder we had met earlier near Short Trail Camp was trailed by his mare's colt, three dogs, and his brother Paul on a tremendous gray horse. Hoping to go to town for a haircut, his first since April, Paul wanted to know if the shorter Johnson Creek trail was open. While Bud called Packwood, I made coffee and cut a huckleberry pie. Learning the trail was closed, they settled back for a visit before returning to camp. The pie was gone in half an hour.

Lean and lanky, George Sellers was the image of a movie cowboy. His brother, Paul, older and softer-spoken, was married but hadn't seen his wife since spring a year ago when she left his sheep camp and headed toward the highway. He didn't seem much worried about her. Traveling with a pack string of six horses, the men herded their band of sheep from the Columbia River north through the Cascade Mountain high country and back. They began in February, they told us, and returned to the river in November. The sheep company packed in supplies every two weeks, but not a barber.

Not long after their visit, George and Paul rode in with mutton for our supper—a bear had found their flock, and they had salvaged some meat. Paul went into town with us for his haircut, but when he didn't meet us at the end of the day we came home without him. Within a week, both brothers showed up to say goodbye. Preparing to move camp, they trailed a calf, a packhorse, and an extra horse. As we sat down for coffee and cake, George, warmed by beer Paul had brought from town the night before, filled us in on his brother's return to the sheep camp.

Paul had found a ride as far as the road into Walupt Lake. But, after zigzagging down the road and up the trail beside the lake, sleep had overtaken him. Paul lay down beside the trail, George said, waking in the night to find a cougar snuggled beside him, snoring away. "When we came back down the trail today to pick up the stuff he'd brought from town," George said, "we saw the tracks of a cougar in that spot." Squinting sideways at his brother, he added, "Or maybe it was a big dog."

The idyllic summer of 1949 ended just as Congress announced the renaming of the Columbia National Forest for the first chief of the U.S. Forest Service, Gifford

Pinchot, who had been an inspiration to foresters since the beginning of the century. Studying in Europe as a young man, he had returned to America full of enthusiasm for establishing in his own country the same sound forest practices that had preserved the forests of Germany. In *Indian Forest and Range*, J.P. Kinney, first chief of forestry for the Indian Service (1914 to 1933), attributed "the intense interest of President [Theodore] Roosevelt in forestry and other phases of conservation to the fire that burned so fiercely in the mind and heart of Gifford Pinchot." For Bud and many other young foresters who had come through a devastating and time-stealing war, Pinchot's enthusiasm offered hope that they could, at last, work toward "the greater good" for the land and the people.

In early September, Bud and I told our new friends goodbye and returned to Iowa State—Bud to complete his war-interrupted education on the GI Bill and I to teach freshmen women about the latest laborsaving household equipment. Unpacking at home in Ames, I came upon the ring I had picked out of the dust that first week at Walupt Lake. Bud's parents urged us to take it to their jeweler neighbor to see if it had any value. Was it glass? "No," Grant Dudgeon said as he adjusted the loupe in his eye. "This is a diamond." He bounced the ring in his cupped hand. "About a carat and a half." I let out a little gasp. "Of course, it's a little yellow," he said, "but some folks like that. Might bring twelve hundred dollars."

That was a fortune to us. Bud looked at me. "I guess it's lucky we didn't take Jim Martin's offer to buy it for ten dollars," he said. I didn't comment on the "we."

Finding Wild Goose Bill

Now and then that first summer, Bud and I had talked about "Wild Goose Bill" Condit. We wondered if the old pioneer had descendants, cousins of some sort for Bud. My father had been one of eight children and I had cousins everywhere, but Bud's father was an only child, born after his own father's death. There were few known relatives.

We carried the Ma's Cafe menu back with us to Ames. Intrigued, Bud's father sent the information to the family genealogist in New Jersey. Yes, Samuel Wilbur Condit was a relative. There he was, number 798 in the 1916 revised edition of *Genealogy of the Condit Family, 1678 to 1885*, listed as "lost at sea en route from British America to California." The genealogist was not surprised to have the black sheep turn up. "Lost at sea" was a common entry for men who went west and presumably went wrong, he explained. We discovered that Wild Goose Bill's father, born in New Jersey, had died in Iowa with no known grandchildren. We wondered if there were any out West.

We discovered the answer in the fall of 1950. Bud had graduated in June, and we spent the summer in Thompson Falls, Montana, where he was the district guard on the Cabinet National Forest. I was relieved when the summer ended with no serious forest fires in the district, especially after learning of the tragic Mann Gulch fire the summer before, when eleven smokejumpers and the district smoke chaser died.[1]

Having taken the civil service exam, Bud waited for a permanent appointment with the U.S. Forest Service, with luck near Thompson Falls. To his surprise, the offer came instead from the Bureau of Indian Affairs for a forester position at Red Lake Indian Agency in northern Minnesota. When Bud learned that the offer was temporary and housing would be "a single government owned, furnished, sleeping room," he wrote the Red Lake superintendent that he was married and needed larger quarters. We both had enjoyed childhood summers in Minnesota, but Bud had known since the summer on the Montana lookout that he wanted to live in the West.

Bud heard next from Klamath Indian Agency in Oregon. He had worked in the woods there for Weyerhaeuser the summer of his air corps discharge and was not enthusiastic about returning. Then, a third offer followed, this time from C.L. Graves, superintendent at Colville Agency in Nespelem, Washington, for a forester at $3,100 a year. "The position involves considerable work in scaling, marking and administration of timber sales [and] some cruising and management work," Graves wrote, "also the inevitable emergency fire suppression work. Quarters are available."

This was the job Bud had hoped for. We knew nothing about the place or the people, but it was only a day's drive away. We figured that with an aging car, our savings dwindling, and a baby on the way, Bud needed to take this job. We left Thompson Falls with regret. Bud had worked here for three summers, and I had known the town from family trips west. We had stopped here to see my dad's uncle, a railroad telegrapher who claimed to be the last person out of town when the famous "fire of the century" swept through in 1910.

We packed our few things into the car and turned the old Ford toward Washington State again. We drove through Spokane, a familiar route to us by now from our many visits to Bud's only aunt, who lived north of the city. Then on to Wilbur where we checked to see if Ma's Cafe was still in business.

Reassured, we turned north toward Grand Coulee Dam to see dust devils dancing across the wheat fields. The broken rocky land suddenly dropped away to reveal the huge dry coulee of the ancient Columbia River stretching away to the west. I remembered then that earlier trip with my family to see the dam under construction and the dust and dryness everywhere. On this day, Lake Roosevelt's blue waters to the east offered relief from the desert. The waters of the new lake were a welcome sight.

We drove down into the construction town of Grand Coulee, still brittle with shacks and dirt from the busy time of the dam-builders. The highway dropped farther, past the west end of the dam, now completed, and through the trim engineers' section of the town of Coulee Dam. We drove along the tree-lined street past identical white houses with green shutters that perched on a narrow bench above the river—a startling contrast to the shacks we had seen above.

The highway crossed the Columbia on a bridge dwarfed by the massive concrete structure beside it. Now free and in its own bed again, the river slipped away from the foam that churned in the pool below the dry spillways. It was dusk. The words, "Best Wishes Mr. Banks," marched in giant lights across the top of Grand Coulee Dam. The chief engineer was leaving this country just as we were coming in.

"Where are the trees?" we asked each other as we headed north out of Coulee Dam along the river and up through the rimrock into the hills. Great haystacks of basalt loomed along the road. Climbing steadily, we passed a few houses—oases in the barren landscape—then finally dipped to cross a creek, green-banked and cool, and on into the dusty town of Nespelem. There were trees, at last, but cottonwoods. A forester expected timber.

Stopping at the lone store across from a Texaco station, we asked about the Colville Agency. The clerk gestured with her thumb. "You passed it two miles back just after you crossed the creek. Looks like an old army post."

Returning the way we had come, we found the agency, the reservation headquarters. We bumped across the cattle guard and entered a shady enclave—a street lined with once-white bungalows around a long park shaded by huge evergreen trees. There were children, and dogs. Frank Gordon, the chief clerk, led us to a house on a side street, across from a two-story building he identified as the Council Hall, where the tribal council met.

The house was much larger than the tourist cabin we had been living in all summer, but on this late afternoon in October it was gloomy. I felt a chill. "We'll put you here for now," Frank said, opening a window. "It's been closed a couple of days—since Pat Brown and her boys left." He paused. "We'll find something smaller soon." It *is* big, I thought, for the two and a half of us—the half not showing yet.

Frank helped us unload the Ford. After a year of marriage, we didn't own much except Nick, our pup. The job offer had included a house to rent furnished. We were glad of that.

"Why did Pat Brown leave?" I asked Frank, following him out on the porch.

"Her husband died in a car wreck."

I rustled up a supper of sorts from the food we carried and some staples left by the widow in her hasty departure. We didn't say much. I could not shake off the ghosts of a family packing up and leaving after a death. Bud was preoccupied with the new job he faced the next day. I put on a sweater.

Steps on the porch, a soft knock. Company? Three small figures stood shadowed by the screen door. They came in with smiles, the youngest carrying a plate of cookies. Two women and a girl, all black-haired, about the same height.

The first identified herself as Donna Mae Rickard. A great crown of hair was braided across her head. Her voice had music in it. "We're your neighbors," she said. "This is my mother, Genevieve LaFonso." She was tiny, wiry. "And this is Jean. She'll be your paper girl."

About thirteen years old, Jean walked in and looked us over. She shooed our pup away from her grandmother and uncovered the cookies. As soon as we all found places to sit in the stark room, Jean passed the cookies.

"Are you from around here?" Donna Mae asked. She knew Bud was the new forester but nothing more. Donna Mae was married to Fred Rickard, a Colville tribal member who had graduated from Oregon State University with a degree in forestry. They had met at Chemawa Indian School near Salem, where she had come from her home at Chico Rancheria, California, for a post-graduate secretarial course. Moving to Colville Agency after Fred's graduation, Donna Mae had become the superintendent's secretary.

Bud told the three women that we were from Iowa but he'd been working in Montana. "With the Forest Service," I said. "We're glad he found a permanent job only a day's drive away." Then it all spilled out. "The baby is due in March, and our car's on its last legs."

Genevieve gave me a close look. "You're a long way from home." The warm tone comforted me. Small in her chair, her feet not quite touching the floor, I liked her at once.

Bud broke in. "But we might have relatives out here somewhere." He described last year's chance stop at Ma's Cafe in Wilbur. "The town's named for a Samuel Wilbur Condit," he said. "Condit was my grandmother's family name."

Donna Mae sat up, her eyes on Bud. He went on, warming to the story. "They called him 'Wild Goose Bill.' My dad found his name, right age and all, in the family genealogy." She broke in. "Then you've got a cousin here—Jack Condon. He's Wild Goose Bill's grandson!"

"And a nice man," Genevieve added. The name had been changed to Condon long ago, Donna Mae explained. Jack, a Colville tribal member, worked for the roads department at the agency. "You'll meet him at work tomorrow." After a bit, the visitors stood and moved toward the door. They turned to shake our hands, each saying, "Welcome to Colville Agency."

Still dazed by the news about Wild Goose Bill and much warmed by the visit, we went out on the porch with them. On her way down the steps Jean said, "I'll start your *Spokesman Review* tomorrow." It was that immediate acceptance by this family and the community in general that made a huge difference in the rest of our lives.

2. BEGINNINGS, 1950-1956

*To start her basket, the weaver gathers a loose bundle of warps together with a long weft strand. ***

The House on the Corner

For a great river that forms the border between the states of Washington and Oregon, the Columbia has a strange beginning. It flows nearly forty miles northward from its boggy source in Canada until the land resists and sends the waters south into Washington. Today, lakes between dams—jewels on a necklace—conceal the river that once surged toward the sea. Just below the mouth of the Spokane River, the long lake turns into the sunset. At the end of that westward reach is Grand Coulee Dam. Here the river drives the generators and then spills into a deep canyon to push northward again before it winds away to the west and south.

It was at this dam that I first saw the Columbia. I was thirteen. My father had brought our family from the green Midwest through August heat and dust to this forlorn place to gaze at what he considered to be the engineering wonder of the modern world. This great concrete barrier would harness the mighty river to bring light to cities and power to irrigation pumps to make the desert bloom. My memory is of astonishing activity above the growing face of the dam—huge trucks, giant buckets of concrete on cables, workers everywhere. In the canyon far below, a small bridge spanned the narrow stream that was the great Columbia.

I wonder now if some life force drags us back and forth across a stage—there have been so many repetitions of place and people, unexpected and seemingly unplanned. Ten years after that family trip, Bud and I crossed the Columbia on that same small bridge now shadowed by the massive face of the dam looming above us, on our way to a place that would be a real home at last. As our three visitors said their good-byes that first evening at Colville Agency, I wondered if it was more than coincidental that we found ourselves so near the spot where I first saw the river.

---

*Paraphrased from Schlick, *Columbia River Basketry*, p. 62.

I wonder, too, if the force was at work on the fourteenth of March the next spring. Someone that day opened the gates that sent the Columbia plunging over seven spillways. The Coulee Dam hospital, only blocks away, rumbled as if a huge locomotive were charging through the streets. It was the day our first child was born.

In the five months in-between, from October to March, we moved twice, an easy thing to do with few possessions. A week or so after we arrived, a small one-bedroom apartment in the duplex a half block away from our temporary quarters was ready. From the big front window we could look across the long tree-covered central lawn known as the campus to the agency office a short block away. The sun set behind the hills that formed a distant backdrop for the low brick office building and for the larger 1910-era houses facing ours on the other side of the campus. We later learned that far beyond those hills, the Columbia bent again, passed the spot where Wild Goose Bill had his ferry, and rolled on westward where it joined the Okanogan River. From there, the river swept south along the foothills of the Cascade Mountains toward Oregon.

Established by executive order in 1872, the land reserved for the Colville Confederated Tribes encompassed all territory below the Canada-U.S. border, bound on the east and south by the Columbia and by the Okanogan River on the west. In 1892, the U.S. government opened the north half to settlement. The Colville Agency was located in an open valley two miles south of the small town of Nespelem.

From our corner, we could hear cars bouncing across the cattle guard at the entrance beside the office. Ray and Bertha Lightfoot, our neighbors on the other side of the duplex, welcomed us warmly. They both worked at the agency. One noontime soon after we moved, I was especially grateful for our shared front porch when I heard a heavy knock. When I opened our door, an Indian stumbled toward me.

"Hey," I blurted out, stepping to block his way. "What do you want?" He began to walk through the doorway. Realizing that he'd been drinking, I grabbed the man's arm and turned him toward the Lightfoots' open door where, by this time, Ray was standing. I gave the man a small push toward my neighbor. "Here's someone looking for you, Ray," I said and slipped back into my apartment, locking the door. It wasn't an hour, I learned later, before the story had circled the campus about Ray Lightfoot opening his door to find a poor confused visitor thrust at him by the new forester's wife. There are those who remind me of it today.

A more welcome visitor was Allan Galbraith, a member of the Spokane tribe whom Bud had met on his first day at work. In Allan, a range conservationist, Bud found an immediate friend, his ideal of a true westerner who knew and loved the woods and all that lived there. We could see the Galbraith house across the campus between the homes of the roads engineer and the superintendent. The other houses on that block were obscured by huge conifers. An occasional dog, sometimes our sociable Springer spaniel Nick, or a couple of children would emerge from the dense foliage and make their way across the campus. Someday soon, I thought, our child will play there.

I walked over to the office each morning to pick up mail from our U.S. post office box. There I met the other wives and talked with Anne George, the receptionist, who later became my next-door neighbor. Her husband, Frank George, was the tribe's execu-

The Columbia, looking west downriver from the mouth of Nespelem Creek. Wild Goose Bill's ferry site is around the bend.

tive secretary and well-known nationally in Indian affairs. Anne was the daughter of Cleveland Kamiakin, son of the famous Yakama leader Kamiakin, one of the Yakama signers of the 1855 treaty with the United States.[1] Anne's mother was from a prominent Nez Perce family who had been sent to the Colville Reservation with others of Chief Joseph's band after incarceration in Oklahoma in the late 1800s.

Among the first pieces of mail to arrive in our box was a postcard from my father, who was recovering from a heart attack earlier in the fall. Not one to waste postage or paper, he had packed the card tight with the cramped lettering of a land surveyor writing field notes. "I've looked you up on the map, but I want to *see* where you are" he wrote. "Herb Ustrud [a colleague] worked out of Republic one winter and says it's rugged country." I sensed my father's delight that we were somewhere that he would enjoy visiting.

As I read the familiar hand, I pictured my dad pushing himself out of the old leather chair, putting on his hat, and heading down the front steps of our house to the post office three blocks away. He would mail the card just before the lobby closed at ten. He had begun this routine during the war, mailing the daily letters from my mother to my brothers in England and Washington, D.C., my sister's to her husband in Europe, and mine to Bud in Texas. He said at our wedding, "Well, good. All that postage finally paid off!"

My dear dancing, singing father's heart, so big that it welcomed the world, gave out in early November. I cry for him today. I had had no pets as a child—my father said it was too hard to lose them. I wished then that I had experienced some loss just to help me handle the shock of his death.

We could not have been among more helpful friends for such a challenge. New on the job and with no accrued leave, Bud told me I would have to go to Iowa alone for the funeral. Hearing the news, Henry Wershing, the forest manager, told Bud to go, that I needed him there. Leave could be advanced, he said. Bud's co-worker, Alec Arcasa, a tribal member, assured him he could get along without him for a few days.

Thinking now about Alec, who had been given this green young forester as a work partner, I realize that he probably welcomed a break from a tough assignment. In those first years, working with this respected man, Bud learned much about the woods and the people he was serving, as well as some choice words in the Salish dialects that were spoken by the Colville groups other than Chief Joseph's people, who spoke Sahaptian Nez Perce (*nimiiputimpt*).

We drove off to Spokane to board a plane for Minneapolis, then on to Des Moines, the closest airport to Ames. Although I had dreaded the funeral, the only really difficult time for me was at the cemetery. As was the custom there, after the final prayer we walked through the fresh snow to our cars and away from the open grave. The workmen would fill it in, but to me the ceremony seemed unfinished.

Bud returned to the agency the day after the funeral and settled into his job. His first monthly scale report, a major responsibility, was due on November 10. Payments to the tribe from the purchaser were based on these measurements of timber taken from the land. He couldn't, he thought, leave the report to someone else. Twice later, in a July and again in a November, others did the job for him when our second and third babies chose the tenth to arrive. But he was home in time that November to produce this first report on his own.

While I was in Ames, Bud sought out Wild Goose Bill Condit's grandson in the agency roads department and told him of their relationship. "I always knew I had relatives back east somewhere," Jack Condon said, and explained that Condit had changed to Condon due to a misspelling in county records long ago. The Condit genes survived better than the spelling, for Jack strongly resembled Bill Schlick, Bud's father. Jack's wife, Eugenia, had a hard time believing our story until the following summer when she saw a stranger coming out of the office. "I stopped still," she told us after the encounter. "I knew he was Bud's dad. He looked just like my father-in-law!"

Bud's dad gave a copy of the Condit genealogy to Jack Condon, who later presented it to the Wilbur, Washington, museum. According to Jack, Samuel Wilbur Condit had come overland to California with an uncle about 1852. He was seventeen. Learning of the "lost at sea" reference in the family records, Jack commented: "He probably disgraced the family name by leaving his fiancée and heading west." By 1853, Wild Goose Bill had made his way north to Fort Walla Walla, where he soon was operating a large pack string into the placer mining country along the upper Columbia. Julia

Basile, a member of the Couer d'Alene tribe, married Condit in 1872; and the next year, Jack's father, also Bill, was born to the couple on the pack trail. Jack learned his love of horses and ranching from Bill Condon.

Reading Jack's collection of newspaper clippings and recollections made me realize that the stories of the Wild West were not all romantic imaginings. Wild Goose Bill's life was as colorful as his name, and, yes, it did end in a blaze of gunfire, over a twenty-one-year-old woman, the sister of Jack's mother. Jack's guess about why his grandfather left New Jersey was probably on the mark.

As winter deepened, the work in the woods became more difficult—scaling on slippery log decks or marking timber in snow. Alec Arcasa continued his education of the new forester on the real world of the U.S. Indian Service and life on the reservation. The good fortune of having Alec Arcasa as a mentor was a gift that followed Bud the rest of his career. Years later, when Bud came to the Yakama Reservation, Joe Jay Pinkham, of Nez Perce descent, introduced the new superintendent by saying, "He learned all he knows from us on the Colville Reservation!"

It was a true statement. Nothing other than the sage tutoring of tribal elders could have prepared him for the career he had undertaken. By an accident of Civil Service selection, he was assigned to a reservation with one of the longest histories of forest management in the Northwest. The United States Congress first authorized the sale of green timber from reservations in 1910. Before that time, Indians in the Northwest who wanted income from logging had to say they were "clearing land for agricultural use," which usually resulted in low payments from the buyers.[2] The Indian Service branch of forestry had been established to ensure fair market value for the Indian owners. The first timber sale on the Colville Reservation had begun on November 11, 1918, one day short of thirty-two years before Bud Schlick filed his first scale report.

I returned at last to the West from Ames just before Christmas, relieved to put those sad weeks behind me and happy to be together with Bud in our new life. I found that Bud had changed his black jeans and checkered wool shirts for the olive drab dress of the agency foresters. He had bought higher loggers' boots to protect him from the timber rattlers he faced in the woods that fall, but he still wore his dad's old felt hat.

Settling In

When I returned to the agency just before Christmas, we bumped across the cattle guard, welcomed by Christmas lights shining in the snow that festooned the huge blue spruce at the north end of the campus. I had heard that the lights went up each year, but this was more festive than I had imagined. Although I had said we were going "home" for my father's funeral, I realized again that our home was here.

The duplex apartment was comfortable for two, consisting of a front room with big windows toward the campus and the side street, a small kitchen behind, and a bath off the corridor that led to the bedroom at the back. I worried about where my mother would sleep when she came to help for a few weeks in March. There was a foldout sofa in the living room, but she would need her own space.

Fortune intervened. Bertha and Ray Lightfoot accepted a transfer to another reservation, and we were offered their sunny furnished south apartment. We would miss them, we knew, but a small enclosed porch at the back of their apartment solved our housing problem. What I remember most from that apartment are the maple furniture and the old Navajo rugs that warmed the cold floors of the bedroom and the enclosed porch at the back. Later, living in the Washington, D.C., area, we could identify those Indian Service families who had lived in agency quarters in the 1950s by the maple furniture and the Navajo rugs in their homes. The government sold the furnishings to residents in the late 1950s, and we missed that opportunity to live the rest of our years with the soft, earth-toned hand-woven rugs from that first agency house.

My mother arrived early in March, welcoming a change of scene after the dark winter in Iowa. She brought a supply of diapers and a tiny hand-knit sweater from Bud's mother. The next challenge was to choose a name for the baby. It had to be William, but you couldn't call a baby that. We settled on Bill.

By the end of the ninth month, I didn't care who arrived, Bill or his sister, just so one of them did and soon. About 4:30 on Wednesday morning of March 14, 1951, only a week late, the baby signaled that it was time. Two and a half hours later, the sun now up, seven spillways open on Grand Coulee Dam, and the hospital still shaking as if a steam train were passing, William Schlick the fourth appeared.

Bud gave his son a long happy look and me a quick kiss, dashed out of the hospital, and raced up the road to the agency. He ran into the forestry office. "I've got a boy," he announced. Then, I learned from my visitors that night, he circled the campus with the news before returning to work. At the hospital that evening, he took a small bundle wrapped in his handkerchief out of his cruiser coat pocket. Opening it, he showed me the crumpled form of a quail. The small creature had collided with the car's grill on the trip into Coulee Dam. It was as if he needed to share this event, to acknowledge his regret for the bird's death on this happy day.

When the time came to sign Bill's birth certificate, we settled easily on Condit for a middle name. We now had our own Wild Goose Bill.

By Mother's Day, I needed a break—not from the baby, but from the tiny apartment and the gloomy skies of a long winter. I had been told that the Columbia River snaked its way toward the west beyond the hills where the sun set behind the Circle grounds— the site of the tribal Fourth of July encampment across the highway from the agency. The Columbia and its tributaries had already played an important part in our short life together, and I yearned to see a new stretch of it. Bud had gone to the Columbia recently with Allan Galbraith, looking for a place to try out their crow calls, and he had located a place for a picnic. "The place reminds me of the Ledges," Bud told me, referring to a startling sunken oasis in the midst of cornfields not far from our hometown.

I packed the standard fixings—hot dogs and buns, carrot sticks, chips, pickles— into our picnic basket along with the red-checked tablecloth my mother had hemmed for me by hand. "Every Iowa girl needs one," she had said.

After loading it into the car with Bill asleep in his basket and Nick wagging his stump of a tail, we set off for our first picnic, feeling like a family. The small dirt track led away from the road about halfway down to the Columbia. Bud turned off there, and the old blue Ford bumped along to the track's end. We parked and followed a trail around a high rock outcropping to a flat place above the edge of Nespelem Creek.

There on the narrow shelf was a table with attached bench built at the base of the rock. The creek whispered just below, frothy from the plunge in the narrow canyon it had carved to reach the Columbia. How did Bud know it would be just right? I wish I could ask him now. The wood smoke, the earthy smell of the rocky cliff at our backs, the tasty food, and the sleeping baby restored my soul. Wanting his son to share this first Mother's Day, Bud lifted him out of the basket to be part of it, but Bill's eyes would not open. I blessed the creek for its lullaby.

After lunch, we drove to the peaceful hayfields and orchards along the river. It was later along this riverbank that we began to understand the meaning of the word "native." The new Chief Joseph Dam was under construction about thirty miles down-river to the west. A team of archaeologists, preparing for the lake that would cover these Columbia lowlands, invited Bud to their study site, where he saw the burial places of the long-ago people who had lived where Nespelem Creek enters the river. I was astonished that we lived so close to a place where ancient bones lay underground, possibly of ancestors of people we knew.

Writing this, I think of the effects of the Grand Coulee Dam that I had taken so much for granted as an engineering accomplishment. The huge blockage of the Columbia was so high that fish ladders allowing salmon to return to mother waters were out of the question. I've seen photographs of Indians dressed in ceremonial clothing standing with state and national leaders at the dedication of the dam. The Indians did not look happy; but when we lived there in the 1950s, no one was talking about the loss of fishing sites or ancestors' burial grounds. I asked a Colville friend about this recently. "My husband and I never talk much about it," she replied. "His family was totally against the dam . . . and on my mom's side they believed that all of the promises would be kept. Some things are best left alone."

While I was in Iowa after my father's funeral, Bud had met Ben Pease, a teacher and coach at Nespelem High School. Son of a tribal leader on the Crow Reservation in eastern Montana, Ben and his wife Marge had come to Nespelem after their graduation from college in Oregon. We became friends and spent many evenings together, mostly at their house in town where we could enjoy "I Love Lucy" and other early television shows. We had no spare funds for a television set, and our Bill was more portable than their two-year-old Janine.

It was Ben who talked Bud into turning out for the Nespelem town basketball team that first fall. Happy to discover the local team, he soon learned that they played a much harder game than he had been used to in high school. It was hard to know which was tougher, the work in the woods or the fast games of basketball, but the combination quickly whipped Bud into shape. Other than Bud and Ben Pease, most team members were from the Colville tribes—Ike Cawston, Nelson Iukes, Matthew Nampooya, Joe Nanamkin, Oliver Pakootas, and Howard Wilson. These are the only names I can remember, beside Jack Barnard who worked at the agency and whose father served as timekeeper. There must have been more—or perhaps not. The small number would account for Bud's exhaustion at the end of every game.

The gymnasium at Nespelem High School had a standard-size basketball court but very little space around it for the fans. Teams from other towns were known to complain that the cheering tribal elders who sat around the edge were the local team's best defense. Visiting players soon learned to keep their feet and the ball away from the sidelines. As far as I know, Bud experienced no discrimination from the Nespelem rooters, but one of their "away" games, at White Swan on the Yakama Reservation, opened his eyes to such possibilities. When his Yakama guard dogged him closely, whispering, "I'll get you, *Pushtan* [white man]," Bud figured it was the same as high school games against Boone, our archrivals in Iowa. For him, the game was worth taking the chance.

We spent many Sundays that first year driving around the reservation in the old blue Ford. Bud wanted me to see where he was working and to enjoy this rugged country where we lived. A special spot was Gold Lake, a quiet place hidden among the mountains near the north border of the reservation.

Gold Lake today is a place of sorrow and mystery to me. A son of Joe and Lucy RedThunder was lost while hunting with a companion in the area during our later years on the Colville. Joe worked for the agency roads department, and Lucy was the Nespelem postmaster. After local search crews could not find the young man, the people of the Nez Perce longhouse brought a Bluejay from Montana to help. This man with special powers announced to those assembled that he could see the missing man "in water." Johnson Simpson, one of the tribal foresters, told Bud later about the Bluejay leaving the longhouse through the window after telling the people of his vision. "He climbed out through the open window?" Bud asked. "No, he flew through the window," Johnson said. "It was closed."[3]

It was not long after that when Bud came home from work and told me that the young man's body had been discovered in Gold Lake. I looked at the baby I held in my arms and could not imagine how a family could go on after losing a son.

Eey'sin — Celebration[4]

It was July, a hot night. I had just dozed off on our airy porch, now screened for summer, when I startled awake. Was I dreaming? The sound insisted, deep and rhythmic like a bass drum but with more authority. I nudged Bud. "What's that?" I whispered, not wanting to wake Bill, asleep in our bedroom around the corner.

"Go back to sleep," Bud murmured. "It's just the dancing at the Circle." I relaxed. We knew that the Colvilles were to begin their annual Fourth of July celebration tonight, but the Circle grounds were out of sight from our house and I hadn't seen even a tepee go up. Nor did I know what to expect.

"The Grand Entry starts about one," Sam Sturgis, the big gentle man who kept the Agency grounds groomed and park-like, had told me that week. "Stop by our tepee for a visit after the parade."

The day was bright and cloudless. We wrapped Bill loosely in a lightweight blanket and drove out the gate, across the highway, and onto the Circle grounds, now transformed into a bustling arena. A great ring of tepees stood where there had been only high grass circling the faint mark of a parade track and a low weather-beaten building. White canvas or striped, a few colorfully painted, many of the tepees had pole arbors beside them looking cool under roofs of fresh, leafy branches.

We parked and, shading the baby with the blanket, walked through the grass and between the tepees to the track filled with riders in gorgeous dress. As we found an opening among the onlookers, we heard the voice of a leader but could not understand his language. A hush fell on the crowd and the horses began to move, the only sound the slow rhythmic cadence of their hooves and the quiet clink of metal touching metal on their gear. Men came first, flags high at the front—an array of banners: Old Glory, the state flag perhaps, possibly a VFW or American Legion flag, a great staff hung with eagle feathers, and others of special significance to the Colvilles. I was too new to this, too moved by the solemnity, to look for details. A riderless horse followed, the saddle turned backward. A man beside us whispered that it was the horse of a Nez Perce leader who had died during the past year.

After the men came the women, each stately rider and her mount beautifully dressed. Several women wore fez-shaped hats that I later learned were traditional headgear for women of the Columbia Plateau.* There were bells, surprisingly quiet on this slow walk—small hawk's bells on the martingales that hung around the horses' necks, sleigh bells on a strap across a horse's chest or attached to the saddle throw.

Babies safe in fancy cradleboards were tied to saddles or held across their mothers' laps. Our baby was awake by now and squirming. I thought how useful it would be to have him laced into such a protective carrier.

After the silent memorial Circle, the pace quickened, as did the sound. Here we were, among people dressed in elaborate clothing and enjoying this festive time. This was not a show for our enjoyment as onlookers. It was a celebration, a gathering of friends. We were privileged to be guests.

When the parade ended, we set out to find the Sturgis tepee, following Sam's instructions to their door—except that there was no door. When we came to the oval opening with a canvas cover pulled to the side, Bud and I looked at each other as if to ask, "Where do we knock?" Sam called us to come inside. Both of us tall, we stooped to enter and found Sam standing to greet us dressed in a crisp long-sleeved shirt, dark pants with a handsome Western-style leather belt. A small gold coin or medal hung from a chain between his shirt pockets. I wish now that I had asked about it, but it was too early in our friendship for such a question. He shook our hands formally and introduced his wife Kate. Mrs. Sturgis acknowledged us with a soft murmur of greeting.

I didn't know where to look first. Because the couple remained standing, I assumed it was all right to look around. Such a scene! The entire space glowed with the soft sunlight that filtered through the canvas. On the far side of the spacious "room," a clothesline stretched between the tepee poles was filled with family heirlooms. I had never seen anything like it. My mother had bought plaited ash-splint baskets from

---

*The twined basketry hat in the shape of a truncated cone is unique to the women of the Columbia Plateau. The earliest known documented example was collected in 1792 by George Hewitt of the Vancouver Expedition and is in the British Museum in London (Cat. VAN197).

the Anishinabe families on the Minnesota-Ontario border, but otherwise my contact with Native arts had been limited to curio shops during childhood visits to grandparents in California and a small display given to the Iowa state historian by Chief Jim Poweshiek. If I had thought about it at all, I would have assumed such beauty existed only in the past.

Mr. and Mrs. Sam Sturgis in their tepee with their display of family heirlooms, at the Circle encampment, July 4, 1951.

We captured some of that first Circle on the Kodak Tourist camera that Bud had given me for a wedding present. He soon saved up for a 35mm Kodak Signet to record this new life in color. Looking at a slide taken in the Sturgis tepee during a later Circle, I re-examine the wonderful display. There is floral beadwork on a man's gauntlets, vest, and leggings; a shawl beaded with flowers, leaves, and tendrils. There are dresses, one with elk teeth or olivella shells; a horse outfit beaded on red trader's cloth; a belt with beaded panels alternating with brass studs. A blanket with beaded strip on dark trade cloth hangs beside a man's buckskin shirt. There is a fringed shawl in a Pendleton plaid. And on the floor are rugs, Navajo and Oriental.*

In the later photo, Mrs. Sturgis stands beside Sam, wearing a wing dress in a handsome flowered print on black background. Streamers from the red satin ribbons tied at her shoulders add color. The underdress, part of the standard dress for a traditional woman on a Columbia Plateau reservation in the 1950s, is bright red with small flowers in the print.

She wears a choker of white clamshell disks, sometimes known in those years as "wampum." English traders in the Northeast borrowed the term from an Algonquian

---

*To refresh my memories of visiting the Circle grounds, I found a photograph Bud had taken of a beautiful young woman in full regalia on horseback. I sent a copy of the picture to Donna Mae Rickard for identification. Now living in Coulee Dam not far from Nespelem, she carried it up to Anne George at the tribal convalescent center. Clear in mind and spirit, Anne looked closely at the photo. "She looks like a Friedlander," Anne said, pointing out her own striped tepee at the side of the parade track and those of her mother and aunt next to that. Strangely, within a month of Donna Mae's report to me, I reconnected with another Colville friend for the first time since those years, Betty Matt Nasewytewa. She had seen the parade photo in my basketry book. "That's Barbara Friedlander on the horse," she said.

word. Many such terms, assumed to be correct for all Native people, continue to be used by non-Indians across the continent. Through the following years on the reservations, Bud and I gradually learned some of the correct words, but our assumptions must have caused much amusement along the way.

To complete her dress for the celebration, Mrs. Sturgis had tied a blue silk scarf over her hair, the red in the print picking up the color of her underdress. In the photo, her eyes are closed, her hands held in repose at her waist. The rope that holds the tepee canvas in place runs from the peak to the floor between them, anchored to something covered with a shawl. The photo is a reminder of the calm dignity of their hospitality and of many such experiences over the next fifty years.

A treasured memento, a gift from Sam Sturgis when we left the agency after six years, is a formal black-and-white photograph of a young Sam standing in a photographer's studio in front of a painted backdrop of the U.S. Capitol. He is dressed in full regalia, complete with eagle feather headdress. On the back in the fine hand of many in his generation, he has written: "To my friends, Mr. and Mrs. William Schlick, Colville Indian Agency, Nespelem, Washington, from Sam Sturgis Nespelem, Washington. Picture was taken in Washington, D.C., either before or after Christmas, 1924."

We were reminded much later of Sam by another of those strange coincidences that bring wonder to life. On one of my mother's visits to Colville Agency, Sam Sturgis had told her that his mother had named him for the doctor who brought him into the world in Pendleton, Oregon. During a visit to a cousin in Michigan years later, my mother met a young doctor friend of the family named Sam Sturgis. "Are you from Pendleton?" she asked. Startled, he said: "Why do you ask?" She told him the story. "That was my grandfather," the doctor said. Sam and his wife are buried in the cemetery where the younger Chief Joseph, the famous Nez Perce leader, lies on a hillside at the edge of Nespelem.*

On the evening after that first Circle celebration parade in 1951, we were eager to see the drums that had startled me the night before. Leaving four-month-old Bill with a baby sitter, we drove back to the Circle grounds. The scene had changed. I had paid no attention to the long building at the center of the area, but returning just before sundown we could see through the open shutters that it was full of people, the dancers bright among them. Settling ourselves into seats on one of the benches that hugged the walls, we tried to take it all in.

---

*A Colonel Samuel D. Sturgis figures in an incident in the tragic Nez Perce War when the great chiefs Looking Glass, Yellow Bull, Tu-huul-huul-hutsiut, Husis-kute, Joseph, and others prevented Sturgis's cavalry from capturing their people and horses in Canyon Creek on September 13, 1877. "Services to honor all veterans," Laurel (Montana) Outlook, September 8, 2004.

Feather bustles flashed as men and boys of all ages "war danced," as someone sitting next to us explained. Everything was new to us—the dance outfits with beaded aprons, cuffs, even ties shaped like a man's necktie. Sleigh bells or small copper cowbells at ankles or knees made wonderful *cha-chang* sounds that echoed the beat of the huge bass drum. Men surrounded the drum, some in flat-brimmed hats with high crowns, leaning into it and beating out the persistent tempo at times gentle and again with great energy. I recognized Cleveland Kamiakin, the high crown of his hat decked with the bright triangle of a bandana. Just as the drum stopped, the dancers stopped—amazingly on the last beat—and sat to catch their breath or walked across the floor, jarring the bells at each step.

A speaker announced the Owl Dance. Women and girls rose from the benches in their beaded dresses and chose partners among the males. Each couple moved into place on the floor, taking positions much like we had learned in our junior high danc-

ing class. Partners faced the direction the dancing would move, counter-clockwise around the floor. Bud and I later learned to recognize the distinctive beat of the dances—Rabbit, Owl, and Circle. We felt welcome to take part but were not bold enough to try. We had danced through the Big Band years of junior high, high school, and college, but this was completely new.

Twenty years later, living on the Yakama Res-

Looking across the Circle grounds toward the Columbia River, where it turns westward again between the near and distant hills.

ervation, we wished we had taken part in the social dancing at the Colville celebrations—we might have been more at ease with the protocol. At Yakama, Bud found himself pulled out onto the floor whenever the drums took up the distinctive beat that announced the women's choice dances. Having been told that only a suspicious wife chooses her own husband as a partner, I saved Bud that embarrassment but could never get up my nerve to invite another prospect. Ben Pease, our longtime friend from Colville days and by then a school superintendent, brought his family to join the dancing at most such gatherings on the Yakama. During a summer celebration at the Toppenish Creek pavilion near White Swan, Ben solved my dilemma by offering to be my partner. By that time, I had learned another lesson the hard way—that a woman is never to turn down an invitation to dance. But that story can wait. It is hard to describe the exhilaration I feel as I write about this dance. I always enjoy watching the stately, formal progression of the couples around the floor, the steady jangle of the men's ankle bells in synchrony with the drum, the swing of fringes on shawls and dresses. But to be part of it is much better.

I found among our keepsakes a dog-eared typewritten and mimeographed program from the Fifty-seventh Annual Indian Encampment at Nespelem, July 7 to July 15, 1956. That was our sixth and final summer on the Colville Reservation. Turning inside, I learned that the first encampment was held in 1899 in the Nespelem town site and moved to the present site west of the Colville Indian Agency in 1934. The parade was "put on for the sake of perpetuating or reliving an ages-old ritual memorial day. . . ." The program described "paraphernalia and artifacts" of those who have passed on, "bringing back memories to those who recognize the finery and view the parade with tear-dimmed eyes." I remembered the hushed parade with the empty saddle that we had seen on the horse belonging to the late husband of Hattie RedStar Andrews. I, too, had memories to rekindle, and tears swelled.

"The ceremonial songs and dances were conceived by the counselors of old," the *Yakama Nation Review* explained on June 20, 2003, "the people of another day who had achieved a harmony with Nature that was never equaled anywhere." I learned much later that such "frequent or prolonged periods of celebration which bring Indians together from remote points" had been outlawed by Bureau of Indian Affairs Commissioner Charles Burke in 1921. The Christian missionary-sponsored ban on dancing remained until the end of World War II, in time to honor returning veterans. By 1950, when we arrived, people were dancing again.

A Gathering of Friends

We had our first taste of Western dancing the summer before we came to Colville Agency at the Saturday night dances in Thompson Falls, Montana. Held in a hall near the old Black Bear Hotel, we had two-stepped and waltzed to a fiddle, a guitar, and a plinky piano played by a woman whose eyes roamed the hall but never looked at the keys. Instead of finding a seat or standing around in small conversation groups when the music stopped, as was the custom in Iowa, couples strolled arm-in-arm counterclockwise around the floor until the music struck up again.

Those dances were lively, but square dancing at Colville Agency was much more so. Our social activities as a couple at the agency included impromptu evening drop-in visits from or on neighbors, get-togethers for dinner, and festive agency potlucks in the Council Hall, a two-story frame building across the street from the house where we first stayed. Named for its use as a meeting place for the general council of tribal members, many events were held in the large, high-ceilinged room, including a memorable concert by pianist Robert Parker, a Wenatchi tribal member from Chelan.

Square dances in that building were noisy, stomping, twirling evenings full of laughter. The caller and his wife brought record player, amps, and mike and taught us to do-si-do, promenade, curtsy, and bow. We learned the Varsouvienne, the polka, and the trotting Schottische. We came to know "Cotton-eyed Joe" and many other tunes that, hearing them today, bring the same warm memories as "Moonlight Serenade" or "Deep Purple" from courting days.

Something about that music and the fast pace of the squares brought out a genuine gaiety that I have rarely experienced since. Jack Condon, straight and gentlemanly in his boots and Western shirt, was right out of a Charley Russell painting. By the time we knew Jack, he'd given up rodeoing, but his performance in the Omak Stampede's Suicide Race was legendary. His grace on the dance floor came naturally—an early pioneer who had known his grandfather during the Gold Rush referred to Wild Goose Bill as "Dancin' Bill." Another dancer, Texan Bill Smith, would let loose a shrill "Y'hoo" at the height of a complicated dance maneuver, freeing us all to enjoy ourselves. When the evening was over, Bud and I walked across the street and down the alley to our house, exhausted but glowing with the fun of it.

One sweltering July night during our second summer at Colville Agency, the group abandoned the Council Hall and we danced outdoors on the tennis court. Our daughter Katherine (known as "Kitty" until she entered graduate school) arrived the next week—earlier than expected, which delighted the doctor. He had been scheduled to move out of town before her due date and hoped I would hurry it up somehow. He hadn't suggested square dancing.

Just before Kitty's birth, we moved to the larger two-bedroom house to the south of our duplex that had been the home of Lou Miller and his family, who had moved into Nespelem. Happy as we were to have the larger house, we were sorry to lose the Millers as neighbors. Donna, their older daughter, had been one of Bill's babysitters. With another baby, it looked as if we would be seeking such help for some time to come.

When the children napped, I had learned not to sleep, for it maddened me to be awakened and I was cranky with them the rest of the day. During those years of concentrated motherhood, I learned to avoid such provocations. The chance to read in the quiet was as welcome as sleep, and it refreshed me.

One afternoon during the children's naps the summer after Kitty's birth, I glanced up from my book, startled to see someone sitting on our front steps—a woman in a plaid Pendleton '49er jacket, the type worn by many older women on the reservation then.* She must have arrived while I was tucking the children in. I stepped out on the screened porch.

"Can I help you?" I asked.

The woman, maybe forty or so, rose slowly, turning to look up at me, her face a warm bronze, hair black beneath a bandana.**

"I was taking rest," she said quietly and picked up her bag as if to go. "Hot day."

Even on such a day, she wore low black rubbers over her moccasins, the wrapped high-tops showing above. Years later, wearing moccasins to the longhouses, I learned that such protection for the soles of the feet was welcome no matter the weather.

I opened the screen door, "Would you like to come in—out of the sun?" I held the door wider and stepped back a bit. She hesitated, not looking at me, then stepped up and onto the porch.

"Come in." I gestured toward the entry hall, with its ancient Navajo rug. "Would you like a glass of tea with me?"

"Cuppee?" she said, moving on through to the kitchen.

"Yes, of course. Coffee." I put on the pot as she settled into a chair. "I'm Mary Schlick," I said. "My husband's one of the foresters."

"I know," she said. By now I was used to this response but always felt I should introduce myself—and always hoped it would elicit a name from the stranger. It rarely did.

I took some cookies out of the bean pot cookie jar, being careful with the lid. The familiar clink would bring my two sleepers out of dreamland. I hoped to have a chance to visit with this woman without interruption.

"Tell me your name," I said. I'd learned by now that it was okay to ask.

"I'm Cecelia Peo." She explained that she had been at the office and was headed for the Indian Health Service hospital at the opposite end of the campus. A hot day, she had stopped to rest on our steps. At first it was hard for me to understand what she was telling me, but gradually my ear grasped the rhythm of her speech. I filled the coffee cups, and we settled into the sociability of the kitchen, dipping our cookies in the coffee.

Cecelia began to talk. On this day and on other visits there and later at Warm Springs, she told of her father as a young man with Chief Joseph the younger. He had

---

*Pendleton Woolen Mills reintroduced the '49er jacket in 1999 "as a testament to the enduring style of Pendleton fashion. It's an item so classic, so genuine, that it still remains popular more than 50 years after its introduction." Linda Parker, Pendleton Woolen Mills, personal communication, 2002.

**Cecelia Peo was born in 1900. I was short by ten years—not unusual, I soon learned.

fought in the long war with the U.S. Cavalry in 1877 that pushed the nontreaty Nez Perce warriors and their families away from their homeland in the beautiful Wallowa Mountains of northeastern Oregon and across Idaho into the Bear's Paw Mountains in Montana. There exhaustion and hunger overcame them before they could reach the Canadian border and freedom.* This close contact with the history of the West continued to astonish me. We had been exposed to little Native history beyond the French and Indian War and Custer's Last Stand, and here we were living among those touched by brutal reality.

Cecelia told of the people's imprisonment in Kansas and Oklahoma Indian Territory and finally, in 1885, the year my father was born, of their arduous return west. They could not return to the Wallowa Mountains, now occupied by settlers. Chief Joseph and more than half of those who survived were brought to live on the Colville Reservation among Salish-speaking strangers. I had known that young Joseph's people became one of the twelve Native groups of the Colville confederation. It was much later when I realized that the Nez Perce spoke a completely different language from that spoken on the Colville. Through the years, we have had many friends among the descendants of the Joseph band of the Nez Perce. The tragic story has never lost its impact.

Over the next couple of years, when Cecelia Peo had business at the agency, she would come by, sometimes bringing letters from her daughter and sons that she asked me to read for her. Occasionally, I wrote replies that she dictated.

Our friendship did not end when Bud and I left the Colville in 1956. We renewed it when our family returned to the West in 1960, to the Warm Springs Reservation in Oregon. It was then that I began to realize what amazing continuity was possible in this life we had chanced upon.

Into the Darkness and Out

The Miller house was a full-sized version of the duplex next door where we had lived for almost two years. It had a large screened porch at the front and a smaller one at the back. An entry hall led into the living room. A wide arch opened into the dining room, and behind that was the roomy kitchen with a vestibule beyond, at the door to the back porch.

---

*According to her nephew, Cecelia Peo's father was Waptis CimuxCimux (Black Eagle), also known as Daniel Jefferson or Jefferson Green. He traveled with his father, Wotolen, in the Nez Perce War of 1877 (Charlie Moses Jr., personal communication, August 19, 2004). Another name for Jefferson Green was Wy-liim-lex, also spelled weyli:mlexs. W. Otis Halfmoon, Haruo Aoki, Nez Perce Language Discussion List, August 8, 2004.

Stored against the wall opposite the back door was an ironer, the amazing piece of household equipment that we called a mangle. To use it, I sat as if at a keyboard and used the knee-activated control to set the roller in motion that carried the pillowcase or other item under the heated plate. It was surprising to find such an appliance—used primarily for flat items—in this house. In those days before "wash and wear," it was a chore to keep men in fresh shirts. My mother had not taught me to iron, but there had been such an ironer in our lab at *Women's Home Companion* magazine. To be able to describe to readers how to use the new equipment, I had to learn to iron a man's shirt on it, no mean accomplishment. Because of that, I was able to send my fastidious husband off to work every day in a freshly ironed khaki shirt with minimum effort on my part and to keep ironed cloths and napkins on the dinner table as my mother had taught me.

In a pantry beyond the vestibule, we squeezed in a new washer and dryer purchased with a small legacy from an uncle. When, with the help of my neighbors, I mastered the skills of a country wife, the shelves above bore rows of canned peaches and pears from the lush orchards along the Columbia, green beans and tomatoes from our garden, and peppery garlic dill pickles made from Donna Mae's recipe. They did not teach canning at Iowa State, and as a town girl I had not had the privilege of 4-H. The display made me proud.

Two bedrooms flanked the bathroom on the north side of the Miller house. The big cast-iron, claw-footed tub proved to be ideal when Bud bathed the children each evening. With a bed on the glassed-in back porch for my mother's visits and a foldout sofa in the living room for others, we were ready for company. By the time my brother Bob arrived from New York to do a story on the new Chief Joseph Dam construction for *Engineering News Record*, we had room for him.

This gave us room, also, for Bud's sister who came to see us after a mission from the Canadian government to the Doukhobors of British Columbia somewhere to the north of us. They had left Russia in search of religious freedom and were marching naked down the main street of their town in protest against the requirement that their children attend public schools. Dorothy, with other members of the Society of Friends in Ottawa, had been sent to help work out a peaceful solution.

Other welcome visitors that summer were Bud's parents, who delivered a much-needed replacement for our 1941 car, a new 1952 Ford. The car was partially financed by the sale of the diamond ring found in the dust on our honeymoon summer at Walupt Lake. The jeweler who had valued it at $1,200 had been willing to take it off our hands for $500.

When Joseph was born in November 1953, Mother did not come to help but suggested what turned out to be the perfect solution. Would our neighbor Maude Friedlander be willing to keep Bill and Kitty at her house during the day for a week or two? Along with the idea came her check. She knew that Maude and Genevieve LaFonso both were willing to help out when needed and that our two toddlers welcomed these grandmothers as caregivers. Maude agreed. Bud dropped the children off after breakfast each day, and I had a restful time in the hospital and a fine peaceful week at home with this placid new child.

There was no trouble about a name. My mother's name was Josephine, and this child was born where the Nez Perce Chief Joseph and his people lived. The honored leader's Nez Perce name, Hin-mah-too-yah-laht-ket, translated as Thunder Rolling in the Mountains, evokes a wonderful image but fortunately did not predict the baby's personality.

Although one nighttime visitor had been startling—a man who appeared at the foot of our bed to report a fire—company was always welcome at our house. There were cookies in the bean pot and coffee and tea easy to prepare. But the time came when my energy for the constant companionship of a close community began to wane.

I've collected the decorated earthenware known as Devon Mottoware since I was four. Those English potters scratched sayings into the red clay ranging from "There's no fun like work" and "Good courage breaks ill luck" to "Many friends, few helpers." My favorite was a fat little milk pitcher I found during our first summer that read "No road is long with good company." A good sentiment, I thought, for beginning a life together. When we moved into the Miller house, I modified the motto to "No *day* is long with good company" and inscribed it in fancy lettering on the wall over the ironer, just inside the back door.

This proved to be one of those "be careful what you ask for" experiences. As soon as the words appeared, neighbors began to stream through our back door for cups of coffee, to cry, to borrow things. One came for the antidote for a child she thought had swallowed bleach. My neighbor brought Bill—he'd been playing at her house—who was choking on something stuck in his throat. I picked him up by his ankles and shook out the tiny wheels and axle of a toy car.

It was a rich life of fellowship, but the company began to take its toll on my own strength. I had lived through three pregnancies in as many years, had two toddlers and a big lively baby who, fortunately, hadn't started to walk, a husband who worked long hours in the woods, and a mind that would not be still. When I learned that the Indian health clinic offered BCG vaccine to agency children to prevent tuberculosis, it reminded of the high incidence of that disease on the reservation. I found myself hoping that was why I was feeling so low. A year in a sanatorium sounded peaceful.

On a dark Saturday morning early in November, a week before Joseph's first birthday, we sat around the kitchen table eating breakfast. Reaching to wipe a face or nose, I knocked over the pancake syrup. Instead of jumping up to find a sponge, I sat like a mannequin, the sticky river running across the table and into my lap. I have a strong memory of the moment, of simply checking out. I neither moved nor spoke. Bud cleaned up the syrup, helped the children finish their breakfast, and called Rickards, asking for Genevieve LaFonso.

My next memories are of traveling north to Omak and on into Canada, where we turned to wind through the North Cascades into the huge city of Vancouver. We had driven nearly three hundred miles, my dark shadow slowly lifting as we moved through steady rain, the heaviest ever for that November date. It was late when we finally found a place to stay, a situation that normally would worry me, but all that was in Bud's hands.

Cousin Jack Condon gives Kitty, Joe, and Bill a ride on Curly, his favorite horse.

By morning, the rain had stopped. As we drove eastward toward the mountains again, I began to realize that the heavy responsibility I had felt for these children, so close in age, was not mine alone. Bud had been sharing it from the beginning.

Hearing of this incident, my mother wrote: "You have a good education, an able body, and a loving family. Now, apply your fine mind to creating a life that works for all of you." I took her message to heart.

We arrived home in the dark, and when we came into the house Bill and Kitty ran to greet us, leading us into their bedroom. Tiny Genevieve was sitting there with husky year-old Joe on her lap, getting him ready for bed. They all were fine. And so was I.

Some September in the 1980s, thirty years after that rainy journey into Canada, Bud and I were on our way home to Oregon from another summer at our three-rooms-and-a-path cabin on the Stanjikoming Reserve on the Minnesota-Ontario border. Stopping in Omak, I called Jean Rickard Berney, who by this time lived with her husband and sons on a ranch in the mountains near Conconully. I was just checking in. "I have bad news," she said. "Grandma died last week. She was ninety-eight." I could not speak. Providence had brought this small strong woman into our lives. Born in a New Mexican pueblo, educated in government boarding schools, married to a concert tenor who was the son of noted Konkow basket weaver Amanda Wilson, Genevieve Avalos LaFonso had shed sunshine on all she touched.

Also greeting us that night was Nick, our high-spirited Springer/Cocker spaniel. Bud had great hopes for the dog during hunting season that first autumn when I was in Iowa. When he opened the door on their first trip out alone, however, Nick climbed across him, jumped out on the road, and was off across the brushy field barking and flushing birds, deaf to Bud's calls. Another time, riding to work with Bud, Nick leaned so far out of the truck bed to watch the road ahead that he tumbled out at the first bump.

After struggles with cockleburs and porcupine quills, Bud gave up on dog companionship in the woods. "Nick's staying home from now on," he told me. "Maybe he'll be good company for the baby." Nick proved to be just that—and contributed to my own peace of mind as the years went on by his loyalty to the children. By the time Bill was four, he seemed capable of being on his own, to have the freedom to play in other homes on that campus where we knew everyone in every house. I could tell where Bill was playing by finding Nick sitting patiently on a porch, hind parts holding the door open, feet on the step below.

I also kept track of Bill by the red corduroy cap I had made to match the red-trimmed jean jacket he had inherited from his cousin. With a baby and toddler at home, I needed to be able to spot him when down the alley at the jungle gym or out on the campus. I could watch both places through the large windows in the old house. Between the dog and the cap, I always knew where he was—except one day when I couldn't find him at lunchtime.

When he came dragging in, face and hands smudged and clothes reeking of creosote, I knew he had wandered off the campus. "We were climbing on those logs behind the hospital," he said. The agency stored their supply of power poles down there, and I realized it was a dangerous playground. We finally set some boundaries on his wanderings.

One of Bill's companions on his sortie was Billy Joe Nelson, a campus kid whose porch was among those Nick guarded. Bill reported that Billy Joe said his grandfather had traveled with Buffalo Bill Cody's Wild West Show, a touring entertainment that thrilled viewers with exaggerated dramas of life on the frontier. I'd been told that Lakota people, as many as four hundred annually, traveled with the popular shows in the late nineteenth and early twentieth centuries but wondered if the Nelsons really were among them. Nearly fifty years later, I found confirmation that they were. John Y. Nelson had performed as the Deadwood Stage driver, and his wife, Jennie, and their children all were part of Buffalo Bill's company. Jennie, an Oglala woman from Pine Ridge, was closely related to Chief Red Cloud. Their youngest daughter, Red Rose, described as "a favorite of the Prince of Wales," later appeared as Princess Blue Waters.[5] How I wish I'd known them.

Working at the kitchen sink on another day, I saw the red cap bobbing up the alley on Bill, followed by a small army of agency children coming to see the small black bear that hung lifeless in our garage. The children stared up at the black furry figure—they had seen deer and elk, but a bear waiting for butchering was unusual. Bud had figured that just once in his hunting career he should try for one. When he skinned it out, the near-human shape cured him forever of interest in bear meat.

Always looking for something that might interest the children, Bud brought home his own bear story one evening after marking trees over in the San Poil Valley. "I heard a noise in the woods today," he told us. Their chatter stopped. "When I heard it," he said, dropping his voice to a whisper, "I looked around. Nothing." Their eyes were on him. "Then, the bushes rustled," he paused.

"Daddy, what was it?"

"And out stepped a bear."

"A grizzly?" they chorused, eyes big.

"Oh, no, just a nice black bear, probably a female." He took a bite, casual. "But I didn't see any cubs."

Bill asked, "What did you do?"

"Well, I gave the tree a tap with my marking ax." He hit the table gently with his knife and leaned back in his chair. "You know," he nodded, "black bears won't bother you if you don't surprise them."

"Did she leave?" Kitty asked.

"Well, no. She said Woof." He spoke the word quietly.

"And?" A chorus.

He hit the table again. "I hit the tree again, a little harder."

This was getting better. "And?"

"She said 'Woo-oof.'" By this time, he said, he really needed to get on with his work so he tried "Hey bear" one more time.

"Did she leave?" By now all three were worried.

"She said, WOOF! very loud." The children jumped. "And she did not move." He waited a minute, then said, "But I did."

It surprised me after that hasty trip to Vancouver how quickly life had simplified for me. With Bud's help and Bill's growing independence, the days seemed calmer and visitors were again welcome. But I feared that we would lose some friends because of the dog. The Rickards had put in a small chicken yard at the corner of their garden. One morning, just after Bud had left for the woods, I had a call from the neighbor across the campus. Nick had gone after the Rickards' chickens, killing several. I feared that this community that had been so welcoming to us would now regret that we had come. Nothing much was said, and I tried to forget it over the years.

In 1999, I rode along as navigator for Donna Mae Rickard when she drove to New Mexico to search out her mother's relatives. She was eighty-six. I finally worked up the courage to mention the chicken incident. She had no memory of it.

"I don't think we even offered to pay for the chickens," I said, the guilt still heavy on my conscience.

"Okay," she said. "You can buy dinner."

The First Farewell

In 1956, after six years on the Colville Reservation, the last three as assistant forest manager, Bud was asked to move to Washington, D.C., to modernize timber sale contracts for the Bureau of Indian Affairs. He had enjoyed the work in the woods, the excitement of fire suppression, and the challenge of managing the large timber resource for the Colvilles, but he looked forward to seeing how things worked at the federal level.

Before we moved, Bud spent a month in the BIA central office in Washington. It was a chance for the rest of us to visit the Iowa grandparents and for the children to have their first train trip. We found Nick a new home and boarded the Great Northern Railway in Spokane to head east—the children and I to Ames and Bud on to Washington.

We all enjoyed the break, and, to Bud's surprise, he found Washington stimulating. Having grown up in a small city and then spending much of World War II at remote airfields in Texas, he liked the feeling of being in a place absorbed in national and world affairs. Still, he hoped not to stay in Washington forever.

Bud came to Ames for a few days before we all returned to Colville Agency in early November. Outside a store near the Iowa State campus, Bill reached to pet a St. Bernard. The dog leaped on him and, rushing the child to our doctor's office, we discovered a long slash across his throat exposing the trachea and windpipe and another at the crown of his head. By the time we boarded the train for Spokane three days later, the twenty-one stitches were well bandaged and healing and Bill carried a large yellow model of a Michigan crane, a gift from the fraternity that owned the dog. The doctor had saved his life.

Because Nespelem was such a small town, the school was the center of community life. We said our goodbyes at a final PTA meeting. Although our children were too young for school, we had made many friends in the little town and on ranches in the surrounding valley because of the Nespelem Parent Teacher Association. When we had first arrived, I told the ten-year-old salesman who came to our door peddling PTA memberships that I was sorry that I couldn't join. I had no children in school. "You don't have to," he said. "In fact, you don't even have to *have* children to belong."

Most families in the valley, Indian and non-Indian, came to the meetings, helped with the dinners, acted in skits, or filled committee jobs. I blush to remember the night in June 1956 when, as the high school graduation soloist, I chose "You'll Never Walk Alone," a song only someone like John Raitt, the star of *Carousel*, should attempt. My consolation is that none of the nine members of Nespelem High School's last graduating class ever complained in my hearing.*

We also had met local families through the small Methodist mission. Not enthusiastic about going to church, Bud had helped with the annual Men's Night chicken dinners. I took the children to Sunday school and Bible school, served in whatever job was needed, and sang occasionally with the choir.

Bud and I knew we would miss these people—our first real friends in our life together. Among our goodbyes was a poignant one to Jack Condon, who rode in from his ranch on his favorite horse, Curly, to give rides to Kitty, Joe, and Bill, his grandfather's namesake. It was because of these friendships that I knew we would be welcomed in 2002 at the Nespelem school reunion. It did not matter that most of us had not seen one another in the intervening forty-six years. We had shared a joyous life in that small community, and we celebrated it. When the reunion was over, Katherine commented: "After a whole life of not feeling that I'm 'from' anywhere, it was wonderful to be in that gymnasium with people who looked on us as belonging."

As we prepared for the move in November 1956, it was hard to believe that Bud and I had arrived at the Colville Agency alone with Nick and what little else we'd carried west in the old blue Ford. Now, six years later, we were a family of five with a load for Mayflower Van Lines. On the day before Thanksgiving, we wedged ourselves into a new-to-us fin-fendered green and yellow Pontiac station wagon, bumped across the cattle guard, and set off down the road toward Virginia.

---

*The high school closed that spring of 1956; future classes attended high school in Coulee Dam.

3. INTERLUDE ON THE POTOMAC, 1956-1960

*Imbrication: Adding interest and beauty
to the surface of a Klikitat berry basket
by folding beargrass back and forward,
securing it with the strong cedar root.**

It hadn't seemed like a long trip in the roomy station wagon, and we were already in the District of Columbia following the signs for Virginia. Ahead we could see the glow from the great marble columns of the Lincoln Memorial lighted in the late afternoon dusk. Traffic was heavy in the circle around the monument, but it was a welcome hindrance. Just before we crossed the Potomac into Virginia, Bill, Kitty, and Joe caught their first glimpse of the Washington Monument and the Capitol down the Mall.

Only a week before, we had left our home near a river that flowed into the Pacific Ocean, and now we were crossing waters headed for the Atlantic. We had exchanged a quiet life in the remote inland West for whatever this place would bring. If we had made this move two years earlier, I would have been on the edge of panic. But this day, with children now three, four, and five, I felt a surge of energy, almost euphoria.

And so we began the first of four sojourns in the nation's capital. It became our other life—a layer folded like the imbrication on a Klikitat berry basket over the foundation we had begun to construct as a family in the West. Each time we made this cross-continent move from west to east over the next nineteen years, we were happy to come but we knew that we were not there to stay. We hoped we would find a way to return to the gentle people we had come to know on the Columbia Plateau. Bud felt that his time in the central office in Washington could be useful to the tribes when he returned to the field.

---

*Paraphrased from Schlick, *Columbia River Basketry,* p. 216. Klikitat is the present-day name for the people of the Klickitat River, a tributary of the Columbia, who called themselves Xwalxwaipum, or "people of the bluejay." They were makers of fine coiled cedar root baskets. According to the 34th Anniversary Washington's Birthday Celebration program (1972), the word Klickitat means "beyond," referring to the mountains.

Kitty and Mary in the backyard of the Bradlee Towers apartment in Alexandria.

By the time Bud opened the front door the evening the moving truck had arrived, the furniture was in place and the table set for dinner. For two weeks, the only place any of us had felt at home was in the car. I had lived in a three-story house as a child, a single room in New York City, a postage stamp-sized cabin in the mountains, an army barracks in college housing, and an old Indian agency house where the plumber took care of a leaky toilet tank by simply drilling a drainage hole in the floor. This was my first apartment. But I had learned that when you walk into your own place and close the door, you're home. The children felt the same way. Now we were at home in Virginia.

January 1957 brought cold weather and President Dwight D. Eisenhower's second inauguration. We bundled up to stand in the throng that filled the park facing the east entrance to the Capitol to see the swearing in. We already felt a connection to this president: Mamie Eisenhower had grown up in Boone, Iowa, fourteen miles west of Ames; and the children and I, with the grandmothers, had waved at the president and first lady from the steps of a church as his entourage passed through Ames in October.

Bill had started kindergarten in Coulee Dam the past September, and I was disappointed to learn that the state of Virginia did not have public kindergartens. When I learned of a cooperative preschool in a nearby church, I called the parent who served as volunteer registrar. There was an opening, she said, and she could interview me the next day.

The children and I walked the two blocks to the church the next afternoon. As we approached the building, a dark-haired woman was also walking up. She looked closely at me. "Mary Dodds?"

I thought a minute and remembered her—Marian Tower from Cedar Rapids. We had been in freshmen classes together at Iowa State thirteen years before. Now Marian Kelso and the preschool's director, she greeted the children and led us down the stairs into the Sunday School section of the church. She took the children along to show them the schoolrooms while the registrar explained the parents' role in the half-day program. Each mother would serve as a teacher assistant one day a month and attend all training sessions. Parents also would form the committees that keep the school going, and fathers were asked to help on special workdays. When the registrar's child went on to first grade, I took on the job and learned how tough it was. I also learned that parents can run a school—if they find good teachers. I had studied child development theory in college, and those unexpected years as a volunteer teacher assistant with four- and five-year olds reinforced what I had learned—that an accepting, nurturing environment offers far better preparation for children going into elementary school than testing, competition, and pressure.

After unpacking and settling in, we began to visit a museum each Saturday. Joining a nearby church to get acquainted, we found a square-dancing group and I tried out for the choir. Aside from giving up square dancing when uniforms were required, my only problem with church arose when a member of the women's society asked me if the Indians "out there" needed old clothes.

"What did you have in mind?" I asked, thinking that good jackets or other wearable items for schoolchildren might be welcome.

"Oh," she said, "I have lots of worn-out jeans that would make good patching material."

At the time of Bill's frightening encounter with the St. Bernard the previous October, Bud's father, a smoker since boyhood, had gone into the hospital in Des Moines for lung surgery. By the time we stopped in Iowa on our way to Virginia, Bill Schlick the elder was home and, we hoped, on the mend. He lived less than two months. As had happened when we first arrived at Colville, we lost a parent after the move. It was a sad repetition. Gentle William Japhia Schlick slipped out of this life seventy years almost to the day after his birth in January 1887.

Bud returned alone to Ames for the funeral. I know how much he had wanted to meet the high expectations of his brilliant father. I never knew if it was a dark time for Bud; he rarely talked about it afterward.

Bud's work revising the BIA timber sale contracts was intense. Learning that the Interior Building was open on Saturdays for National Park Service children's programs, he brought us along for those while he worked upstairs in the BIA offices. If there was no program, the children and I would leave Bud at the office and walk the few blocks to the National Museum of Natural History to see the replica of the Blue Whale that hung from the ceiling, the great dinosaur in the rotunda, and the necklace of fingers in the Native American wing.

During our four-year stay, we tried to see everything. We took the trolley from the Interior Building to Glen Echo Park to ride the Ferris wheel. We picnicked with friends on the Virginia side of the Potomac near the giant carousel at Great Falls Park. When young Queen Elizabeth II and Prince Phillip visited Washington in 1957, Bill and I stood at the Lincoln Memorial and watched the royal couple returning from Arlington Cemetery sweep past in a limousine, returning our waves. Bud made good friends at work. The Bureau employees, Indian and non-Indian, had come from reservations across the country, and we were to cross paths frequently through the years. The graduates of Haskell Institute, a Bureau of Indian Affairs boarding school in Lawrence, Kansas, knew several of our Colville Agency friends.* There was little chance of anonymity. We saw many more of Bud's co-workers during the holidays, their lively parties reminiscent of agency days.

From the day I met Bud's boss, Forestry Branch Chief George Kephart, I felt that he was an old friend. His father, Horace Kephart, had written *Camping and Woodcraft*, my constant companion during childhood summers in the wilderness of the Minnesota borderland. I had learned to build a lean-to, make a raft, and start a fire with a magnifying glass by reading Horace Kephart.

It was not until four years later when we were leaving Washington to move to the Warm Springs Reservation in Oregon that I learned the full scope of Bud's job. In March 1960, Glenn Emmons, the commissioner of Indian Affairs, presented a superior performance award to Bud, praising him for "work far exceeding the requirements of your position, superior ability, initiative, and resourcefulness," and, of most importance to Bud, "valuable contributions to the Bureau's forestry program." Of most interest to me were his specific "important accomplishments"—preparing material for congressional committees on BIA and two other federal agencies' forest management practices, developing the handbook of information for college students and other potential forestry employees, developing standard contract forms for larger sales of Indian timber, and revising pertinent portions of the Indian Affairs manual. Reading the first item, I realize now why he was so eager to return to the reservation, where at least part of his work would be for the benefit of a tribe rather than for a member of Congress trying to make points with a constituency.

For my part, I hoped to do some freelance writing and found my first job through the American Home Economics Association (AHEA). My initial freelance assignment was as editor of the AHEA Home Economists in Homemaking section newsletter. The job was truly "free," but it gave me good experience and eventually led to other work.

One day, after delivering an editing job to AHEA near DuPont Circle, I walked up the steps of the Interior Building to meet Bud and catch a ride home. Coming toward

---

*Now Haskell Indian Nations University, Haskell Institute was founded in 1884 and became Haskell Indian Junior College in 1965.

me were Frank George, the Colville tribal secretary, and Lucy and Johnny Covington, who
had rescued Bud from a snowy ditch one winter
night. The trio was in town, I learned later, on
urgent business—an intense battle to prevent
Congress from terminating the federal trust responsibility for the Colville Reservation.

It was not an empty threat to the Colvilles.
The trust responsibilities had been guaranteed
by nineteenth-century treaties and compacts,
but in the 1950s Indian Commissioner Dillon
Meyer—the man responsible for administer-
ing Japanese-American concentration camps
during World War II—began urging Congress
to end federal obligations to American Indians
and their land.[1] In 1954, Congress passed House
Resolution 108, which allowed "termination" of,
among others, the Grand Ronde and Siletz reservations in 1956 and the Klamath in 1961.* A

*The Schlick family poses on the mall for a
"monumental" Christmas card in December 1956.*

strong, committed servant to her people, Lucy
Friedlander Covington—the granddaughter of
Chief Moses, the last recognized chief among
the Colville tribes—had heard her grandmother say, "If an Indian does not have land,
he has nothing." The threat to the Colville subsided when the tribal election brought
in a new slate in 1968, thanks to Lucy Covington. She was given much of the credit for
saving the reservation.[2]

Another visitor to Washington was much less welcome to us. In September 1959,
I learned that Nikita Khrushchev was coming to visit the United States. Khrushchev
had denounced Stalin in 1956, but in the context of the long Cold War most of us
considered the Soviet leader an enemy of our country. I felt compelled to see what he
looked like. With Bill and Kitty settled in elementary school and Joseph in preschool,
I could go into the city for the morning welcoming parade. Or so I thought. The only
hitch was Bud, who said "No" when he heard my plan. "You cannot honor this man
with your presence!" Astonished, I explained that I felt we needed to see such people,
to judge for ourselves, but he was adamant. I held my peace.

---

*Federal trust status was restored to the Confederated Tribes of Siletz Indians in 1977, to the
Confederated Tribes of the Grand Ronde in 1983, and to the Klamath Tribes in 1986.

On the day of the Russian delegation's arrival, I boarded the bus for the District and made my way to 14th Street. Being tall, I settled behind a group at the curb and began to listen for the band. It wasn't long before I heard the subdued throb of marching feet and drumming. The honor guard approached, followed by a company of very young soldiers.

I don't remember music, just the eerie sound of boots on pavement. I felt the sharp bite of tears rise when I realized that these marching boys were the sons of mothers like me. No one spoke; the hush was palpable over that insistent tramp of the soldiers. Then came the open presidential car, with our war-hero president squeezed between the ample figures of Khrushchev and his wife. The sunlight was intense.

I remember the sound of rolling tires as they passed and a rush of something like fear at seeing our president so physically overshadowed. This man, I thought, is the reason our children have learned to "duck and cover" and why I outfitted our preschooler with his "survival bag" in case he had to be evacuated without me. I turned away and slipped behind the crowd toward Constitution Avenue, where I boarded a bus for home.

Bud was shocked that I had gone downtown that day but softened when he saw the trip's effect on me. We rarely mentioned it afterward. I was sobered by the experience, both by my husband's unusual demand and by my own reaction to seeing President Eisenhower sandwiched between the Khrushchevs.[3] The parade remains a sobering memory.

Even if we hadn't know that Alexandria was part of the South when we arrived in December 1956, it soon became clear to us. Everywhere we heard the soft unhurried speech that we called a "Southern drawl," and we soon learned to understand most of it. People stood as the strains of "Dixie" announced the beginning of movies in Alexandria theaters. All notices for parent meetings of the preschool ended with "Y'all Come!" in big letters.

Although the poll tax had been removed, the clerk at the courthouse handed me a page of confusing questions to answer before I could register to vote. I had to ask for help, which she gave willingly. An African American man came in while I was there and he, too, approached her with a question about the form. "I'm sorry," she said, "You'll have to figure that out for yourself." The man left without registering.

Bill was in the third grade in the winter of 1959-1960 when his teacher told the students that four black children would be joining the class. "Mrs. Levin asked us to put our heads on our desks and close our eyes," he told us. "All of us willing to sit beside one of the new children were to raise our hands."

I asked how many children raised their hands. He frowned at me. "I don't know, I had my head down."

"Well, did you raise your hand?"

"*Mom*," he said. "Of course I did."

Alexandria schools would not be fully integrated until 1971, two years after we lived in the city for the second time.

Through the years, my association with other home economists opened some doors for us, including the doors to the White House. The first time, none of us entered in person, but an Easter egg tree made by our children purportedly did. The food editor of the *Washington Evening Star* had asked if she could write an Easter feature on our family, "moved here from an isolated Indian reservation." A friend at AHEA had told her about the children painting "blown" and dyed eggs and hanging them on a bare tree branch to make a special Easter centerpiece.

Fascinated by the process of removing the contents of the egg while keeping the shell intact, the editor asked the photographer to document the process. We enjoyed the interview and the resulting article—which included recipes for venison curry, huckleberry buckle, and other favorites—but I was less happy with the photos.[4] There I was on the food page of a major metropolitan newspaper, leaning over a kitchen counter "blowing" the slimy contents from a raw egg into a small bowl. It may have caught the reader's eye, but it was hardly flattering.

One whose eye the story did catch was Mrs. Marie Lingo, a Washington socialite who, as a friend of former President Truman, had friends on the White House staff. She called to ask if we would like to have the Easter egg tree displayed at the White House. Of course we would, I said, and she arranged to meet us at the National Capital United Service Organization Center, which faced Lafayette Park. We set up the wobbly structure in the lobby of that famous USO "home away from home" for men and women in the armed services. She assured us that the tree would go to the White House on Easter Sunday. We never knew if the tree made its White House appearance, but we've had a lot of mileage out of the claim in the years since.

In early 1960, Bud was offered the job of forest manager for the Warm Springs tribes in Oregon. Allan and Annette Galbraith, good friends since Colville days, were there, Allan as reservation superintendent. We both looked forward to reservation life again, to the smaller world that allowed a stronger sense of community, even of identity.

We drove north to the Pennsylvania Turnpike and then west toward Oregon. The green grass around the Lincoln Memorial had been covered with snow as we left, as was everything on the two-day trip to Iowa. The following morning, Bud and Bill left Ames for Warm Springs. Kitty, Joe, and I stayed behind to fly to Portland in a few days.

It was a great luxury to have some time with my mother and to be spared that three-day drive across a snowy country. Bud and Bill met our plane late at night, and we awoke the next morning to see camellias blooming outside our motel window. We would be home in Warm Springs by noon.

4. AT HOME IN THE CANYON, 1960-1964

His own village . . . more easily sensed
than described. — Patrick O'Brian*

Crossing the Deschutes

A warmth spreads through me when I think about descending the steep grade into Warm Springs that first morning in Oregon. The same thing happens when someone talks of the tundra in the high Arctic or when I enter the village of Ranier, Minnesota, and see the blue waters of Rainy Lake at the end of the street ahead. There are places in the world that are our heart's home. Warm Springs is one of those for me.

Two hours before, we had loaded our bags into the Pontiac, checked out of the Portland motel, and made our way through the blossoming city toward Mount Hood and central Oregon. Greening acres of strawberries and other row crops lay on both sides of the road. The sweet clean pungency of the conifers filled the car. We were back in the woods at last.

A corridor of ancient firs carried us through the small communities of Welches, ZigZag, and Rhododendron. As we came out of the tall trees, the mountain gleamed directly in front of us. Bill was ready for this. "That's Mt. Hood," he said, "eleven thousand two hundred and forty five feet high."

The road was wet at Government Camp, the highway's summit, but only from the snow at the edges. We were soon out of it and on the downhill slope into central Oregon. When we saw the Warm Springs Reservation sign, Bill was proprietary, having three days' advantage, and he filled in Kitty and Joe on what to expect when they reached their new home.

"My friend Steve Duck," he said, "took me down to Shitike Creek where we'll swim in the summer."** I looked at Bud when I heard the creek's name. He gave a tiny nod, assuring me, "It's an Indian word." Bill had told us about his new friend the night before. A year older, Steve, the son of the principal at Warm Springs Boarding School, had come over to the house to greet Bill as soon as he and Bud had arrived.

*From Patrick O'Brian, *The Hundred Days*, p. 113.

**"*Shitike* means that people stayed here to pick roots, camped here, Shatash—for picking roots." Mae Queapahma John and Matilda Queapahma Mitchell, personal communication, 1963.

After crossing a couple of smaller summits, the road took us downhill and out of the woods onto a plateau. The day was clear and offered a view across the sagebrush and junipers of the reservation to the farmlands beyond the canyon of the Deschutes River, the reservation's eastern boundary. Bud said the farmers called that high dry flatland beyond the Deschutes "The Plains," a Bureau of Reclamation project that had opened newly irrigated land to farming. "Like the Columbia Basin, mint's their big crop right now."

Here and there in the distance, volcanic buttes rose from the flat land. To the south we could see a chain of snow-covered mountains, more of the familiar giants of the Cascades that dominate the skyline from British Columbia into California.

Bill had learned about these, too. "Jefferson," he pointed to the peak closest to us. "That's the reservation corner. Then Three Fingered Jack and Mt. Washington." He touched Bud's shoulder. "What's next, Dad?"

"Three Sisters, Broken Top, and Mt. Bachelor."

The volcanic cones continued south to Mt. Shasta in California and through the Sierras, all part of the great "Ring of Fire" that once circled the Pacific Ocean. Somehow I felt as if we were closer to an ancient world here than in those gentle rolling hills of Virginia.

At last we approached the canyon of the Deschutes and began to descend a winding grade. At the bottom was a green oasis, the community of Warm Springs—a church, some tennis courts, and brick buildings, which Bill explained were the boys' and girls' dormitories and the school.

"It's a boarding school for the Indian kids," Bill said to Kitty. "We have to take the school bus into Madras."*

Soon we spotted another red brick building—"The office," Bill said—a store— "That's Macy's"—and, most important, a large grassy square surrounded by trees and houses. "The campus," he announced. "We're here."

Turning to cross the cattle guard and enter the agency, we drove along one side of the square and passed a small court where some boys were shooting baskets. When we came to the corner where Bud turned, a big white dog lifted his head and barked at us.

"That's Ting," our tour guide said. "He's a Samoyed." And then, "There's our house." Bill pointed to the last of three small green-shuttered white houses. Next to the brick office building, ours was shaded by a beautiful blue spruce and a ponderosa pine.

---

*The BIA had operated a residential school at Warm Springs Agency since the early 1870s. See Stowell, *Faces of a Reservation.*

Bud turned the Pontiac into the gravel roadway between the house and the office and then into the garage driveway behind the house. Waiting by our back door was a small boy.

"Oh, that's Bobbie Smith," Bud said. "He's looking for Joe." We piled out of the car. "Bobbie Smith from Colville?" I stared at the child. The last time we'd seen him he was a baby in a stroller.

The movers had set up the beds—Kitty's small four-poster in the back bedroom, our big oak bed that Bud's dad had made for him as a boy squeezed into the other, the boys' bunks in the basement. The rest waited for us to arrange. After leading us through the house, Bill left with Steve Duck and Joe went off to the Smiths with Bobbie. Too shy to go outside, Kitty unpacked her clothes from the trip and then came into the front room to watch Bud help me move our things around until they suited us both.

No larger than the living room in our Virginia apartment, this room had the advantage of light from two windows on the street and a French door that opened onto a glassed-in porch that covered the west side of the house. It didn't take long to settle in, and soon Bud headed out the back door and across the alley to his office. I was glad for the chance to get at unpacking the kitchen.

While I worked, I watched Kitty slowly move out to the side porch, then to the steps, and finally to the curb where she could watch some girls playing in a yard on the far side of the campus. My heart ached for her.

"Hi, Mary." It was a woman's voice. I could see a head pass below the kitchen window.

Opening the back door, I was startled to see someone I knew. It was Sue Stimpson with a small boy in her arms and three little girls in tow. Kitty skipped along beside them, beaming. Our families had met briefly at Colville, and here they were six years later, neighbors across the Warm Springs campus. Knowing I was busy, Sue handed me a loaf of bread still warm from the oven and left, taking Kitty with her.

Bud had seen to it that there was food in the house, and by the time the noon firehouse siren called everyone home, I had lunch on the table. As the children talked, we learned about our new place—there's an amazing snake slide in the playground behind the girls' dorm, children are to stay away from the engine at the firehouse, the jail is on the street behind us, and kids choose pomegranates at Macy's Store over candy bars for snacks.

We were still at lunch when the knocks began at the back door. One by one, our three excused themselves and ran out. By mid afternoon the troops were back, full of excitement about the bucket of mud puppies they'd caught in Shitike Creek below the hill. Busy unpacking boxes, I was happy they had brought their friends in, but noticing the ugly salamanders in their hands I shooed everybody out. During the days that followed, the dried-up bodies of brown salamanders turned up in corners, under beds, behind the sofa, and, most of all, in the hot air registers of that little white house with green shutters at Warm Springs Indian Agency.

On the Monday after our arrival, I drove into Madras to enroll Bill and Kitty in school. Going up that long winding grade on the far side of the Deschutes River to the farmlands above, I was happy that winter was behind us. It seemed a dangerous road for the school bus in bad weather.

With Joe as my companion, I explored Madras, now our nearest town. U.S. Highway 97, which connects British Columbia with Northern California, was the main street. Seven blocks long at the most, the business district was anchored at one end by a supermarket and a motel and restaurant at the other.

We drove back to Warm Springs, a sixteen-mile trip across the high irrigated plain dotted with homes and outbuildings of young farms and ranches, then down the winding grade to the bottomland along the Deschutes River. Following the river north, the highway turned to cross the Deschutes where the canyon narrows. Coulee Dam had been the same distance from the Colville Agency. There seemed a nice symmetry to that. It wasn't long before we began to know that highway well—driving to Little League games and Bluebirds, school, church, and 4-H activities, to the doctor or dentist, and for needs not met by Macy's Store.

Cleaning up the kitchen one morning, I heard a knock on the glassed-in porch door, which faced the campus and served as our front entry. A formal call, I wondered? Up to now visitors had come around to the kitchen. As I walked through the living room, I could see a small woman about my age standing on the porch steps. She held a bundle in one arm and carried a notebook. The paisley bandana tied neatly over her hair identified her as a tribal member. I opened the door. "May I help you?"

"I'm the census taker," she said. I invited her into the living room and told her my name. "I know." She took a chair. "I'm Lizzie Rhoan." I said I was glad to see her. We had wondered if, by moving, we had missed the chance to be counted.

"Well," she said, unwrapping the bundle. "Here's one who just made it!" She held up the baby. "This is Felicia." The baby made a small sound and Lizzie opened her Pendleton jacket to adjust her clothing. She slipped the baby under the garments to nurse. The interview began, as did a long friendship.*

Another early contact at the agency was Ivy Hilty, an energetic Oklahoman who was the reservation's new Oregon State University Extension home economics agent. Her job was to bring the newest information on homemaking to the women of the res-

---

*Lizzie McBride Rhoan died in 2002 at the age of eighty-five.

ervation. Ivy shared an office with longtime agriculture agent George Schneiter in the corner of the administration building across the alley from my kitchen. The secretary was Lillian Starr Smith, originally from the Muckleshoot Reservation in Washington State and married into one of the Smith families at Warm Springs.

George Schneiter's years of experience at Warm Springs and the flow of tribal visitors to their office shortened my getting-acquainted curve considerably. One of the first elders I met in the office was Mary Hote Tom, a woman of indeterminate age with a strong voice and a contagious chuckle. Her eyes smiled through thick glasses. She had a place about five miles up Tenino Creek, and her old pickup was often parked at the office or over at Macy's Store, which also housed the post office.*

Hearing a knock at our side door one morning, I looked out to see someone climbing down from Mary's truck. I opened the door to find Mary, with Cecelia Peo coming up the sidewalk behind her. Each wore a headscarf and Pendleton jacket over a cotton dress. I had seen Cecelia last at Colville Agency four years before. I thought about our photo of Sam Sturgis taken in Washington, D.C., and of meeting Lucy Covington on the steps of the Interior Building. It began to dawn on me that the Indian people I was living among were themselves great travelers—and that they seemed at home anywhere. It reminded me that children on the reservations would ask me "Where do you stay?" rather than "Where do you live?"

The two women returned many times when Cecelia came over from the Umatilla Reservation at Pendleton. It was always a treat to share coffee with these longtime friends as they talked together at my kitchen table, with Mary translating a word or two when she remembered I didn't speak the language.

On one visit, Mary told me of making deer hide gloves. I showed her a much-worn pair made by Mary Gwa at Nespelem ten years before and asked if she could replace them for me. She nodded but said she had lost her pattern. Remembering a pattern from a college crafts class, I asked my mother to find it among my treasures at home. Mary was pleased to have it. Not long after, she and Cecelia came by to examine the decorative stitch on the Gwa gloves, handsome in black thread on the white buckskin. The stitch was new to Mary, and she wanted to try it. She took a glove with her and returned soon with the finished pair, perfect for my needs.

Mary had an imposing presence. Years later, when I learned that she had served as whip lady for children of the community, I was not surprised.** As we sat together

---

Tenino, a Sahaptian word, means river channel confined by rock ledges. Brought with the people from the Columbia, the name originally referred to the fishing grounds a few miles downstream from Celilo. See Shane and Leno, *Historical Map.*

**A whipwoman or whipman is the traditional role of disciplinarian. See Stowell, *Faces of the Reservation*, 10.

over coffee, she began to talk about her family. In her grandfather's time, she said, her Tenino people were moved away from the Columbia to the Tygh Valley, where they continued to find plenty of salmon on the Deschutes River. But there was no wood or deer, so they moved farther south and settled in a village up Tenino Creek about five miles from Warm Springs Agency. There they found what they needed. In my notes from that conversation, I spelled the names of the roots as I heard them: "*pe-a-chee*; *locksch,* for biscuits—grind roots, form in hands, dry and store for winter. *Cowsch*—a round bulb, very good when cooked and served with butter and sugar. *Pe-a-chee* is long, fingerlike, when peeled and cooked tastes like macaroni, they serve them without salt, almost tasteless to the uninitiated."*

Mary told me she was in boarding school at Warm Springs when the flu epidemic swept through in 1907 or 1908. "About three girls weren't sick, and a few boys. The girls cooked and the boys took the meals to the sick children. Many died, some lived." She described the school as strict. Every child had a job—mornings in the kitchen and laundry or mending, cleaning, gardening, or taking care of the animals. In the afternoon, they were in class and were required to study an hour each evening. She had hoped to go to high school at Chemawa, she said, but the flu took eleven of her parents' twelve children.** Their only child, they wanted her to stay home after that.

When we lived on the Colville Reservation, my main contact with women other than my neighbors had been through the school PTA, the women's society of the small Methodist mission church in Nespelem, and the Civic Club. Because the south half of the Colville Reservation had been opened to homesteaders in 1915, there were often more non-Indians than Indians at public meetings.[1] Consequently, my first meeting of Little League mothers at Warm Springs was notable because I was one of a very small minority of non-Indians in attendance.

Describing the meeting to my mother, I wrote: "Last night we met in the VFW Hall to plan a potluck supper in honor of the teams and the coaches. We were to start at seven. By 8:30 enough were there to begin. This is Indian time.‡ The women were of assorted ages and spoke very softly, listening to every comment. We laughed, had coffee after the business was over. It was delightful. I didn't say a word. One young girl had her baby with her on a cradleboard. She doesn't have a child on any team but

---

*We talked on March 15, 1963, Warm Springs, Oregon. The words are spelled "pe ah ke," "luksh," and "coush" in *Nutritive Value of Native Foods of the Warm Springs Indians.*

**Chemawa Indian School is a BIA boarding school in Salem, Oregon.

‡My favorite definition of Indian time is "when the event starts."

is a member of this very active post of the Veterans of Foreign Wars. They provided the refreshments."[2]

As each day brought new contacts, I realized how fortunate we were as a family that the agency, which had been established arbitrarily in this spot in 1855, also had become the reservation's major settlement. We knew BIA families elsewhere whose homes in towns adjacent to reservations offered little opportunity for contact with the people they served.

Our Own Village

Ivy Hilty's first task in the new job as an extension agent was to revitalize the home extension group. With advice from George and Lillian, she traveled around the reservation, inviting women to attend or hold educational meetings. From Ruth Estabrook's house on the south end near Seekseequa Creek to the homes of Sadie Brown and Agnes Wells in the Simnasho district to the north, we met each month for lessons on homemaking subjects.* Expert at food preservation and other household arts, the Warm Springs women also welcomed the latest information from Oregon State University.

An important result of Mrs. Hilty's work at Warm Springs was an unusual booklet, *Nutritive Values of Native Food of Warm Springs Indians,* published a decade later. Through that project, Warm Springs women documented the importance of the foods the earth had always provided their families. For example, the booklet reports that one cup of bitterroot (*Lewisia rediviva*) provides the full daily recommended allowance of vitamin C.[3] Huckleberries also are recognized for their significant contribution of vitamin C. In 2002, the public health nutritionist at Warm Springs added to this. She reported that the natural substances giving huckleberries their deep-blue color are the source of many of their surprising health benefits, such as improving and protecting eyesight, preventing and treating urinary tract infections, and helping prevent cancer.[4] The berries' powerful antioxidants—the highest content of over forty common fruits—help protect the body and brain from the effects of aging.

We learned much more at these meetings than homemaking tips. We learned about one another. At a Food Fair, we each brought our family and a dish that had been a childhood favorite, and we talked about it. It was there that I first tasted the favorites, bitterroot and barbecued "eels" (Pacific lamprey).

---

*Seekseequa is the coarse rye grass that grows on the banks of the creek. See Shane and Leno, *Historical Map.* Simnasho is the name of a small community on the northern part of the reservation and the surrounding district. The name is derived from the Indian word *sinemassa,* which means thornbush.

Another local food looked slippery, like chocolate cornstarch pudding except it was greenish-black. "What is it?" I asked, as the woman next to me scooped up a small serving and put it on her plate. "K'nch," I thought she said. "Pudding made from black moss, baked in the ground. It's good."* I remembered that Sam Sturgis had brought some of this moss to us on the Colville after it had been baked in the ground, but it was not cooked into a sauce like this. I tasted it, surprised to find that I liked it. Later, on the Yakama, when little bowls of this delicacy appeared on a longhouse table at dinner, it was gone before reaching me.

Manuelita Smith brought sopapillas from her New Mexican Pueblo background. Our Joe was so taken with the puffed "pillows" served with honey that he asked her for the recipe. Our family contribution was corn on the cob, not a new dish for anyone there, but our description of Iowa and the rows of tall cornstalks stretching off to the mountainless horizons was new information for many.

One evening, the extension group met around the dining table at the superintendent's house to work on quilt blocks, piecing them by hand. As we sewed, the conversation drifted to a subject I had heard only vague references to—*Sta-ya-ha*, stick Indians.[5] Voices hushed as the women told the stories from their elders about those mysterious dwellers of the woods that take on different shapes and carry away children who wander from camp.

"They make bird sounds at night when birds are asleep, or hoot like an owl," someone said, "or push sticks into the tepee" or "imitate sounds of water splashing or assume different shapes." One woman remembered her grandmother putting out soap and matches at night to keep them out of camp. As with the ghost stories my sister and brothers told each other on summer nights at Rainy Lake, I couldn't decide whether to enjoy the fearful thrill that these new tales engendered or to hum so loudly that I couldn't hear. I chose to listen.

Caught up in the storytelling, we all startled when one woman slapped down her sewing, pushed her chair back from the table, jumped up, and said, "That's enough!" Her voice was urgent with fear. "Those 'people' terrified me when I was little, and I

---

*Black lichen (*Alectoria* species), or "koonts," means hair. The lichen grows on fir, pine, and juniper trees. It is gathered, cleaned, soaked in water, placed in a clean burlap bag, then placed on top of and under layers of green pine boughs and dry pine needles in a rock-lined pit heated by a fire. A wet sack, then dirt are placed on top and water is poured through a small opening. The lichen cooks for twelve hours, then is cut into smaller bars and stored in the freezer or ground and dried. It is cooked in water with a little flour, sugar, and possibly raisins for a dessert that is high in iron. See Oregon State University, *Nutritive Value of Native Foods of the Warm Springs Indians*, July 1972, 16.

don't want to hear about them now." Gathering up her things in a rush, she asked if someone would ride with her.

"I'll go," said the woman beside her. Picking up her sewing, she took the frightened woman's arm and moved her to the door. Others looked concerned. No one laughed. The idea of stick Indians has great power.

Over the years, I have held these dwellers of the deep woods in respect. After we settled in Oregon's Hood River Valley many years later, we were in Portland attending a reception for some Warm Springs leaders. I carried a small twined purse. I had woven into the design a traditional face motif from the Wasco twined root-digging bags. While talking with Wasco Chief Nelson Wallulatum, I opened this bag to take out a handkerchief.

"Ah," he said, looking at the face in the weaving. "Stick Indian."

"Oh, no!" I cried. "It's not *that*, is it?"

He looked at me closely. "Have you had any trouble lately?"

"Well, no," I said.

"Then it's okay." And he walked off. Figuring that he'd know if anyone would, I carry the bag today.

We had little consciousness of the ceremonial life that was alive among the Warm Springs people until we learned of the Huckleberry Feast held every August at the longhouse at HeHe Butte.* Through the extension group, I had met Freda Wallulatum and her sister Romagene Knight, who lived at Simnasho, a small reservation community about fifteen miles north of the agency. "Come on out to HeHe on Sunday," they said. "Everyone's welcome."

We had heard of the small rodeo grounds and wooded camping place beside the Warm Springs River there but had never driven off the main highway to see them. By this time, Bill was old enough to be in charge for a few hours, so Bud and I drove out in the early evening. We could hear the throb of the big dance drum as we entered the grounds. Daylight was fading. When we went into what appeared to be a dark building, we found the place full of people seated on bleachers along two sides and standing everywhere. It was our first visit to a longhouse. I was nervous as, I suppose, was Bud. Dancers in full regalia filled the center of the room. By the time my eyes adjusted to the low light, Freda and Romagene were at my side. Leaving Bud to fend for himself, I followed them through the crowd and climbed up on the bleachers to squeeze in next to them.

---

*HeHe is a Chinook Jargon word for laughter, "where the good spirits or He-Hes abound." See Shane and Len, *Historical Map*.

"Where are the huckleberries?" I asked, looking around this new place. They laughed, explaining that the feast itself had been held at midday following the Wáashat service.

"We celebrated Friday night and Saturday," Freda said. "This is the last night." It was more of an event than I had imagined. No wonder people had been talking about it for weeks. "Now everyone can go out and pick berries," Romagene said.

I must have looked puzzled. They explained that after the people thank the Creator at each of these seasonal first food feasts they are free to fish for salmon or dig roots or gather berries for their winter's supply, depending on the season. Through the years that followed, I began to realize the importance of these foods to the Columbia River peoples. They not only provided subsistence, but the ceremonies themselves—

Warm Springs tribal councilman Sam Wewa on a timber tour in the reservation backcountry in about 1962.

giving thanks to the Creator for the gift of the natural abundance of the land—contributed to the well-being of the people both socially and spiritually.

Some of the women at HeHe Longhouse that night were wearing the distinctive wing dresses that I first noticed on older women on the Colville Reservation. I could tell that there were two garments—an overdress with short, open sleeves made in a plain or printed fabric and an underdress with sleeves covering the arms to the wrists in a contrasting fabric.

By the following spring, I was so curious about these dresses that I asked my friend Mary Ann Arthur if she would help me make one. Mary Ann delivered our Portland *Oregonian* newspaper and often stopped by after completing her route when our children were in school. Our visits on the sunny glassed-in porch where I sewed or did other work were high points in my days. We talked about the usual things—our children, the families we'd grown up in, reservation goings-on, and life in general. "All right," she said, with no hesitation. "We'll talk about it next time."

Mary Ann came by a few days later. I didn't see any dress pattern in her hands, but I had pencil and paper ready and a tape measure. I figured she would have to measure me to tell me how much material to buy. "Lie down on the floor," she said.

Puzzled but willing, I stretched out on the rug and she walked around me, measuring with her eyes. "It'll take about four yards for each part." As the mother of daughters, she must have made such dresses many times but never one so long, I realized. She told me to pick out a plain cotton fabric and a print that would look nice with it. I had forgotten that I'd be making two dresses—the wing-sleeved dress itself and the long-sleeved underdress. At Hatfield's store in Madras, I found a plain light blue cotton and a sprigged print that looked like those I'd seen Indian women wear.

In a few days, Mary Ann appeared on my porch. Pulling the print material out of my Hatfield sack, she took a packet of pins from the drawer of my sewing machine and carried the cloth into the living room. Four yards was a great deal of fabric. She opened it out lengthwise on the floor, where it nearly reached the door to the kitchen.

"Now, lie down beside it," she said, "with your feet here," pointing at one end of the cloth. She worked around me, placing pins in the cloth as needed. I stood as she cut off the extra yardage that would make the wings and gussets. Except for the lying down, the process was much like my mother's dressmaker draping and pinning my wedding dress.

When Euro-American traders first arrived on the Plateau early in the nineteenth century, Native women welcomed the new yard goods, but they had to figure out how to create from a rectangular length of fabric the comfortable shape of the traditional dress made from two hides of antelope or deer. The wings and gussets compensated for the extra width offered at shoulder and hem by the animals' upper legs.*

True to my nature and training, and to her amusement, I had to sketch out on paper the pattern and instructions for assembling the dress before I could begin to sew it together. The underdress was next, the only difference being the longer sleeves that would be gathered at the wrist much like the dresses worn by white pioneer women in the nineteenth century.

When Mary Ann came to see the finished dress, she brought a gift, a piece of Indian celery she had picked near Simnasho. It had a stiff stalk, thinner than a celery plant, and an airy blossom and tasted just like its namesake. This first fresh greenery, known as *chum-si,* she said, was especially welcome after a long winter eating stored foods.

---

*In pre-reservation days, dresses were made from two hides attached at the shoulders with the tuft of hair from the tails folded to the outside at the center of the neckline. This formed a decorative trim as it acknowledged the animals whose hides warmed the wearer. Later, this tuft was outlined with beads in a diamond or triangular form. When trade cloth became available, the maker would work the beaded diamond or triangle at the center of the neckline of a cloth dress, front and back, to honor this important feature of the original garments. Many traditionalists include this detail on beaded dresses made for ceremonial and celebratory occasions today.

When I made that first wing dress, I had no expectation of wearing it. I simply wanted to understand a garment that I had first seen older women wearing on the Colville Reservation. It was not until the early 1970s on the Yakama Reservation when I felt I could part with it. When Julia Sohappy's family brought her "out of dark clothes" a year after the death of her husband Frank, she asked Bud and me to come to her home. This ancient ceremony marked a new beginning for the widow. Family and friends brought brighter clothing and new household goods to replace the old and drab she had been given at the time of the funeral. The wing dress was the only thing from my own hands that seemed an appropriate gift. I hoped it carried the joy of the day of its making.

I have long since learned that there are many ways to make a Plateau-style wing dress. To help this memory along, I examined dresses given to me on the Yakama Reservation by Elsie WakWak and the Sohappy family. I studied notes from Julia and her daughter Laritta Yallup, as well as from Theresa Sampson, Esther Wilkinson, and Mary Cloud. I have a set of miniature pattern pieces cut for me by Rosalie Bassett. All of these have slight differences but result in essentially the same garment. All use the fabric with impressive efficiency.

Many years after my sewing session with Mary Ann, when we both were grandmothers, I saw her wearing the traditional dress. I asked if she had learned the skill from her mother. "Oh, no," she laughed. "When you asked me that day, I had to go to Caroline."

Caroline Tohet had grown up in a family well versed in traditional ways. In the 1950s, when we first moved to the West, two new federal policies interfered with the transmission of cultural knowledge. The first was the relocation program, which moved Indians to cities, away from their family elders. This coincided with the second policy, termination of the federal trust relationship with some tribes.

The Warm Springs and the Colville reservations were not "terminated." It was a time of great uncertainty for Indians everywhere, however, when they realized that the United States was preparing to abrogate the terms of treaties that the tribes had been told would hold "as long as the mountain stands and the river flows." As in the days when children were sent off to boarding schools, many families did not or were not able to carry on the traditional teaching. By the 1960s, when the threat of termination ended, it was too late for many tribal peoples to recapture the old knowledge. Caroline Tohet was one of the Warm Springs women whose role it became to retain and pass along knowledge that was slipping away. Thanks to these "keepers of wisdom," the traditional arts experienced a revival in the last quarter of the twentieth century that continues today.[6]

I treasure a photo that Mary Ann brought to me in 1987. Seated between grandsons Taylor and Christopher, she is dressed, as any proper grandmother should be, in a wing dress. The lavender underdress sleeve picks up a color in the print, as does the blue of her headscarf tied above two eagle fluffs tucked into one braid at the back, signifying a married woman. She wears an embroidered shawl over one shoulder and across her lap, where a beaded handbag lies decorated with the portrait of a horse. The boys are standing, dressed in calico shirts decorated with satin ribbons. These handsome shirts came into fashion for Plateau males sometime after 1970, possibly inspired by the long-established ribbon-work tradition of the Great Lakes peoples.

The first wing dress that I could examine closely was worn by a doll. Kitty had wanted a small cradleboard made like those carried by Warm Springs mothers. One of the first women we had met when we arrived in Warm Springs was Alice Florendo at Macy's store. Each day when we picked up our mail, Alice visited with us, making the children feel especially welcome. I suggested that we could ask Mrs. Florendo about a cradleboard. We walked over to the store. "Yes," Alice said, "I could make that for you." Kitty told her she had six dollars. "Is that enough?" Alice said it was.

Soon the board was ready, and we returned to Macy's, Kitty with money in hand. Alice brought out a perfect replica of the cradleboards we had seen in use. The bow that arches out to protect a baby's head was covered with seed beads; short strings of larger "pony" beads hung from this to entertain the infant. The cover and hood were in bright pink corduroy edged up the front in scalloped buckskin and with buckskin lacings. Made in a size that would hold a small puppy, we were astonished to see that it held a doll. This was more than Kitty had hoped for.

"I figured," Alice said, "that for six dollars I would make a doll baby, too." Kitty beamed. As we looked closer, we could see that there was something odd about the baby whose small face peeked out above the lacings. She wore an old lady's silk bandana. Alice laughed. Unlacing the doll from the board she said, "I forgot that babies have big heads." Lifting out the doll, she added, "This is the baby's *cuthla*."*

That was exactly what the doll looked like—dressed in a wing dress in dark blue striped cotton, ribbons at her shoulders, the pink sleeves of her underdress peeking out at her wrists. She wore plain high-topped buckskin moccasins and a choker of beads around her neck. Her body was made entirely of velvety smoked buckskin. The hand-drawn face had the placid look of the elders we saw going into the agency office. Kitty could not have been happier with the cradleboard—and the new doll. She named her Cecelia for our friend Mrs. Peo.

Cuthla means maternal grandmother.

Occasionally we saw wing dresses at Sunday services at the Warm Springs Presbyterian mission church, where I joined the choir. There I met Louis Pitt, a tribal member of Wasco descent with an exceptional tenor voice. It was an important friendship for me. His gentle explanations of his peoples' customs and expectations helped me understand more about those we were living among and seeing every day.

An important lesson came one day when I heard a great mournful sound swelling up from a stake truck that rumbled past our house. I ran to the door to see women in dark clothes on benches in the back, weaving back and forth and wailing. At choir practice that night, I asked Louis Pitt about it. He explained that they were mourners following the hearse from a funeral that day at the Shaker church.* They were going to the burial in a tribal cemetery.

"It isn't done every time anymore," he said. "You're privileged to see it."

I agreed. There had been a kind of beauty to it, a reality. I could not have expressed my grief in that way in the car that followed the hearse carrying my father's body to the cemetery. It might have helped.

The first funeral I took part in as a choir member at Warm Springs was for a child, a girl about eleven years old whom I knew only as one of several sisters who walked past our house to school. She had fallen from the back of a pickup, not an unusual place for a child to ride at that time. As I sat with the choir facing the congregation across the flower-covered casket, I tried to steer my mind away from the pain of her parents and siblings. How could they bear to be here? At the end of the service, the congregation filed past the open casket. I wondered if I could slip down the hall when it was the choir's turn to follow, but that did not seem right. My memory of the black-haired child in a ruffled yellow dress lingers today.

Louis Pitt offered me a ride to the cemetery, and when I asked what would be expected of us, he sensed my discomfort. "Just watch me," he said, "and follow the women."

We walked across the rocky hillside to the place where the grave lay open, a mound of dirt piled at its foot. As we approached the assembled people, Louis gestured for me to stand over with the women. He joined the men. When it was time for the music, he nodded and our small choir gathered near the grave to sing, led by his true clear voice. After the song, I returned with the women to our place. Several ministers spoke, Presbyterian, Baptist, and Nazarene, as well as Shaker and Wáashat

*The Shaker church at Warm Springs is one of several Native congregations that formed after John Slocum of the Squaxin band at Mud Bay, Washington, established the religion in 1881. There is no connection between the Indian Shaker Church and the Shaker religion of the eastern United States.

leaders. I knew little about the Shakers or the Wáashat, and I thought it unusual that so many would take part in the ceremony.

After all of the speakers and a Wáashat song, the men filed along to the foot of the grave, where each in turn took a handful of earth from the shovel held out to them and tossed it gently onto the casket. They returned along the other side to their places.

I followed with the women, doing the same. I had been a child the only other time I witnessed such a personal gesture of farewell. At my Uncle Rob's funeral in Minnesota, each member of his Masonic Lodge had plucked a sprig of evergreen from his lapel and tossed it into the grave. It had seemed very strange to me then. But somehow taking part in this act felt natural, allowing each of us a chance to bid farewell to this child.

We stood silently as men picked up shovels and filled the grave, leaving a long smooth mound where people laid the flowers they had carried from the church. After a final prayer, we left the graveyard. I thought back to my father's funeral, where we had left the cemetery with his grave still open. I returned to the car on this basalt-pebbled hillside above Warm Springs Agency with a sad sense of completion but a new sense of peace.

Fitting In

On the Colville Reservation, the tribal members I knew were those who worked at the agency or were active in the tribal celebrations or the school PTA. At Warm Springs, we lived *in* the community—met at the store, at 4-H and Cub Scout events, at PTA movies and carnivals, Little League games, and Extension Service activities. Whenever someone new sat by me in a group, I would muster up my courage and mention my name. "I know," they would reply and would talk with me but rarely give their names. Once I understood that there was little need for people to introduce themselves in a place where everybody knew everyone, I learned to ask.

There was no "town" basketball team, but in this job Bud would not have the time or energy for all that travel anyway. He did discover that a group of young Warm Springers played volleyball every Tuesday night at the school gym, and they welcomed us both. It proved to be great fun—and exercise. They were good sports and good players, and it didn't matter what I did wrong. Someone was always there to keep the ball in the air. I was never very graceful and not much of an athlete, and there was only one other time in my life when I enjoyed team sports so much. That was a few years later when we returned to the Washington, D.C., area. Bud signed us up for a BIA bowling group that met near our home in northern Virginia. There, again, the Indians' enjoyment of the game and the complete acceptance of all skill levels made me look forward to the nights. Best of all, my consistently low scores and lack of handicap gave my team of hotshots an advantage, something I never quite figured out.

When fall came in 1961, a year and a half after we arrived in Warm Springs, the Bureau of Indian Affairs with the concurrence of the tribal council agreed to consolidate the boarding school with the county school district. We were much relieved that our children would be attending school—by now in the second, fourth, and sixth grades—in their home community. What nature had failed to do, the school system rectified. Our children, born in 1951, 1952, and 1953, at last were two years apart. We soon became acquainted with many more Warm Springs families, as almost everyone on the reservation showed up for activities held at the school.

Cascades Cook 4-H Club: (from left) Judy Kalama, Kitty Schlick, Bernyce Courtney, Geraldine Smith, Kathy Short, Delores Galbraith, Sharon Miller, Annie Smith, Pinky Courtney, Teresa Switzler (missing: Coy Stimpson).

There was an active 4-H cattle club at Warm Springs, and one of Ivy Hilty's goals was to revitalize the 4-H home economics program on the reservation. I agreed to take on an after-school foods and nutrition group. To my surprise, all three children wanted to learn to cook, and we set up three separate clubs that met on successive days after school. On Tuesdays, Kitty and nine other girls about her age trooped into our small living room. The Cascade Cooks were Adeline and Vivian Arthur, Pinky and Bernyce Courtney, Judy Kalama, Sharon Miller, Geraldine Smith, and Theresa Switzler from Warm Springs families. Kathy Short, Annie Smith, and Coy Stimpson were daughters of non-Indian BIA employees.

At each meeting, we had a cooking lesson. If it was a baked product, the girls took turns setting the oven temperature (exactly), measuring ingredients (carefully), stirring (gently), and pouring batter into the pan (without licking fingers). The reward came when we took the day's project out of the oven. The girls crowded into chairs around the table in the kitchen window for the taste test.

One of my goals was that these youngsters would be able to go anywhere to eat and feel comfortable. Although many had learned at home and at the longhouses such courtesies as waiting until all were served before beginning to eat, they were patient with me about other lessons in table manners. I tried to give them the tips that my mother had passed along to me. Possibly a few were useful, but in retrospect the most useless was the lesson on finger bowls that my mother had given me when I was twelve before a visit to her socialite aunt in Chicago. The irrelevance of the lesson didn't appear to bother anyone, and the girls treated it as a party game.

Our family adopted one relaxed policy as a result of a Cascade Cooks meeting. As long as the members of the group knew the basics of biscuits and muffins and other products they would enter in the Jefferson County fair, I was free to elaborate on the food preparation lessons in the project book. Next to a 4-H fresh lemon pudding, their favorite was huckleberry buckle adapted from a blueberry recipe I had found in *Sunset* magazine.

My lecture on manners for the huckleberry lesson probably had been a reminder to put their napkins in their laps and to use them on hands and face. After Pinky Courtney polished off her huckleberry buckle, she picked up her plate and licked it clean. I gasped. It was something I had always wanted to do, but never dared try. As the girls turned to see what had startled me, I thought, "That's wonderful applause for a cook!"

"Okay," I said, hoping I hadn't embarrassed Pinky. "We have a new manners rule. What is a food that's so good that we are forced to lick our plates?" They began to giggle, eyeing the purple marks on their dishes. "Yes," I said. "Huckleberries." And we all picked up our plates and licked them clean. I can't speak for the families of these girls, but at our house no sign of a huckleberry was ever left unlicked on a plate again.

Joe Schlick, Ronnie Chestnut, Mark Jackson, and Wayne Smith—members of Wednesday afternoon's World's Greatest Chefs—chose outdoor cooking for their project. Our most successful lesson, the amazing hobo stove, was an upside-down gallon can with holes punched with a wedge can opener in one side near the top for a chimney.[7] The unopened end was the cooking surface. A three-inch door cut at the bottom on the opposite side gave access for the "buddy burner," an empty tuna can filled with tightly rolled newspaper strips and candle wax. With great excitement, the nine-year-olds set up their stoves in the driveway beside our house and cooked bacon and eggs. Forty years later, Joe, now a restaurateur, can describe every step of making that stove.

Bill and three junior high classmates—Delores Galbraith, Diana Richardson, and Nicea Stimpson—met on Thursday afternoons as the Cascade Chefs. No one ever missed a meeting. I never knew whether to lay the club's success to the cooking or the attraction for him of being in the same room with three girls, or for them, with the boy. Many years later, Nicea told me it was the latter.

We had known of the Warm Springs Boy Scouts because of the spectacular Indian dance performances they presented all over the Pacific Northwest. These had begun under the leadership of Irving Shepard, an Alaska Native, when he was boys' advisor at the Warm Springs Boarding School.

When asked if he would take a turn as Cub Scoutmaster for the younger boys, Bud agreed. It was his first opportunity to participate in an activity that would serve his sons, and the once-a-month pack meetings took little time. He volunteered me as den mother, which meant weekly Cub Scout meetings at our house. Tony Suppah, a gentle Boy Scout assigned to me as den chief, kept the boys in line. My memories are of boys tromping down the basement stairs to our makeshift recreation room followed by a lively hour of blue and gold in motion.

Many years later, a well-known Warm Springs family dance group came to the Maryhill Museum of Art to perform during our museum week for schoolchildren.* When I heard one of the drummers identified as "Big Rat" Suppah, I introducing myself and asked if he was related to Tony. "I am Tony," he said, shaking my hand. "I was your den chief at Warm Springs." The man who performed a spectacular hoop dance that day turned out to be Joe Tuckta, a classmate of Kitty's and one of my cubs. Later, at a Portland Art Museum opening, Olney Patt Jr. introduced me to his associates as his den mother. By this time, the boy I knew as Junior Patt had become executive director of the Columbia River Inter-Tribal Fish Commission.

When Little League began at Warm Springs, Joe went with Bill to sign up for the Warm Springs Veterans of Foreign Wars Post team. Three laid-back men were the volunteer coaches—tribal members Elmer "Sheriff" Quinn and Milan Smith and James Selam, a Yakama whose children were enrolled at Warm Springs. From that time on, our spring and summer life adapted to the schedule of baseball practice and games. Opponents were the highly motivated Papooses, also from Warm Springs, and teams from around Jefferson County.

The boys loved the games, except for one notable contest with a farm community southeast of Madras, one of the few Bud and I missed. When the boys banged into the house after that game, we knew we should have been there. Bill came in first, furious with Joe for catching a Warm Springs player's fly ball. "He put Lewis out!" he said, "He caught his home run." We heard the story. Culver had been short two players, and Warm Springs had given them Joe Schlick and another rookie, know-

---

*Maryhill Museum of Art is on the Columbia River near Goldendale, Washington.

ing they wouldn't do any damage. "And the ball came right to me!" Joe said. When I see James Selam today, the coach recalls that great catch that lost the game for Warm Springs. "Joe was so proud of himself," he chuckles, "and Bill was so mad."

At a game at Metolius, a community west of Madras, I sat with parents and other supporters along small bleachers at the edge of the field, our little group just down the benches from the home rooters. We were all a noisy bunch, cheering on our boys. But each time the umpire—Si Katchia from Warm Springs for this game—made a call they didn't like, a couple of Metolius mothers filled the air with scathing abuse. For a while, Si ignored them. Finally, he stopped the game, turned, and walked slowly toward

Willard Suppah and Lucille Geary Owl dancing at the Boy Scout carnival in December 1961.

the bleachers. As the place fell quiet, he gave the hecklers a long steady look. In Little League, the players were to learn sportsmanship; that look was his only reprimand. Riled by the disapproval, one of the women stood up, her words clear in the stillness, and shouted: "Go take a bath!" I sucked in my breath. As Si turned and walked back to his spot, I turned to Prosanna (Prunie) Katchia, Si's wife and the mother one of my Cub Scouts who also was a teammate. "Did you hear what she said?" I asked.

"Ignore her," she told me. "We hear that all the time."

The incident shocked me. The taunt was blatant racism, and I had never witnessed anything so personal and direct. Alice Florendo had told me earlier of hiding under the blankets as a small child when her grandfather's wagon passed through Madras on their way to Prineville for supplies. "People yelled at us sometimes," she said, "and called us names." She smiled, but I knew it hurt to remember. "If we did stop in Madras, the clerks followed us around to see that we didn't steal anything."

"And in Prineville?" I asked.

"Indians were treated better," she said. "They were glad to have our business there."

"But your James," I said, "is in Bill's class at Madras."

"Yes," she agreed. "The town has changed, and we wanted him to learn to get along in the outside world." She paused, as if deciding whether to say more then added with a tone of wistfulness, "But attitudes die hard."

From the time Bud and I came to the Colville Reservation as newlyweds, we had never been treated with anything but kindness. The only reminder at Warm Springs that I was "different" came when I picked up the phone and found our multi-party line in use. I apologized and hung up but not before I heard a boy hiss, "*Báshtan!*" in great disgust.* Later, I asked Mary Ann what that meant. "White man," she said, and gave a little laugh.

True, I thought, I am *Báshtan*. It was time I learned that word. I began to wonder if by coming here we were subjecting our children to pain because they were

One of many colorful family floats that passed the Schlick house in the Fourth of July parade.

white. All I could do was hope that this place offered them, as it did to Bud and me, a rich and comfortable place to be. In a school of 347 children, only 17 were non-Indian. Our three faced the normal challenges of school life, but as far as I know, incidents stemming from the fact that they were different arose only twice, and they, too, were understandable.

The first happened the day Bill came home excited about getting a calf to raise for 4-H. One of his friends was in the cattle club and told him to sign up. "Joe Warner's the leader," Bill said. Bud stopped him. "The tribe buys the calves. It's part of the BIA range program and open only to tribal members."

"Oh!" Bill said, "I guess I won't then."

Kitty figured in the other incident. I was surprised when she marched into the kitchen after the school awards assembly fuming about her classmate, Junior Patt. I had gone up to the school for the assembly but hadn't noticed anything disturbing. "What did Junior do to you?" I asked.

She slid into the chair by the window. "He won the award for the best essay on patriotism!" she complained.

"Well, honey," I said. "I heard him read that essay. It was great."

"Mine was better."

---

*Báshtan derives from "Boston Man," the Chinook Jargon word for Americans. On the Yakama Reservation, the word sounds more like "Pushtan."

"Okay, you can read it to us tonight," I said. "But you knew this was a tribal award . . . for a Warm Springs student's work."

"Oh, I know that," she said. "I just liked mine better."

In March 1962, the National Congress of Parents and Teachers held its annual convention in Portland. When Prunie Katchia made her report at our next Warm Springs PTA meeting, she rubbed her forearm with her other hand as she spoke. This was unusual. Prunie, like most tribal leaders, was an excellent speaker who chose her words carefully and used few hand movements. When she finished speaking, someone asked if she had injured her arm.

"Oh, no," she smiled, suddenly aware of what she had been doing. "Talking about those meetings made me remember something." She described how a few people at the convention had touched her arm "as if they wanted to know what my Indian skin felt like." I was struck by her generosity. What she might have taken as an intrusion she had accepted as the simple reaching out by one human to learn about another.

The Fourth of July was a day when the entire community of Warm Springs turned out—from early morning, when agency branches, churches, organizations, businesses, and families readied their entries for the much-anticipated parade, to late evening when it was dark enough to show off an amazing fireworks display.

Bud left for the agency garage, where the forestry crew and the roads department brought out the big equipment for the parade. The boys went with him to join their friends who would ride in the trucks and pumpers, front-end loaders, and other rigs. Girls, to Kitty's never-forgotten disgust, were not invited. "It's the same thing," she said, "as me not being able to win that essay contest." To be excluded, whatever the reason, seemed unfair to her.

By ten o'clock, the rest of us had lined up with chairs and blankets on the curbsides in front of the houses that faced the campus to wait for the drumbeat that accompanied the color guard's flag-carriers. The parade route led around the square, past the office, turned before Macy's store, and descended the hill to the baseball grounds along Shitike Creek below.

It was like no parade I had seen before—walkers and horseback riders and their mounts in full beaded regalia, dressed-up pets, kids on bikes and trikes and pulling their dogs in wagons, families on cars draped with blankets and shawls, trucks where elders sat in style on chairs and benches. Bill waved from his perch high on a huge bulldozer atop a long lowboy and Joe from the back of a fire truck.

When the last float had passed, we picked up our chairs and, like the children of Hamelin behind the Pied Piper, followed it down to the ball field below the hill for the barbecue. The yellowed "Schedule of Events, July 4, 1960" that lies before me as I write this lists "12:00 Noon . . . Lunch (Bring Your Own)." (By the next year, the sponsoring Warm Springs Recreation Committee was serving an all-you-can-eat barbecue.) In the early afternoon, the games began. For those not playing baseball, there were twenty-six other games—for every age and with prizes for all winners. There were penny and toy scrambles for the toddlers; boys' and girls' sack races; one-, two-, and three-legged races; orange (under the chin) relays; and a tug-of-war for the men (with cigars for prizes). No child cried at losing; nobody took offense at shouted comments and jokes. The noisy competition ended with a series of cracker-eating contests for every age group, followed by the watermelon-eating contest. We laughed until we ached.

On the back of the dog-eared copy of the 1960 program are my penciled notes describing one of the elders: "Blanche Tohet, a beautiful woman." We had lived at Warm Springs only four months, and this was my first contact with many of the people. I sketched a high-topped moccasin with the lacings tied around the leggings, then noted that the wing dress in lavender matched the colors in her Russian-style head-scarf. I described Navajo turquoise jewelry, a long strand of beads, and her floral-beaded handbag. Her belt was covered with small blue beads and was tied in front with a strip of hide.

The games ended before sundown, and we trooped back up the hill and home, to carry chairs over to the rim beside the jail when darkness fell. I think of those hot nights with a feeling of contentment. Families perched at every overlook to watch the fireworks. Water trucks, we knew, sat in readiness near the staging area beyond the creek below. From the dark shadow of Warm Springs Mountain, great sighs of wonder rose as bursts of sparkling color lit up the ever-starry sky.

Into the Woods and Out

It was a nice change from our life in the Washington, D.C., suburbs to have Bud come home for lunch on the days when he was not in the woods or in Portland at the BIA area office. From our kitchen window I could watch him leave the office building and come up the walk to our back door. On one of those days, I was standing at the sink scrubbing carrots for salad when he approached the house holding something in his hand.

"I have a present for you," he said, coming into the kitchen, "from Alfred Smith." Smith was a Wasco rancher who lived out on Sidwalter Flat and the father of several of our volleyball teammates. Wrapped in a paper napkin was a black lump about the size of a shriveled-up hamburger patty. "What *is* it?" It smelled good, sort of smoky, and something else I couldn't identify. "It has a strange smell."

"It's barbecued bear. They build a fire in a pit, stones on top, then a layer of bear, layer of fir."

"Stop," I said. "Fur?"

"Smell it again." I did. It didn't smell like burned fur—something more familiar. "Look closely," he said. "What do you see on it?" I held it up to the light. "Needles. Fir needles!"

When the children came in, Bud told the story and divided the small piece of barbecued bear among us. I only wish I had known then about Meriwether Lewis eating the same food cooked by Nez Perce Indians in the same way. Lewis wrote in his expedition journal on May 14, 1806, "I taisted of this [bear] meat and found it much more tender than that which we had roasted or boiled, but the strong flavor of the pine distorted it for my palate."[8]

Lunch together was only one way life had changed for us with the move to Warm Springs Agency. In Washington, as a specialist in sustained-yield timber management, Bud had developed procedures and standards to provide the greatest possible cash return to Indian owners. Because of frequent contact with tribal representatives, his position description called for "a sympathetic understanding of the Indians' needs" as well as "good judgement and tact in relations with the public and the Indians." I was surprised not to find this advice repeated in his position description at Warm Springs, where BIA employees and their families had daily contact with tribal members. Sympathetic understanding and good judgment and tact were critical to every employee's success.

As forest manager, Bud's mission was focused on the land. The Confederated Tribes of the Warm Springs had entered into their first timber sales contract in 1942, and from that time on the standing forest became their major economic resource. Bud's responsibility was to see that it continued to provide for the tribes' economic and social benefit, as well as enhancing "water, fish, wildlife recreation, grazing, long range planning, fire prevention, presuppression and suppression." All of this was to be done by coordinating the forestry branch work with the tribal council and other BIA agency branches. The closeness of the community in school, workplace, and social life made such coordination possible. On a personal level, living in the community allowed our family to develop a greater understanding of Bud's job and a warm relationship with the people for whom he worked.

Through the years, Bud had hoped that young members of timber-owning tribes would become foresters to serve their own people. On a visit to Warm Springs in 2003, Joe and I stopped in to see Bob Macy who had taken over the family store after retiring as general manager of Warm Springs Forest Products Industries. I wanted to check on his father, who, with his mother, had been good friends.

"It's your dad's doing," Bob said to Joe, "that I went into forestry." He described a long night in the 1960s when he and Bud were working on a fire somewhere out on the reservation. Just out of high school, Bob had a summer job with forestry, and to his surprise Bud asked him what he planned to do with his life.

"Oh," Bob said, "I told him I was set to go down to Bend to take a mechanics course. I was pretty good with cars." I could predict Bud's reaction to that.

"He took that in," Bob said, "then suggested that I go on over to Corvallis and enroll in the forestry school. 'You're smart,' he told me, 'and the tribe needs you.' "

Bob grinned at Joe. "So that's what I did."

Summertime meant fire—and danger to the magnificent forest that covered the northern and western slopes of the reservation. Although it was the major economic resource, the forest had great social and spiritual significance to the people as well. Protecting it was a responsibility everyone at the agency took seriously. Located on the dry side of the Cascades, it was rare for a lightning storm to work its way through the mountains without at least one strike smoking up and alerting the lookouts.

When that happened, the radio in the bedroom hall in our house would begin to crackle. Then we would hear the calm, familiar voice of Zelma Smith on Eagle Butte or her sister Catherine Courtney on Shitike Butte or Adeline Miller on Sidwalter reporting a smoke to the dispatcher over in the forestry office.* When Bud was home, he would listen to the chatter as long as things went well. Terry Courtney, the fire control officer, and, later, Vic Sisson, had radios in their houses also. But in the night, if the calls sounded ominous, Bud would pull on his clothes and dash across the street to the office to be there if needed.

That radio was a constant and, usually, reassuring presence in our house. It was especially welcome when Bud was out on a fire and his "10-8"—the radio code for "in service, subject to call"—told us he was back in his pickup and heading home. If he returned from a fire late in the night, which happened many times, Bud would undress in the hall outside the bedroom, the sour pungent odor of his clothes an affront when we entered the hall in the morning. The only word I can think of that describes that smell is "fetid," and looking it up in *Webster's* I find it perfect: "akin to the Latin *fumus,* smoke."

---

*Over the years since, I have had many opportunities to see Catherine and Adeline. Zelma Smith, however, remained only a remembered voice to me until November 2003 at an exhibit of Native artists' views of Lewis and Clark at Maryhill Museum. Her niece, Wasco artist Pat Courtney Gold, was curator and brought Zelma to the closing ceremony. I identified myself as Bud Schlick's wife and told her that her voice checking in on the radio from Eagle Butte lookout started each summer day for me in the early 1960s. We discovered then that we were nearly the same age. "I liked Bud Schlick," she said. "He was a nice man." "Yes," I agreed, "he was."

Kitty, too, could hear the messages from her bedroom, and there were times when I wished the radio had been farther from her room. Late one night when the Simnasho police officer was on patrol in Warm Springs twenty miles from his home, his wife radioed him to report a prowler outside their house. She had arrived home and, seeing the stranger, locked the children in the car and ran into the house to make the report. We could hear the frustration in the young officer's voice as he raced for home, trying to give her advice.

Another time, about daybreak, we were awakened by a patrolman's call for an ambulance and police support on the highway just above the agency. From his voice, we could tell there was more to the emergency than he could report over the air and learned later in the day that it had been a brutal murder that affected a family we knew well.

Kitty was fascinated by the two-way radio, and, in an unusual way, the medium brought her closer to her father. From childhood, when he had brought the scratchy voices of the world into his bedroom with a homemade crystal set, Bud had wanted to go into amateur radio. No longer working until dark as at Colville or commuting into the District of Columbia, he had time at Warm Springs to build a Heathkit high-fidelity tuner. With the help of a new turntable and yards of wiring, he brought his favorite George Shearing records into our living room and bedroom and to his workbench corner of the basement.

With that finished he had moved on to ham radio equipment, took the exams, and was on the air. Through this process and in the years that followed in other houses, Kitty would sit with him and talk about her day or simply listen to "Hello, CQ, CQ, CQ. Hello, CQ. This is N7CLQ" and wait for the fish to bite. This, she told me later, took the place for her of playing catch or shooting baskets or hunting, the activities he shared with the boys.

Because of forest fires, we took no family vacations in the summertime. Bud was nervous about planning even a quick trip to the Oregon Coast for a break. The few times we did slip away, any relaxation gained evaporated when he saw thunderclouds piled up as we approached home. Fortunately, we did not need to leave the reservation for recreation. At work, Bud had scoped out places that we all might enjoy—picnics among wildflowers under the Ponderosa pines along Tenino Creek; camping at Trout Lake, a popular fishing place for the Warm Springs people at the headwaters of Mill Creek; and Breitenbush Lake, a gorgeous setting just north of Mt. Jefferson.

The children had free run on the campus and nearby, within limits. There was a fine swimming hole not far up Shitike Creek from the agency that families enjoyed and the old concrete pool at the Hot Springs ten miles into the red hills to the north

Forest Manager W.T. Schlick; J.P. Kinney, first chief of the BIA branch of forestry; and Superintendent Allan Galbraith, with Mt. Jefferson in the background.

that later became Kah-Nee-Ta Resort was always available. Even warm water is refreshing in the hot, dry summers of central Oregon.

The road to Hot Springs was dusty and rough. The small resort had been built in the late 1920s on one of the few tracts of nontrust (non-Indian owned) land on the Warm Springs Reservation. As the children grew older, they rode bikes to the Hot Springs pool to swim—although the gravel road was long, hot, and brutal on bicycle tires and steep on the return trip.

Our favorite Christmas Day activity was to drive across the snowy reservation to the Hot Springs, rush into the open-air dressing booths, peel off winter clothes, climb into swimsuits, and then scurry across the concrete and into the delicious waters that give the reservation its name. The major trial was leaving frozen footprints across the deck as we headed back to dress. By the time we returned with grandchildren to relive the Christmas custom, the tribes had purchased the land and built Kah-Nee-Ta Resort with a fine new pool and tiled and heated dressing rooms.

The swimming hole on Shitike Creek was a perfect place to cool off after a hot day, where children could play on the sandy shore of the creek just above where we swam. Below, large rocks forced the water into a short twisting channel that gave the swimmers a chute-like ride that ended in a stretch of calm water. One summer evening, Kitty had waded across the stream below this place and was heading back along the higher rock on the other side to watch the swimmers pass through the chute. We heard her scream, then stand immobile, arms in the air, her eyes fixed on a rock beside her path.

"Daddy," she cried, her voice shrill, terrified. "A snake!"

Before she said the word, Bud was running down the shore. He jumped across and raced to where she stood, grabbed a stout stick, and struck the coiled rattler with a great "thwack." He continued to hit at it, adrenaline pumping.

"Stop, Daddy," she grabbed his arm. "It's dead now."

He picked up the shaking child and carried her back across the creek, his face white. It was then that I understood with what fury he had dispatched those timber rattlers on the Colville Reservation. Their rattles lie as trophies in a box on my coffee table today.

The Warm Springs tribes in those years gave BIA employees permission to hunt deer on the reservation in season. Bud and Allan Galbraith had enjoyed hunting together a decade before on the Colville and were glad for the chance to try it again. By the last day of the season, however, they had had no success and headed toward the rugged Mutton Mountain country above the Deschutes River.* Finding what looked like a good spot, Allan decided to try the ridge and, turning to Bud, said: "If I chase one down, shoot it for me." Bud said okay and headed off the other way, soon spotting a nice buck at the edge of a clearing. Just after he dropped it, another came bouncing down through the hillside brush. "Well," Bud thought as he raised his rifle, "this is good luck," and shot it for Allan. "Now we've got our limit." In the meantime, up on the hill, Allan's approach flushed out a pair of bucks. He shot, hitting one, and the other spooked and headed down the hill.

The shock came when Allan appeared carrying a buck and found Bud standing over two dead deer. Both men, scrupulous since their late teens about observing rules, were stunned. "We were pretty quiet about it," Allan recalled when I asked about it recently, "except in family gatherings." Living where all parents worked for the same employer, our children fortunately had learned to be discrete about what they over-heard at home. "The statute of limitations must have run out by now," he said.

During the fall after we arrived at Warm Springs, Bud and Allan spotted the tracks of a black bear in the woods. Thinking they might like to go after bear, the men applied for a tribal permit. But no furry rug decorates my house today. The only trophy from that brainstorm is a framed permit dated October 7, 1960, that hung over Bud's desk for many years:

> TO WHOM IT MAY CONCERN: This is to advise that William T. Schlick, Supervisory Forester, Warm Springs Agency has been granted permission by the Tribal Council to hunt bear during 1960 within the boundaries of the Warm Springs Reservation. Very truly yours,
>
> Vernon Jackson, Secretary-Treasurer

---

*The Mutton Mountains were named for the big horn sheep that lived in the area. The name was in use before 1855. See Shane and Leno, *Historical Map.*

When we lived in Virginia, Bud had continued the target rifle competition that he had enjoyed in Coulee Dam. After attending a few gun club meetings in Madras, however, he found his evenings tied up with work and community activities at Warm Springs and gave it up. I had been wishing for one of the new tape recorders to capture the voices of some of the women I was meeting on the reservation. To my surprise, he sold his fine rifle and bought a portable Sony reel-to-reel tape recorder for me for Christmas.

I asked Mae John Queahpama from Simnasho and her sister Matilda Mitchell if they would be willing to be taped. When they agreed, we set the date. Dressed in wing dresses with silk bandanas tied over their hair, they sat on the sofa in our living room, the recorder on the coffee table in front of them, with me on a facing chair. I asked questions, and they talked. They sang—the words unfamiliar, the course of the melody completely new to me. They tapped the table to provide the drumbeat.

"That song is from a long time ago," Mae said at the end. "I think it was how the religion started. It was sent from God." She paused. "Because we're Indians, we have one language, Priest Rapids, Yakama, and us. We talk one language, we understand one another. Priest Rapids, that's where our grandfather used to go." There was one man, she explained, who died, then returned to tell the Wanapum people at Priest Rapids about God who created heaven and earth. "Everything," she said, in her soft, certain voice. "The rivers where he put salmon for the Indian people. Roots would grow wild, without cultivation."

"Wanapum?" I asked Mae. The name was new to me.

"That's where it comes from," she said. "Just a tribe—of Priest Rapids Indians." Then she added, "Some kind of half moon in the rock right in the island there. That's where this happened. That's where the dam was built.* It's covered up now. So we have to worship," she said. "Seven of these round drums. We worship with that."

"Does the religion have a name?" I asked.

"Same religion as Wáashat," she said. "Has no kind of name. Just praising to God."**

"These songs?" I asked.

"They're just like hymns, in praise," Mae said. "My people were great worshipers; they taught people to worship one God."

I've attended many Wáashat services in the years since that day. The songs, the ritual, the words spoken—I could not understand most of them—have brought comfort and filled me with the peacefulness I felt as a child in our brick church in Iowa. I thank the Queahpama sisters for their gentle introduction.

---

*Priest Rapids Dam is on the Columbia River about sixty miles east of Yakima, Washington.

**Wáashat, the Sahaptin word for worship or "Indian religion" also means dance.

Several of their songs were sung, I was told, when Indian people gather around a campfire late on a summer night to sing courting songs and other favorites. As the two women sang along in "Indian," as they described their Sahaptin language, all of a sudden they would break into English. It startled me to hear "Come up and see me so-o-ometime, come up to see me when I'm alone" or "Take me out in your one-eyed Ford." Their laughter rang out at the end of the song. When we began to talk about Indian foods, I mentioned the baked moss that Sam Sturgis had shown us at Colville. "Oh Sam," they said. "His wife is our first cousin." It pleased me to think we had mutual friends. It was a lovely afternoon.*

One evening, Mae John called on us and brought her sisters Nettie Shawaway, who was visiting from the Yakama Reservation, and Sylvia Sahme, mother of one of "my" Cub Scouts. Our family gathered around for a memorable visit. Bud asked Nettie if she liked living in Washington. "Yes," she told him in her high sweet voice, "but I miss the juneepers and the sagebrushes."**

"Yes," I say today when I talk about Warm Springs. "I miss the juneepers and the sagebrushes."

Moving and Shaking

Three distinct groups form the Confederated Tribes of the Warm Springs Reservation of Oregon: the Warm Springs, Wascos, and Paiutes. Each has its own language and hereditary chief.‡ Those known as Warm Springs—the Tygh, Tenino, Wyam, and John Day Indians—speak a form of the Sahaptin language. The Chinookan-speaking Wascos had been their closest neighbors to the west, living from just above The Dalles west to the Cascades of the Columbia and beyond.

The United States government, in the June 25, 1855, treaty with the Confederated Tribes and Bands of Middle Oregon, removed the Warm Springs and Wascos nearly a hundred miles to the south of their ancestral homes along the Columbia River and its tributaries. This left the river open for growing commercial traffic without threat of Native interference. By treaty, the Warm Springs people retained the right to fish in their "usual and accustomed places." Hoping to settle in Tygh Valley, a wintering

---

*The tape and recorder are in the archives at The Museum at Warm Springs, Warm Springs, Oregon.

**Nettie Queahpama Shawaway, widow of Yakama leader Alba Shawaway, returned to the junipers and sagebrush at Simnasho for her final years among her sisters and their families. A much-revered tribal elder, she died on October 20, 2003, as this chapter was being written. She was 102 years old.

‡Nathan Heath was Warm Springs chief and Raymond Johnson was Paiute chief during our years there. Wasco chief Nelson Wallulatum continues to serve today.

place for one of their groups that was closer to the Columbia, they accepted the present reservation farther south "under threats and intimidation." Loss of the abundant life that fishing had provided the river people for at least ten thousand years caused great hardship.* In 1879, the Warm Springs agreed to the settlement of over a hundred Paiute U.S. Army prisoners in the Seekseequa area on the south end of the reservation. A Shoshonean people, they spoke a Uto-Aztecan language related to that of the Hopi in the U.S. Southwest and the Aztecs of Mexico. Paiute bands had a long history of intermittent raids on the River People of the Columbia. The raids had increased with the Wasco and Warm Springs move to the new reservation, an area traditionally used by the Paiutes. The raids ended with the Paiute treaty with the U.S. government in 1868. Cynthia Stowell writes that sharing the reservation with former enemies was "an uneasy marriage at first," but the resident tribes extended all rights and privileges to them to form the Confederated Tribes of the Warm Springs Reservation of Oregon.[9]

The governing tribal council on the Warm Springs includes the chief of each tribe, who serves for life, and eight members elected for three-year terms from reservation districts. When we arrived, Vernon Jackson was the secretary-treasurer for the Warm Springs Tribe. The son of a longtime tribal leader, Jackson was sent to college by the tribes to prepare for this newly established position. Later, his son Charles Jackson held the same office from 1998 to 2004. The Bureau of Indian Affairs superintendent on the reservation, the position held by Allan Galbraith when we were at Warm Springs, is responsible for carrying out the federal government's role as trustee. Since the Indian Self-Determination Act of 1975, however, the BIA role is much reduced.

Bud met regularly with the tribal council on forestry matters. My only meeting with that body came two years later in the company of tribal members Mary Ann Arthur, Lizzie Rhoan, and Aridonna Seyler. That meeting led to action important to the success of our PTA's plan for starting a kindergarten at Warm Springs, a project that led in 1992 to the opening of the modern Early Childhood Center that provides services from infant care through after-school programs.

Work toward the local kindergarten began in the spring of 1962 after the National Council of Parent and Teacher Association's annual meeting in Portland. Our Warm Springs delegates came home from the conference with an idea for reducing the worrisome number of Warm Springs students who dropped out of school after entering junior high in Madras. Kindergarten, the delegates had been told, could give children the skills they need before they're ready to read or do arithmetic or take the other steps that lead to higher learning.

---

*The great floods that scoured the inland Northwest at the end of the Glacial Period would have erased any evidence of much earlier habitation.

"How can we provide this," our delegates asked at our first PTA meeting after the convention, "in a state with no public kindergartens?" The question struck a chord in me. "We can start a kindergarten here at Warm Springs!" I described the parent cooperative preschool in Virginia where I had worked so hard for four years. No one thought it was a crazy idea. This small tight community was accustomed to providing what it needed for itself. When television became available, a couple of local men put together a cooperative, built a tower, and brought the cable into this canyon for everyone. When the tribes decided to purchase the old Hot Springs spa and develop it into a first-class resort, volunteers jumped into action and Kah-Nee-Ta was born. A kindergarten was just one more collaborative project the people and the tribes might be willing to take on.

We formed a planning committee that night. I sent to Alexandria for procedures, bylaws, and anything else the Fairlington Cooperative was willing to share with us, and we worked out a preliminary budget. Our first task, we agreed, was to find out if there was real interest among the parents of potential students—those children who would enter the first grade in 1964. That would give us just over a year to have the classes ready to go.

Part of the committee volunteered to be interviewers. We wrote a description for them to take to the parents that explained how the children could benefit. If we can start a kindergarten class, would you send your child? Would you be willing to pay as much as fifteen dollars a month per child? Would you or someone else in your family be willing to help in the classroom at least one day a month? Would you attend evening parent meetings monthly? On the whole, the response was enthusiastic. Of fifty-four families with children of eligible age, forty-seven expressed interest. Some parents wanted to send their children but could not afford the tuition or the volunteer time.

The Presbyterian mission church agreed that the new kindergarten could meet in their large Sunday school room. Furnished for children's use, with bathrooms and a shady yard, it was an ideal location. We planned for two classes, a morning and an afternoon group. Committee members worked on other arrangements—professional teachers, insurance, physical exams, and transportation for Simnasho children. We agreed that some financial as well as time commitment from each child's parents was important. It could lead to greater interest in the student's school life later on—one key, we had learned, to a child's success in school. It seemed important to us that, in a cooperative venture, each family should pay something, but we didn't want any child left out. Acknowledging the hardship for some families, we decided to ask the tribal council for half-scholarships for all children of tribal members.

Our committee requested time on the council meeting agenda and obtained permission from Tribal Chairman Ed Scott to include me. I was nervous, and Bud suggested that local mothers should discuss the benefits of kindergarten to Warm Springs children. If a councilman spoke directly to me, I should neither take it personally nor respond to any critical comments. Very likely, they would be meant for someone else at the table—and that person would get the message. "They'll probably like your idea of half-scholarships," he said. "They're all for education here."

And that's the way it turned out. The council considered our proposal at length, each councilman speaking in turn. Several commended the PTA for undertaking the project. The tribal education committee agreed that families should be helped with the tuition but also felt that parents should assume responsibility.[10] The vote for our proposal was unanimous.

The Warm Springs Cooperative Kindergarten opened in September 1963. Dakota (Coty) Soules, an experienced teacher and wife of the administrator at the Indian Health Service clinic, was head teacher. Irene Stiles, a kindergarten teacher who had recently moved to Madras, taught the second class. Mary Ann Arthur had earned her high school credentials through the new adult classes taught at the agency in the spring, which qualified her as a teacher aide.

I remember standing at the door of the church on the first day of school to watch the children arrive. When Freda Wallulatum brought her Lisa in from Simnasho and up the sidewalk to the church, without thinking I commented on the child's beautiful beaded moccasins. Her mother told me later that after school Lisa had insisted on being taken to Macy's to buy a pair of sneakers. It's hard enough, I realized, for a child to come into a strange place for a new experience without someone making her feel different.

At least I hadn't discouraged her from staying in school. As I write this I have before me a dog-eared photo clipped from the June 11, 1964, edition of the *Madras Pioneer*. There is Lisa Wallulatum sitting in a row of eleven girls in frilly dresses, with thirteen boys standing handsome and scrubbed behind them. Counting Lois Lessert, who was ill and missed the ceremony, twenty-five children graduated in the first Warm Springs Kindergarten class. Those children represented a milestone in education at Warm Springs.

In 1965, a year after that first graduation, the U.S. Office of Economic Opportunity launched Project Head Start. Many of the child development specialists who set up the Head Start guidelines had been active in the cooperative preschool movement. The Warm Springs Kindergarten, already established with parent participation and teachers and facilities that met the new program's guidelines, became one of the first tribal Head Start programs in the nation. In 1983, nearly twenty years later, an article in the tribal newspaper listed 110 children enrolled in Head Start with 12 teachers, two cooks, a bus driver/cook, a curriculum coordinator, a parent/health and handicap coordinator, a secretary and director.[11]

By 1987, the program served 215 children with 89 on the waiting list. Having outgrown the space at the Presbyterian church, classes also were held in trailers, at the community center, and in the former boys' dormitory.[12] The parent education component, which our committee had addressed through child

Arlene Boileau (left), the "helping mother" for the day, and teacher Irene Stiles work with one of two classes that inaugurated the Warm Springs Cooperative Kindergarten in 1963.

development programs at the monthly parent meetings, also was part of the national Project Head Start blueprint. Staff and parents participated in regular early childhood education classes, in many cases earning college credits for the training. This, in turn, helped meet the growing need for qualified teachers at Warm Springs.

In 1992, the Warm Springs tribes opened the $5 million Early Childhood Education Center. In addition to the Head Start program, the complex includes an infant care center and an after-school facility for school-age children. "I think some of our people have been looking forward to this for more than twenty years," Warm Springs Chief Delvis Heath Sr. said at the dedication.[13] His comment reflected the strong support tribal leaders have given to the education and development of Warm Springs children.

Through the years, the early childhood education program has developed a significant cultural component, including the teaching of all three languages. Looking through the tribal newspapers, searching for a photo of Head Start graduation at Warm Springs to compare with that first event in 1964, I find an article on a special day held at the Early Childhood Education Center in May 2002. Instead of a frilly dress, young Cyrelle Frank wears a ribbon-trimmed wing dress in a floral print over a bright cerise underdress. In another photo, Brandon Lucei and friends are in paper vests they have made and feathered headbands.[14] Their feet are not in view, but many are undoubtedly wearing moccasins. The children's comfort in wearing traditional clothing for public events is one more indication of the pride in Native heritage that became more visible on Northwest reservations in the 1970s.

Mary, Kitty, Bill, and Joe crossing the Columbia on a family trip to Toppenish from Warm Springs, looking west toward Celilo from the Maryhill Ferry.

By the time Coty Soules retired as director of the tribal Head Start program in January 1987, Bud and I had settled in the tiny community of Mt. Hood in the upper Hood River Valley, only seventy-five miles from Warm Springs. I wanted to give Coty a gift that honored her critical role in bringing that long-ago dream to an unimagined reality.

In the twenty-three years since the kindergarten opened, I had mastered the technique used by early Wasco and Wishxam weavers to twine soft bags to use when digging bitterroot, wild carrot, camas, and other foods.* The unusual feature that distinguished Wasco/Wishxam weavings from those of their Sahaptin-speaking neighbors were the images—fish, birds, animals, people—that they twined into these handsome bags. For Coty, I chose to weave boys and girls, hand in hand, around a small bag. I had never seen such a design, but it seemed appropriate.

It was the first time I had shown any of my weaving at Warm Springs, and I was a little nervous about how it would be received. A dear friend, an elder on the Yakama Reservation, had taught me to twine several years after we left Warm Springs, but she was not Wasco—I had had to figure out that distinctive technique for myself. Did I have the right to do this, I wondered? As I was leaving the party for Coty, Viola Kalama, the sister of the Wasco chief called me to her. "Uh-oh," I thought, and went over to tell her goodbye. "You know that little bag?" she said, pointing at the table where Coty's gifts lay. "Ye-es?" I steeled myself for her criticism. "The little Wasco?"

"Yes," Viola said. "We used to do that." I told her I had been searching for some-

---

*The north shore of the Columbia is the aboriginal territory of the Wascos' relatives, the Chinookan-speaking Wishxam people. They are enrolled on the Yakama Reservation today. The earliest documented example of the distinctive ancient Wasco/Wishxam full-turn twining technique is a round root-digging bag 11.5 inches high and 6 inches wide. The bag was collected by the Lewis and Clark Expedition on the Columbia River in 1805-1806 and is in the collection of the Peabody Museum, Harvard University, Cambridge, Massachusetts.

one who still did that Wasco twining. "No, not the weaving," she said. "We *danced* like that, boys and girls together around the fire, in camp." She smiled at the memory. I relaxed and thanked her for telling me about it. "I'm heading over the mountain right now," I said. "I'll start a little bag for you when I get home." I twined a small bag with children dancing around it and hung it with some beads on a string of buckskin for a necklace. Viola wrote after it arrived and told me she'd been wearing it on different occasions. "Everyone likes it, they ask who made it. Thank you."

She added a poignant note that carried the sentiments of all the River People I've known: "I got to look across one day at Spearfish [on the north side of the Columbia], my old playground and where our swimming hole was. In a way I feel sad how all of it was ruined—for the sake of progress." The note ended on the upbeat: "I'll be going thru on my way to Mowich Mt. for huckleberries. Always a friend, Viola Kalama." After these long years with Indian people, the combination of regret and hopefulness of Viola's note did not surprise me. Life simply *is*, to be acknowledged for the bad and the good. Accepting this has given me much peace.

We had arrived at Warm Springs in 1960 just as researchers from Oregon State College (now University) completed a report on reservation assets, development needs, and strategies for reaching goals. The study was funded by the tribes' share of federal compensation for the loss of the centuries'-old fisheries on the Columbia River caused by building The Dalles Dam in 1957.[15] The dam changed the wild ten-mile stretch of river between The Dalles and Celilo Falls to a docile lake. No longer would Indians dip a generous living from the churning waters when the salmon returned upstream to spawn.

There had been great excitement among the Warm Springs people about proposed projects. As 1964 began, the tribes were building the first phase of Kah-Nee-Ta Resort and had begun to buy back lands lost through sales of private allotments—both projects the result of the economic development effort. The reservation buzzed with plans for other tribal and individual opportunities. The new cooperative kindergarten was functioning smoothly. Tribal members were improving their social skills in dealing with the outside world by attending Dale Carnegie's "How to Win Friends and Influence People" classes. Although laughed at by some, Carnegie's stories and simple, well-phrased rules helped many learn to be effective public speakers. As I think

---

*The Dalles Dam, completed by the U.S. Army Corps of Engineers in 1957, flooded countless traditional home sites along the Columbia River. Although Celilo Falls is the best known fishing grounds, every family settlement along the Columbia River was a productive and deeply mourned fishing place.

back on that singular community education idea, I'm impressed with its logic. The Warm Springs people already were skilled in working with others, but Carnegie's tips helped arm them for the greater role in state and national affairs that would be coming.

Life changed for us in January 1964 when Bud was selected for a six-month Interior Department manager development program at George Washington University. We moved, temporarily, we thought, across the continent to a furnished apartment in Bradlee Towers, the Alexandria complex where we had lived before coming to Warm Springs. When I enrolled Kitty and Joe in school, Kitty was thrilled to be instantly recognized by the grade school principal after four years. Bill joined Alexandria eighth graders at Jefferson Middle School, the city's only fully integrated school, and I connected with both social and professional friends.

Although depressed by President Kennedy's death, Washington, D.C., was stirring with that same energy we had felt at Warm Springs. Vice President Lyndon Johnson had stepped into the presidency, and the War on Poverty was the major thrust of his legislative agenda. The administration had sent the Economic Opportunity Act to Congress. It was a major attack on the roots of unemployment and poverty and included Head Start, Job Corps, and many other community development programs, including those focusing on American Indians.

During that spring, Bud told me of an "Indian Day" being held at Washington's National Cathedral to discuss ideas for reducing poverty among Indians. I remember little from the day other than the beauty of the cathedral grounds and meeting Alvin and Betty Josephy. Alvin M. Josephy Jr. was editor of *American Heritage* magazine, and the couple's cordiality and commitment to Native issues impressed me in the discussion group on Indian education.

When Bud's program ended in June, we returned to Warm Springs. Congress passed the Economic Opportunity Act in August. Sargent Shriver, who had drafted the legislation and was the director of the new Office of Economic Opportunity, asked the Agriculture and Interior departments to set up Job Corps centers on lands under their jurisdiction. That included national forests, Bureau of Land Management, and Bureau of Reclamation lands and, with tribal approval, Indian reservations.

Commissioner Nash contacted Bud at Warm Springs, asking if he would be willing to return to Washington to head up this new effort for the BIA. As Job Corps officer, he would work with the tribes to establish conservation centers on Indian lands for men and women, ages sixteen through twenty-one. The goal was to increase their employability through education, vocational training, and work experience, which would include natural resource conservation on Indian-owned lands under federal trusteeship.* Bud enjoyed pulling such operations together, and the challenge of spending the next two years setting up centers to prepare young workers for jobs appealed to him. After talking it over with us, he agreed to accept the position and to report to Washington at the end of August.

When the time came to say goodbye to all of our good friends at the end of our fifth fine and busy summer on the Warm Springs Reservation, the employees' club planned a farewell party for us. It was a picnic at the shady park and boat launching place on Pelton Lake where the children had taken Red Cross swimming lessons and learned to water ski. The gifts we received that day would change my life.

To explain the gifts, I have to go back to our second summer at Warm Springs. My contacts with George Schneiter and Ivy Hilty in the reservation extension office had led to a career of sorts for me—judging at county fairs in our part of Oregon and eventually at the state fair. The reservation lies in two counties, the north part in Wasco County and the south in Jefferson. I was invited to judge that year at the Wasco County fair held near Tygh Valley. A long way on a rough road, George offered to give me a ride.

Before we headed for Tygh Valley, he stopped at the home of Blanche Tohet, the elder I had admired at that first Fourth of July celebration, to pick up items for her display at the fair. Bringing out their family keepsakes for the annual event was a custom among some traditionalists. When Mrs. Tohet showed George what she was sending, he called me to the back of the truck. There, open on the tailgate, was a tin suitcase full of large, flat, hand-woven bags, heirloom textiles that rivaled Oriental rugs and fine Navajo weavings for their beauty in craftsmanship and design.

"They're called cornhusk bags," he explained, "for storing dried foods. They're only made by the people of the Columbia—nowhere else in the world." It was my introduction to a completely new art. To think that such beautiful weavings were in Warm Springs, and I had known nothing about them. During the rest of our years there, I saw a few more of the bags, but it was not until our farewell picnic that I held one in my hands.**

---

*By the end of 1966, the BIA had trained 1,600 young workers in nine Job Corp centers across the country.

**Archaeologists have confirmed that weavers on the Columbia Plateau have used an ancient off-loom weaving technique to make such storage bags for at least nine thousand years. This complex method is known as "false embroidery" or "external weft wrap." The earliest documented example is a large root storage bag collected at Lapwai, Idaho, in the 1840s by the Rev. Henry H. Spalding, Presbyterian missionary to the Nez Perce. Oberlin College returned this bag to the Nez Perce people in 2002. *Yakama Nation Review*, June 5, 2002.

When the time came for gift-giving at the picnic, Bud's coworkers presented us with a large, flat package. A tablecloth, I thought, or a photo album. We opened it, and there was a beautiful old cornhusk storage bag like those Blanche Tohet sent to the Tygh Valley fair. With it was a handsome handbag with a design similar to those on the woven bags, but the design was worked in tiny glass beads. The uniqueness of the gift, the connection to this place that we had loved so much, and the amazing thoughtfulness of the choice astonished me. The bags have had an honored place in our home ever since. I treasure them even more now, for that gift inspired me to begin a study of the rich history and basketry of the Columbia Plateau people.

The day came at last to leave Warm Springs for Virginia. We took a final look around the empty house where we had had such good years, then climbed into the 1963 Ford for our third trip across the continent that year. Giving a last wave to the kids on the basketball court, Bud tapped the horn to salute Ting, the Galbraiths' big white dog, barking in their yard. We bumped across the cattle guard and out the gate onto U.S. 26. Turning east down the hill, we passed the old Heath house, then Madeline St. Germaine's and the Brunoes and Quinns. I looked for Mary Ann at her house in the trees beside the creek. My beaded bag and necklace and a little beaded sewing kit for Kitty were safely packed, but I had hoped to give her a last wave in thanks for the gifts.

We came to the bridge and the sign, "Leaving the Warm Springs Indian Reservation." As we crossed the Deschutes River, I had a sudden sensation of loss, of leaving something important behind. I turned to look at the children and then, beside me, at my husband. I could only imagine their thoughts—Bud eager for the challenges of the new job, the children sad at leaving friends. They could picture, at least, where we were headed—back to Bradlee Towers, Kitty and Joe to the school they knew and Bill to Hammond High School where he would meet friends from the past spring. I was confident that something interesting would show up for me.

As we followed the beautiful river and climbed the familiar winding grade toward Madras, I began to feel better. I knew without a doubt that we would return. This place and the people we knew here would continue to be part of our lives just as the Mt. Adams country of our first summer and the people of the Colville continued to be. Yes, I thought as we paralleled the chain of mountains south toward Bend, where we would spend the night, we had come into this country to stay. We would be back.

5. RETURN TO THE POTOMAC, 1964-1969

*False embroidery: The weaver wraps
each stitch with a strand of cornhusk,
adding beauty and strength as she
twines the bag.**

For the second time that year, we drove through our nation's capital and crossed the Potomac into Virginia. It was the end of August, as hot as it had been in Warm Springs the week before, but the humidity was higher. Neighbors greeted us with surprise; in June, they thought they had sent us home to Oregon for good.

Before tackling supper, I unpacked the cornhusk root bag and beaded handbags and hung them together on the living room wall to remind us of Warm Springs. Studying the cornhusk bag before I put it up, I puzzled over the weaving. The bold designs that gave it such distinction were only on the outside. Inside was a tightly woven surface with small ends of the decorative cornhusk showing here and there. Somehow the weaver had created the pattern on the surface as she wove this sturdy bag. It was a metaphor for what I hoped was ahead for our family. I wanted this time in the East to provide another rich layer of experience over the strong foundation that life on the Colville and Warm Springs reservations had helped us build.

The kindergarten project at Warm Springs and the needs of young children had captured my attention. John F. Kennedy's assassination and the growing unrest in the country made me realize there were human needs more pressing than my college education had prepared me for—saving time and energy or having easy-to-understand use and care manuals for household appliances. I was looking for direction.

On our trip from Warm Springs we had visited my mother in Iowa. I also had talked with Glen Hawkes, a child development professor at Iowa State, about the Warm Springs kindergarten project. When I asked about studies on Indian children and culture change, he suggested I contact Elizabeth Hoyt who was teaching for a year at Howard University in Washington. An economics professor at Iowa State when I was in college, Dr. Hoyt had conducted a study with the Mesquakie Indian children near Tama, Iowa.

---

*Paraphrased from Schlick, *Columbia River Basketry*, p. 216.

"And while you're in Washington, find out what you can about the new 'Head Start' program," Dr. Hawkes said.

Much had happened in the world during our years at Warm Springs—the first lunch counter sit-in in Greensboro, North Carolina, in 1960 and the following peaceful protests against racial discrimination by thousands of white and black students. We read *Stride Toward Freedom* by Martin Luther King Jr. and other books on race and civil rights and watched Dr. King's "I have a dream" speech from the Lincoln Memorial on television. Television had brought other news to Warm Springs—the Soviets' downing of the U2 reconnaissance plane, Kennedy's inauguration, the Bay of Pigs, Alan Shepard's first manned trip in suborbital space, and John Glenn's triple-circling of the globe.

The summer of 1964 had been sobering. In June, Congress passed the Omnibus Civil Rights Act. Within days, three civil rights workers were murdered in Mississippi. While we were driving east in August, Congress finally authorized President Johnson to send troops into Vietnam. We knew by returning to D.C. we were diving into a whirlpool. We hoped we could swim.

And so we began an intense five years in the nation's capital. Bud and his assistant, Harry Rainbolt, began to work directly with the tribes to find locations for the new Job Corps centers and to get them up and running. The Economic Opportunity Act, which had created the centers, was landmark legislation, an important milestone in federal and tribal relations that "empowered tribes by building capacities, creating independence from the BIA and knitting tribes together." Prior to the act, the BIA had administered all monies for programs affecting Indians. Through the united effort of Indian leaders nationally, the new Office of Economic Opportunity allowed grants to go directly to tribal governments and mandated the establishment of new Job Corps conservation centers on federal lands. In the case of the BIA, though the land was Indian-owned, it was under federal trusteeship.

According to the legislation, a specific number of Job Corps centers were to be fully operating on Indian lands within two years. Not only would the centers help Native American youth become employable, but they also offered a way to improve and rehabilitate tribal lands and resources. Because of the success of the "Indian CCs," the Emergency Conservation Work projects the BIA operated in the 1930s, many tribes welcomed the program.[1]

It wasn't long before we found a house in a wooded area that we liked. School opened soon after, and I suddenly had time to myself. I called Dr. Hoyt. "Yes?" An abrupt, no-nonsense voice. "Elizabeth Hoyt." I pictured her as I had seen her many times, striding across the campus, her dark eyebrows in a scowl of concentration. I described my experience with the Warm Springs kindergarten. "I'm not sure where I fit in the picture," I said, "but I want to know more about Indians and education."

"Why don't you come up here? I'll set up an independent study for you," her voice still gruff, but encouraging.

"Howard University?" I thought. "Why not?"

Each week from then until late January 1965, Dr. Hoyt and I spent a half-day of intense discussion in her office, always starting with my assigned readings. She challenged me to puzzle out solutions for the issues we raised, based on my reservation experience. I came away believing we had been on the right track at Warm Springs with emphasis on meeting each child's developmental needs and the close involvement of the parents and community. Teaching needs to be personal, I believed—with teachers designing their lessons in ways that relate to the lives of the children who face them each day. The semester's readings on the history of Indian education and children in the midst of culture change had a profound effect on me, leading to a change in my professional direction toward work with teachers in culture-based learning. Just over ten years later, during our third and last posting to Washington, D.C., I commuted twenty miles to night classes at Dulles Airport to complete work on a master's degree in child development and adult education from Virginia Tech.*

Through Elizabeth Hoyt, I met Sue Sadow, a well-known East Coast nutritionist charged with developing a corps of consultants to work with the new Head Start programs across the country. Intrigued with my story of the Warm Springs cooperative kindergarten, she told me to stay in touch. Within a year, she asked me to serve on the nutrition advisory committee for National Capital Head Start, which led to volunteer work with the nearby Fairfax County (Virginia) community action program.

Margaret Morris, a former graduate student of Dr. Hoyt's at Iowa State, was setting up consumer action programs in ten neighborhood development centers for the United Planning Organization (UPO), the District of Columbia's new community action agency. She offered me a halftime position as her assistant to work with the graduate home economists and "indigenous" neighborhood workers in each community center.

Indigenous—having originated in a particular region—had become a key word in community action parlance. The goal of community action was to change the institutions that contributed to poverty and to institutionalize the change. The belief was that the push for change had to come from inside the community; those living there would develop an active interest in seeing that change took place and was lasting.

---

*Virginia Polytechnic and State University is located in Blacksburg, Virginia.

At the UPO, I coordinated the consumer programs with public agencies that could provide information and training opportunities. Among our projects were comparing prices in neighborhood stores, offering stretching-food-dollar classes through the gas and electric companies, and teaching residents to use neighborhood credit unions, a new concept for those who had never had bank accounts. Within a year, Margaret Morris went on to set up a new national program to upgrade the status of household workers, and I stepped into her coordinator's job.

On occasion during these years, the UPO filled whatever hall it could find, usually one of Washington's large black churches, for all-staff meetings. They were always stimulating and sometimes rancorous, as when our director, educated as a social worker himself, raked the UPO social workers over the coals as "lily-livered bastards" for acting as if they were too good for their clients. To keep us fired up about the importance of the work, Roy Wilkins, executive secretary of the NAACP, and other black leaders spoke to us on civil rights. Daniel and Philip Berrigan spoke to us about civil disobedience. Sol Alinsky, a founder of community organizing, came from Chicago and warned us "never do for another what they can do for themselves." Each step people take on their own makes them stronger, he told us.

When the chance came to write training materials as a consultant for the household employment program led by Margaret Morris, I welcomed it. The new job offered an opportunity to draw on my training in technical journalism and household equipment. When completed, the product of my labors—which I soon gave the presumptuous title of *How to Care for the Home and Everything in It*—would be put to use in the training and employment centers in eight cities. Of most importance, as it turned out, I could do much of the writing at home.

I was at home one morning in February 1967, at work rewriting instructions from manufacturers' use and care booklets to make them easier to follow. Bill, now a junior in high school had been ill for several days and was asleep in our bedroom, closest to where I was working.

I heard him stir, then "Mo-m!" I ran to the bedroom and what followed was a nightmare. At four the next morning, surgery for a hemorrhaging duodenal ulcer was over. It had been a complex and exhausting night, and the surgeon had saved Bill's life.

Because of the surgery, Bill had to give up rowing—he and Joe had enjoyed the high school crew together—but he returned to work on the school's literary magazine. He had already arranged for interviews with two syndicated columnists, Jeane Dixon, the famous clairvoyant who had predicted President Kennedy's death, and the internationally known Art Buchwald. He found Dixon interesting, but Buchwald was his all-time favorite. Bill and fellow writer Nancye Caskey visited Buchwald in his Washington office—"from which fly some of the funniest political barbs in Washington," they reported. Buchwald told them of a childhood in foster homes, his work in Paris, and returning to Washington to write about politics. His goal, always, he told them, was "to get a response . . . good or bad."[2] What they thought were diplomas decorating the office wall proved to be framed copies of nasty letters.

By the time I finished writing the training manual in September 1967, our employment projects were geared up and accepting trainees. I was promoted to assistant director and, when Margaret Morris took a position at the American Home Economics Association headquarters, I succeeded her again as project director. Like the D.C. consumer action job, the new position required frequent visits to our program's centers. Instead of driving all over the District of Columbia, however, I flew to Boston, New York, Philadelphia, Pittsburgh, Chicago, and Lawrence, Kansas. Luckily, two of our training centers were nearby, in the District and in Alexandria, neither very far from our office on DuPont Circle.

By this time, the new Job Corps centers were serving 1,600 corpsmen in six western states with plans underway for a special center in Alaska. Harry Rainbolt was now in charge, and Bud had moved on to positions in the office of Robert Bennett, commissioner of Indian Affairs. For a year, he coordinated BIA contacts with Congress and other federal agencies. Then, in 1967, he was given the task of setting up a new division of program planning and budgeting for the bureau. Both of those positions required less travel.

On the top floor of the Interior Building, Secretary and Mrs. Stewart Udall had established a Center for the Arts of Indian America, which exposed us to a new dimension of the world we had come into. Through the exhibitions, Bud and I began to develop a deep appreciation for the work of Native artists from the past as well as contemporary artists. Among those we met were Yeffe Kimball, an Osage artist whose thirty-year retrospective show filled the gallery, and potters Maria Martinez and her son Tony Da, who came to Washington from their home at San Ildefonso Pueblo.

Exhibiting artists Solomon McCombs (Creek) and Edna (Kitty) Massey (Cherokee) were BIA employees whom we knew. One of Kitty's responsibilities was to seek out and purchase work by contemporary Native American artists to add to the fine collection that graced the Interior buiding's walls. Not long after we left Washington in 1969, the Bureau of Indian Affairs moved into its own headquarters on Constitution Avenue, a block away, where it continues to offer visitors the opportunity to see the work of Native artists.

Yakama Tribal Council visit to Washington, D.C., in January 1969: (from left) Yakama Superintendent-elect Schlick; Chairman Robert Jim; James Hovis, Yakima, Washington, tribal attorney; Watson Totus; Secretary of Interior Walter Hickel; Harvey Adams; Stanley Smartlowit; and Paul M. Niebell, the Washington, D.C., attorney for the Yakama (courtesy of the U.S. Department of the Interior).

The time in Washington had been hopeful for us. We felt our work was important, and Bud could see a shift in federal policy toward more tribal involvement in their own affairs. I had begun to accept a few consulting assignments from Sue Sadow working with teachers in nearby Head Start programs on developing culture-based nutrition education programs.

Then the spring of 1968 brought two incidents that completely changed our feelings about living in Washington, D.C. On Thursday afternoon, April 4, I left the National Committee for Household Employment office in the DuPont Circle building at five and followed my usual route south along 18th Street to meet Bud at the Interior Building twenty minutes away. I nodded and smiled at those I had come to recognize through the years of walking along that sidewalk. Going up to Bud's office, I found people at the window watching dark smoke billow up from the east side of the city. "Martin Luther King has been murdered," he told me. "We'd better head for home."

Late into the night, we watched the television coverage of the riots that had erupted in Washington and other cities. In the morning, as we drove into town, we saw the smoke again rising in the neighborhoods north of the Capitol. This time on my walk up 18th Street there were no smiles, no eye contact even, from pedestrians black or white. Most difficult of all was entering our office and meeting the same guarded looks from my colleagues, all of whom were African American. For the first time in Washington, D.C., I felt like an outsider.

Two months later, on June 5, Senator Robert Kennedy was shot in California, where he was celebrating his presidential primary victory. He died the following day. Bill graduated from Hammond High School that evening. The speaker was Louis L. Mitchell Jr., the deputy regional director for the Peace Corps. A friend of Kennedy's, the grieving speaker challenged the young men and women to continue the difficult work for peaceful change in our time.

At the time of John Fitgerald Kennedy's death I saved a quotation from Senator Daniel Patrick Moynahan: "To be Irish is to know that, in the end, the world will break your heart." I thought of it again that day and hated for our son, descendant of Irish immigrants, to begin to learn this truth so early.

Just after the Nixon inauguration in January 1969, the BIA sent Bud to the Yakama Reservation to interview for the position of superintendent. No stranger to the Yakama, he had worked with the tribal council to establish the Fort Simcoe Job Corps Center on Yakama land and more recently had worked with them in his current position in the commissioner's office. We agreed that we had been away long enough and were eager to return to the Northwest. I knew I could continue the Head Start consulting from anywhere. Bud had completed a two-year advanced management seminar and felt ready for the new challenge. The job sounded interesting, but he wondered if the tribe would accept him. "I still wondered this," he told us when he returned from the interview, "as I stood at the council table before the fourteen stony-faced men who represented the signers of the Yakama Treaty of 1855."

Bud knew from earlier council meetings that it is customary for each member to speak in turn, and he was prepared for this formal routine. But as the council members spoke, he could not judge from their faces or their tone of voice what the decision would be. The last man to speak, Bud said, was a serious, dignified leader who began very slowly, and Bud was afraid the councilman was letting him down gently. After a few words, the councilman said: "Washington will send this man no matter how we vote. We might as well accept him."

And that was that. The council voted to approve Bud's appointment. I was delighted. The move to the Yakama Reservation offered welcome respite from the social upheaval that seemed so palpable in the city. But more than that, it brought us home to the country that Bud and I had embraced when we first spotted the Goat Rocks from the porch of that tiny cabin at Walupt Lake twenty years before.

6. IN THE SHADOW OF PÁTU, 1969-1970

*Coiling: Building strength by binding sturdy roots together in an unbroken coil as on a Klikitat basket.**

Crossing the Columbia

The day was much the same as it had been twenty years before when Bud and I first crossed the Columbia River together—too hot for comfort. This time we were in an air-conditioned car, but instead of two honeymooners, there were five of us, three over six feet tall.

We had crossed the river at Umatilla and headed northwest through the Horse Heaven Hills that rose voluptuous and treeless above the river. As we came over the summit we saw the green valley of the Yakima River stretching toward a startling backdrop—snow-covered Mt. Adams. Mt. Rainier loomed to the north. Bud pulled to the side of the road, and we stepped out to stretch and to gaze at the place where we would live. Bud said the Yakama called Mt. Adams "Pátu."** The tribal chairman had explained that it meant "put there for our use, to provide water, the source of all life."

Many years later, I asked Joe how he felt that day when he looked into that beautiful valley. "I thought," he said, "my life is saved." Just five months before, Joe had taken our camera into D.C. to take photos of Richard Nixon's inaugural parade. It had been a dark, rainy day. When he pulled the images out of the developer, all we could see were glimpses of passing dignitaries between the shoulders of storm troopers who lined Pennsylvania Avenue, guns ready.

"Things didn't seem very easy to me in Alexandria," Joe said, in answer to my question. He had loved being at Warm Springs. "Coming over that hill, it looked to me like we were back in the same kind of country—freer, friendlier, easier." I think we all felt the same relief.

---

*Paraphrased from Schlick, *Columbia River Basketry,* p. 215.

**Pátu is the word for mountain or snowpeak. See Virginia Beavert, *Yakima Language Practical Dictionary.*

We left the highway at Toppenish to show the children where we would live.* The town had grown along the Northern Pacific Railroad, where it cut across what had been Yakama Reservation land. When Bud had arrived in February, leaving the rest of us in Virginia for the children to finish school, he had found housing scarce. He had arranged for a local contractor to build a house for us in a neighborhood near the agency headquarters. Winding our way through the tree-shaded streets, we found the house well started. We should be in by August 15, the builder told us. To find a place to stay until then, we drove on to Yakima, nineteen miles to the north.

The first place we stopped was the Columbia Motor Court on Fruitvale Boulevard. We found a row of red-trimmed, white-frame units just off U.S. 12, the highway that leads over the mountains toward Seattle. The motel was small and old but shady and clean, and it allowed long-term rentals. Best of all, there were two adjoining units available. We agreed we could squeeze in for a couple of months. I saw the tiny bathtub of a swimming pool in front of the office. "Bud," I said. "We've been here before!" The place was little changed from June 1949 when it had sheltered us the night before we drove into the mountains to Packwood to begin the job at Walupt Lake Guard Station. We had passed the place again at the end of that summer, heading home to Iowa. We had closed a very big geographic circle.

Each child had needed something special, something that would make this sixth move in thirteen years more palatable. Joe had parlayed a Christmas gift darkroom kit into a full-blown interest in photography and, when asked what he would like, chose a good camera. Kitty had come home from school in Alexandria one day excited by a presentation on the wilderness experiences offered by Outward Bound. Learning of a summer Outward Bound School in the Oregon Cascades, she had asked for an application and we had agreed to finance it. Bill hadn't decided what he wanted yet. As soon as we reached Yakima, he found work in a fruit warehouse. My sister in Oregon asked Joe to go with her to the family cabin at Rainy Lake as camp man, and they headed off to Minnesota. As soon as they left, Bill knew what he wanted as a "moving" gift—a ticket to International Falls. With much effort, we located Aunt Katherine and Joe en route, and she agreed that two camp men would be even better.

Soon after Bud had arrived on the Yakama Reservation in February, he had begun to research tribal history to better understand the people he had come to work with. A member of the tribal council suggested that he get in touch with Click Relander, a Ya-

---

*Toppenish is a town in the central Yakima Valley. The name is taken from a Yakama word meaning "sloping down." See 34th Anniversary Washington Birthday Celebration program.

kima newspaperman and friend of the tribe. Click welcomed Bud's interest, probably hoping the new superintendent would serve the Yakama well—they needed an effective connection with the often-inscrutable Bureau of Indian Affairs in Washington. Bud shared that hope.

Relander was generous with his library as well as his knowledge. He directed Bud to A.J. Splawn's *Ka-Mi-Akin, the Last Hero of the Yakimas*, published in 1898. This book, told largely from the Indian point of view, recounts events in Yakama country from before the treaty of 1855 to about 1917. Bud also read Relander's

Watson Totus (left) gives Bud a drumming lesson at the Satus Longhouse. Longtime tribal councilman Eagle Seelatsee is seated at center back.

Drummers and Dreamers and two smaller books about the Wanapum people of Priest Rapids whose ancestors had refused to move to the reservation. When I arrived, I started in on the reading list and, now steeped in local history, was eager to meet this writer.

The opportunity came soon. On the Fourth of July, Bud, Kitty, and I headed toward Mt. Adams to the Toppenish Creek encampment grounds near White Swan. As we parked in the field above the grounds, we could hear drumming, deep like that at the Circle near Nespelem or in the Warm Springs gym when the Boy Scouts danced. Above that and closer were other sounds—conversation, laughter, children's voices—all coming from the jumble of small stands that stood between us and the dance building. Warm smells of frybread, hotdogs, and chili led us through the crowd.* Bud spotted Click Relander sitting with a couple of other men on a bench outside the big building, and he introduced us. As we walked into the big frame building toward the drummers, I could see that Bud recognized some men sitting behind the big drums.

---

*Frybread is a standard specialty in Indian Country, best when served with huckleberry jam. Recipe from Kah-Nee-Ta Resort at Warm Springs: 3 cups flour, 2 tablespoons baking powder, 1 tablespoon sugar, 1 teaspoon salt, 1 teaspoon fat, cold water, fat for frying at 350 degrees. Mix all dry ingredients. Cut in fat and add water to make a thick dough. Knead well. Break off handfuls and fry in deep fat until golden brown.

"Join them," I said. "We'll watch from here." We settled on the bottom step of the bleachers. Males of all ages in beaded and feathered outfits danced across in front of us toward the drummers. They bobbed and turned, twisted and dipped, their steps on the drumbeat. Women and girls in beaded buckskin dresses sat in the audience or hovered on the sidelines waiting for their time on the floor.

It wasn't long before a woman about my age or slightly younger stopped near me. She wore street clothes and beaded moccasins and carried a fringed shawl over her arm. I watched as she arranged a small blanket as a cushion on the seat near us and sat down, making some comment about the evening. I responded in kind. Then, hoping she would introduce herself, I mentioned my name and Kitty's. I waited to hear her name, but she said instead, "We knew you'd be all right."

"What?" I said. Had I heard that right? She leaned forward a bit to look past me to Kitty. "They told us you had good kids." Astonished, I asked, "Who?"

"The folks at Warm Springs."

When I asked her name, she told me she was Marie Shilow and pointed out her daughters just stepping out on the floor. "And," she continued, "that's Hadley, my husband, up there with Bud."

The tempo from the next drum seemed slower. The singers seated around it leaned into their task, their voices high and plaintive. We watched together as the procession passed in front of us—women and girls wearing beaded buckskin or wing dresses with shell and ribbon trim, and most carrying soft, silk-fringed shawls over their arms. Fancy dancers, men and boys, even very small ones, in feathered war-dance outfits dipped and turned as they wove among the others. I couldn't keep my eyes off the beaded leggings and moccasins. This great mass of color streamed by as a single organism held together by the deep throb of the drum.

Reading the Sunday *Yakima Herald* the following day, I came upon an article by Click Relander that described in detail the memorial that had been held at Toppen-ish Creek Longhouse on the day before the Fourth of July celebration began. At this ancient ceremony, the names and the heirlooms, dance gear, other personal belongings of the departed are bequeathed to family members and friends. He described the scene: two men walking the length of the building, speaking so all could hear. "Here, for the first time," Relander wrote, "the names of the dead are spoken so relatives and friends may hear."

He told of the families bringing in large bundles of heirlooms and new goods gathered all year for the give-away and of the dinner with "Creator-given food only found now deep on the reservations." On such occasions, other rituals could be part of the day—name-givings, first deer and first berry-picking ceremonies, welcome-home or leaving dances. The memorials clear the longhouse for other activities, he explained.

It was September, the long summer ending, our children home from their adventures and settled in high school and college. I stood at the kitchen sink pulling supper together. Bud drove in, stepped down from the pickup, and, passing the open window, said, "Click Relander has died." I waited for Bud to come into the kitchen. "We're going to the funeral." He pulled up the kitchen stool. "Tonight." A tiny pinch of anxiety rose in my chest. I don't like funerals. "It's over at Wanapum Longhouse." We had not been in a longhouse here, but, I thought, at least it won't be far. "Where's that?"

"Way off the reservation." As I cooked, he explained. The tribal chairman, Robert Jim, had come to his office to tell him of the death. New to this reservation and to tribal expectations of the superintendent, Bud, fortunately, took this notice for the summons it proved to be. It was several months before he realized that being told about an event usually meant he was expected to appear—and, if not a strictly political occasion, with his wife. "Where is the Wanapum Longhouse?" I asked again.

"It's over above Hanford."

"So far?" He saw my face and began to recite the directions Bob had given him. "We go past Zillah to the highway out of Sunnyside." There, he said, we hit the road from Yakima and follow it to the T at Hanford's closed area. "We'll drive north to Vernita, cross the bridge, and follow the river on north."

"What river?" I said. He'd lost me.

"The Columbia. We turn in at the sign for Priest Rapids Dam and cross the dam."

"Cross the dam? How?" I hate heights.

"We'll figure it out. The Wanapum people have lived over there at Priest Rapids forever."

That rang a bell. I'd learned about that place long before reading Relander's book. Back in Bud's gun-club days, we had gone from Nespelem to Wenatchee for a rifle match. Bored with the novel I had taken, I picked up a leaflet in the hotel lobby and read of a Wanapum prophet at a place named P'Na somewhere farther down the Columbia River. The story stayed with me. Smohalla had inspired a spiritual revival among his people, and the place then became known as Priest Rapids. I put the two stories together—the place I had read of and the people Click Relander had described so vividly in *Drummers and Dreamers*.

Rex Buck, Bob Jim had told Bud, was the longhouse leader, the son of Puck Hyah Toot, the famous prophet's successor. Smohalla's bones lie, I knew from reading the book, in Satus Point Cemetery in the hills south of Toppenish. He had died on a visit

A Wáashat service at Priest Rapids Longhouse in about 1954. James Rayner took this photograph for Click Relander with the permission of Wanapum leader Puck Hyah Toot (courtesy of the Wanapum of Priest Rapids).

to the valley in the heat of summer when they could not return the body to P'na for burial. We would see this ancient place for the first time because of a funeral. In spite of uncertainty about the long drive to an unknown place and ceremony, the feeling of stepping into history intrigued me.

It was barely dusk when we headed for Priest Rapids. After winding past orchards and hop fields to the highway north from Sunnyside, then through the hills to Vernita Bridge, the high rimrock along the west bank of the river blocked all remnants of the warm twilight. There was no moon. We crossed the Columbia and turned upstream to watch for Priest Rapids Dam in deep darkness. At last, a few lights on the dam, then a sign appeared and we turned off the highway toward the river. We slowed to find the ramp that Bob Jim had said would lead up and onto the dam, and the headlights picked up another sign in huge block letters: "KEEP OFF THE DAM."

"We can't do this," I said. "There's no road." I began to open the car door. "We'll have to walk across." Without a pause, Bud drove up the ramp, took a sharp turn left, then right. We were on top of the dam, the Columbia churning below us. I held my breath, letting it out when we came to the far end. But where were we? As we drove down into the darkness, our headlights picked up the faint haze of smoke. An unpainted frame house stood near the river's bank. Nearby, toward those cliffs that loomed to the west, we could make out a long frame building, its door in the end toward the river.* There were other houses behind.

We pulled in beside the pickups and cars parked in front of the building and turned off the headlights. A dim lightbulb shone above the door, and we could see a few people gathered there. "This must be the longhouse," Bud said. The soothing smell of wood smoke, the deep sound of drums and singing, high and urgent,

---

*This frame longhouse had replaced the Wanapum's traditional mat lodge in 1952 and was destroyed in a windstorm in 1972. A World War II Quonset then served for many years and is now replaced by a modern building.

seeped from the building. I hoped Bud was feeling braver than I was about walking into the place. In all our years of living on reservations, this was our first venture into such a ceremony. The darkness, the remote place, the unfamiliar singing increased my anxiety. I pulled on the sweater I had brought; there was no remnant of the day's warmth.

"We'll be intruders," I thought. "We'll be fine," Bud said, putting his hand on my arm. I knew he was as nervous as I was.

As we walked up to the group at the door, a young woman turned from the others and came toward us. "Superintendent," she said quietly, "I'm Delores Buck." She gave his hand a small shake, then mine. "I'll take you in as soon as the song ends." My apprehension ebbed a bit at her welcoming tone.

When the sound inside died, she opened the door and led us past a kitchen and into a long space where people sat on benches along the walls. Men stood at the far end holding large hand drums and waiting. I could see linoleum around the edges of the floor where people walked, but the entire center area was the hard-packed earth it had been in Smohalla's time. Shelves held bedrolls and bundles high above the benches. Hats and other garments hung from pegs beneath the shelving.

Delores murmured to Bud, "Go along there," and gestured toward the left side where the men sat. "Find a place toward the singers." He turned and walked along in front of the seated men and boys. Touching a woman standing nearby, Delores said to me, "This is my mother—Josephine. She'll take care of you." I looked at my guide in the dim firelight. Her sleeves were softly gathered at the wrist beneath the dark wing dress. A black silk kerchief tied tightly across her forehead covered her graying hair. No smile on the lined face, but no judgment in the dark eyes either. I hoped it was a good sign that my own mother and this woman had the same lovely name.

Delores said something in the Yakama language, and her mother led me down the right side past the women and girls toward the place where the drummers waited. Eyes downcast to be as inconspicuous as possible, I realized all were wearing moccasins and hoped I wouldn't step on any toes. Later we learned to wear moccasins in a longhouse, especially if we would need to step onto the Mother Earth of the center floor. About halfway to the front, Josephine stopped beside two women who moved to make room for us. We sat down. As the night progressed, I was grateful to my unknown neighbor for leaving part of her folded blanket to soften my perch on the hard bench.

A fire burned in a shallow pit in the center of the earthen floor near the covered pine casket, and by its light I searched the men's faces across from us. I found Bud watching me from the back row a little closer to the front of the longhouse where the seven singers now sat resting. He gave me a slight nod.

I had read of the Plateau peoples' tule mat-covered lodges, the forerunners of present-day longhouses, where extended families spent the cold months. They were snug homes. Each family group had its own fire, as many as seven down the length of an A-frame structure. This frame wooden building served the same purpose—a place of shelter, warmth, and sociability, Smohalla's Wáashat service made it a sacred place. Somehow this setting, so new to us, seemed just right. The reassurance of the close-packed mourners seeped into me.

As I sat there looking at the pine box, I thought about Mr. Relander, a man I had met only a few weeks before. These people had taken him into their lives and had become his family. They gave him the name Now-Tow-Look. Tomorrow they would bury him as a son. Relander's book about their history and beliefs had helped Bud develop some insight into the complex culture of the Plateau people. As a forester at Colville and Warm Springs, he had needed only to understand the best way to manage the timber resources for the benefit of the tribes, but in this new role he needed to know about the people. I realized that Bud saw this funeral as a time to honor the man who had prompted him to begin this study. He also saw it as a start toward learning more about the Wanapum people.

After we were settled, seven singers raised their drums. Each held a flat wafer-shaped hand drum about the size of the wheel on a child's bicycle. In the other hand was a drumstick with a soft end of cloth or buckskin. One of the men hit a few soft beats, then began to sing. I could not understand the words; the melody, even the scale, was unfamiliar, plaintive, and sweet. As if at a signal, the other singers picked up the beat, their drums raised in front of them at shoulder level, and joined the song the drummer had begun. Most of the onlookers stood up. Josephine put her hand on my arm to say we could sit. I relaxed.

Above the singing, I heard the high, strong voice of a woman coming from my right, across from Bud. "Superintendent," she called across the longhouse, "stand up." Bud rose, his face immobile, serious. I felt a sudden rush of admiration for this man I had known as a fractious teenager, a young soldier, a son hopeful of pleasing a silent father, and a tender father himself. I admired his dignity and courage in taking on this new phase of his life. The tribal chairman had told Bud that women elders were important, that he sought out their counsel. This now was being offered to my husband, and he responded.

At a certain point in the song, the leader rang his small handbell and people raised their right hands, palms open. The voice rang out again. "Superintendent," the woman said, "raise your hand." Then later, at the end, with all hands lifted high, the sweet strong voice said, "Superintendent, say 'Aiii.'" And he raised his hand and voice with the others.

As the music died away, I marveled that we were here in this ancient village in the early hours of morning among people offering an ancient farewell to a dear friend. The Columbia River flowed past just a few feet away, but we were a great distance in time and custom from anything we had known up to now. Our younger two slept in the new house in Toppenish, their brother in Seattle. I was content to be here.

At the end of seven songs, it was time for a break. The bare bulbs in the ceiling came on. Blinking at the brightness, I roused from reverie and looked over to catch Bud's eye. Someone added wood to the fire; the singers propped the drums nearby to keep them supple for the next set of songs. Two young boys came along with white china restaurant-style cups in a big laundry basket. A man followed, calling, "Cuppee?" He filled our cups from a huge graniteware coffeepot. Two young women carried another big basket, this one full of sandwiches wrapped in paper napkins. We had eaten supper at home, but it was nearly two in the morning and I reached for a sandwich. They both smiled as if they knew who I was. Word had traveled.

As we ate together, I asked Josephine if the service was over. She shook her head. The woman on my other side explained that the service would go on until dawn. After a last set of seven songs, she said, they would open the casket for a final goodbye to their friend and would carry Now-Tow-Look to the cemetery not far off, where he would be buried facing the sunrise. Following a final meal and according to custom, his name would not be mentioned again until it was brought out a year later at a memorial and give-away.

By the time we finished our sandwiches and the singers picked up the drums again, I saw Bud stand and make his way toward the door. Someone had told him it was all right for us to leave, he told me later. Thanking Josephine and Delores, I slipped out to join him. Wordless, we stepped into the still and chilly night. A bullfrog rasped over toward the river, and the drums began again.

The drive home seemed short. We talked a bit as we crossed the dam—a low, easy remembering. Relieved of the earlier anxiety and warmed by the sense of inclusion felt in that close company, we settled into a comfortable silence. Safely awake, we crossed the Columbia at Vernita and drove on through the now-dark maze of hop fields and orchards toward home.

Discovery

Bud had driven to Toppenish from Virginia in our 1965 Volkswagen bug. Handy for city traffic, it offered challenges on a three thousand-mile road trip, especially through a vicious Montana winter wind. As soon as we arrived in Yakima with the other car, Bud replaced the VW with a brand-new yellow Ford 100 pickup. He had always wanted his own truck. "Now," he said, "we're ready to explore the reservation."

For years Bud had yearned to do some hiking along the summit of the Cascades. No longer directly involved in fire protection, he could leave on summer weekends. Although not yet outfitted for backpacking, we began to explore the foothills of Mt. Adams in the new pickup, checking out Medicine Valley and up the Klickitat drainage to get the lay of the land.

Late that first summer, one of the councilmen suggested Fish Lake. "An easy trail in," he had said, "up near Mt. Adams." That sounded good, and we set off with Kitty, now home from Outward Bound. Following directions, we found the trailhead, put on our boots, and started off through the woods—downhill. It was an easy two miles, but our concern about the climb out grew as we lost elevation. We ate our lunch on the shore of the small lake with no view but trees. As we trudged uphill, a Yakama fisherman came along. He showed no surprise at seeing us, but when he learned why we were there, he asked, "Whose idea was this?" When Bud told him, the man gave him a soft slap on the back. "I've gotta remember that one."

As soon as we heard that huckleberries were ripe in the mountains, Bud suggested that it was time to take the road through the closed area to Mt. Adams and over into the Gifford Pinchot National Forest on the west side. We had been intrigued by the road that first summer at Walupt Lake. Choosing a day that promised good weather and, with tribal council permission, we drove up through the grassy hills and into the deep forest toward Potato Hill. We saw tepees everywhere when we reached the open country around Potato Hill, and the bushes were heavy with berries. Knowing that this picking area was reserved for tribal members, we drove across the reservation boundary and stopped on national forest land to pick enough huckleberries for a pie.*

After this jaunt, I knew there would be no more time this summer to return over the summit to pick again. Not wanting to spend another winter without huckleberry pie, I asked Bud if he could put out the word that we would like to buy a gallon of huckleberries. This simple request opened a door for me that has never closed. But it wasn't the berries that had such an effect on me; it was what they arrived in.

---

*The berryfields located in the Gifford Pinchot National Forest next to the reservation boundary are open to all, but a portion of the well-known Sawtooth berryfields in the national forest a few miles to the south toward Trout Lake is reserved for exclusive Native use. This area was used traditionally by the Indian people who lived along the Columbia River on its westward reach and set aside by the U.S. Forest Service in an unusual Handshake Agreement in 1932 between Chief William Yallup and Forest Supervisor J.R.Bruckart. See McClure and Mack, "For the Greatest Good," 47.

Within a day or two of his request, a call came from Gracie Ambrose, a Yakama woman whose daughter, Theresa, I had met. "I'm at Savin' Sandy's, and I have your berries." I grabbed my purse and drove over to the huge general store at the busy intersection where Highway 97 meets the Fort Road. Spotting a small Yakama woman standing by a pickup, I stopped. She smiled and turned to lift something out of the pickup—not the plastic ice cream bucket I had expected nor even a two-pound coffee can like

Mt. Adams at the end of summer, looking south over the huckleberry grounds from Potato Hill.

the one I picked into. She held out a beautiful coiled Klikitat-style berry basket, strings laced across fresh huckleberry foliage to hold the berries in place. I gasped.

I had seen these baskets in museums, but never full of berries. I took it from her—the first such basket I ever held in my hands. She watched me examine the basket's design. "Mountains," she said, "and stars." Then, "Did you bring something to put them in?" It hadn't occurred to me that they would arrive this way. There was nothing in the car but a blanket. That won't work, I thought. "Can Bud bring it to Theresa at the office?" I realized I was asking her to trust me with something precious She nodded and turned to go. "Don't throw away the leaves," she said. "They need to go back to the mountains." I must have looked puzzled, for she added, "So there'll be a crop next year."

The encounter with this handsome basket brought the work of an unknown Klikitat weaver into my consciousness for the first time. Reaching home, I unlaced the loops, removed the foliage on top, and emptied the precious berries into freezer cartons, saving a quart to make a pie. I examined the basket and marveled at its sturdy construction with some kind of shiny grass covering the outside only. I set it on the table in our cozy family room near where the Warm Springs cornhusk storage bag was displayed. Taking this basket's picture would not do, I thought. Drawing, however primitive, was the only way for me to connect with the work.

The sketch is now faint from years in a file drawer, but it continues to evoke the pleasure of that day for me. I read: "Huckleberry basket, Yakima. Holds 1 gallon berries." I've noted the materials, beargrass and cedar root, and sketched some leaves on a twig: "huckleberry foliage to hold in berries and keep cool." Then my version of Gracie's warning: "return to the berry fields or some natural disaster will ruin next year's crop." I have never looked at a coiled berry basket since that day without visualizing it full of berries protected by leaves.

At the first hint of a thaw in the mountains the following spring, Bud got out the lists of backpacking equipment he had been working on all winter. With a permit from the tribe to travel in the closed area of the reservation, he looked forward to getting into the mountains on weekends. He asked about trails that would take us toward the crest of the Cascades and into the country near the Goat Rocks where we had spent our first summer. Bill, now in college in Seattle, had discovered REI, a place that carried "durable outdoor gear," and we drove over to pick out backpacks, sleeping bags, tent, Primus stove, and freeze-dried foods.*

Unloading the car in Toppenish late that evening, Bud pointed at the air mattresses in my hands. "Don't take them in," he said. "We'll try the tent out tonight."

"Oh, no." I wanted to put off the torture of sleeping on the ground. "Let's wait until we're in the mountains and really need it." He picked up the packaged tent and headed around the house to the backyard. "We've got to see if this works." The tent worked fine. Odd as it must have looked to the neighbors, it was cozy but not uncomfortable. The night was surprisingly cold for May, and we were glad for the new down-filled "mummy" bags Bud had chosen for high-country camping.

I awoke the next morning completely disoriented. From the neighborhood sounds, I knew it was time to get up—but it was strangely dark. Opening the flap I realized we were in a murky, brownish fog, something I had not seen before in the sunny Yakima Valley. "Smudging," Bud said. And that's what it proved to be. Orchardists still using the soon-to-be-outlawed oil-burning pots were protecting their fruit from an untimely frost.

The only thing on our calendar the next weekend was Kitty's high school baccalaureate on Sunday. She and Joe had Saturday plans of their own and, leaving the refrigerator full, Bud and I stuffed our gear into the new backpacks—forty or so pounds for Bud and thirty for me—and took off for the hills. "We'll be home early tomorrow," Bud told the kids, "in plenty of time to get dressed for baccalaureate."

Bud wanted to start our explorations in the far northwestern finger of the reservation, where it poked up between the Snoqualmie and Gifford Pinchot national forests. Donnie Sampson at Satus had told him of a trail that followed the Klickitat

---

*Recreation Equipment, Inc. is an environmentally conscious consumer cooperative founded in Seattle in 1938.

to its source below 8,201-foot Gilbert Peak near Cispus Pass. This was a section of the Cascades that had intrigued us both since our summer at Walupt Lake twenty-one years before.

Driving out through Medicine Valley that Saturday morning, we connected with the upper Klickitat and followed the stream to the road's end. We parked the pickup, hoisted on our packs, and set off uphill toward the crest of the Cascades. Coming upon a meadow that Donnie had described, we stashed our gear under some brush. It was unlikely that anyone else would come this way or bother our packs, but city habits are hard to shed. After a quick lunch, Bud slipped on the daypack that Bill had given us, and I followed him up the brushy trail beside the Klickitat, now only a small stream cascading down the rocks from the snowfields above. As the trail steepened, I stopped more frequently to catch my breath.

"You go on," I finally said. "I'll just perch here in the sun." Once alone, the noise of the place began to fill what I'd thought was silence. The river was loud and unfaltering, punctuated by high calls of hawks. Beneath this was a steady rasp of "Whiskey Jacks," the ever-present Canada jays, quarreling somewhere nearby. I watched the meadow far below for signs of life—a bear, maybe, or cougar. But no such luck. I stretched out with my cap over my face. Awakening suddenly, I saw Bud coming down the trail, gravity pushing him along, a big smile on his face. "It's lucky you didn't go," he said. "There's a snowfield up that way. You would have hated crossing it." Obviously he had loved it. "We need to wait a week or so before we try for Cispus Pass."

We climbed back down to the meadow, pitched the tent, and rustled up some supper. Thinking there might be mosquitoes, we built a small fire to cook over. As soon as the sun began to drop behind the mountains, we burrowed into sleeping bags, exhausted by the unaccustomed exercise, the fresh and rarified air, and the unremitting schedule of the past months.

Heavy breathing beside the tent wakened me, and I nudged Bud. "What's that," I whispered. "Maybe a bear?"

"Maybe elk," he murmured, not wanting to disturb them. "Donnie said we might see some." We lay still, listening. A deep, throaty noise next to my ear made me jump. "That sounded like a 'moo'," I said aloud.

Bud scrambled across his sleeping bag to the foot and looked out the door. "Yup," he said. "We're surrounded by cows."

After breakfast, we decided camping in a pasture with cows was not what we'd had in mind, and Kitty might need some help getting ready for this important senior event. We stuffed the packs, slipped the still-unfamiliar frames on our shoulders, and set off down the four-plus miles to the pickup. The day was heating up, and it was a great relief to throw our packs in the back of the truck and settle into the comfortable seat.

Bud turned the key. The starter growled, but nothing happened. He tried again. Flooded, he thought. We got out, walked around, got in, tried again. No better. Bud lifted the hood and stared at the engine. He checked the oil, checked the water—the limit of his ideas. After repeating these steps, we decided we'd better start walking—seventy-five miles was a long way, but fortunately all downhill.

We figured we'd gone about three miles when a pickup approached. "Need help?" the man said. A tribal member, he identified himself as a Lawrence from up above White Swan. He was coming out to do a little fishing. "I can do this later," he said. "Hop in." We asked him to take us to a phone, realizing even that was a long way away. He wouldn't hear of it and carried us the seventy miles back across the reservation to our house in Toppenish. Kitty had gone. Jumping into more presentable clothes, we made it to the high school gymnasium and into seats in the balcony just in time to see her march in with her class. "I figured you'd either make it or not," she told us when we found her at the close of the service. "It didn't occur to me to send out the tribal police."

Later trips to that meadow were more successful, with day trips to the summit minus the heavy packs, and mountain goats, elk, and deer in sight on the steep hillside above our campsite. But none gave Bud's coworkers more entertainment than the story of the cows and the seventy-five-mile "walk."

It was about this time when the tribal council denied U.S. Supreme Court Justice William O. Douglas permission to bring a party through the closed area of the reservation. The action made us value even more our backpacking ventures and, later, the lifetime permit given us when we left the reservation in 1975.

Over the five summers on the Yakama, we worked our way south along the Pacific crest. On one trip, we camped on 6,600-foot Lakeview Mountain—the mysterious dark image we had seen reflected in Walupt Lake a quarter-century before. When we climbed to the summit and entered that heady world among giant mountains, the only jarring note was the sight of our dusty yellow pickup parked far below.

In June 1970, Bill began the first of three summers working for the U.S. Forest Service on the Snoqualmie National Forest. He was stationed at Tieton Ranger Station just below White Pass on the highway between Yakima and Seattle, fairly close to Toppenish. A strange coincidence, he found himself working under the direction of our friend Walt Tokarczyk. We had known Walt and Shirley since 1949, when we were at Walupt Lake and they were our nearest neighbors at Midway Guard Station, ten miles away.

Joe found a job with a hop grower and Kitty worked briefly in the cherry harvest and represented Toppenish as Miss Friendliness, riding on the community float, the Arrow of Unity, with two classmates. Miss Yakima Nation, Karen Jim of Celilo, Oregon, joined the Toppenish court on the float when she was in town. When the float broke down on the way to a parade in nearby Mabton, a U.S. Navy recruiting unit invited the court to ride on the long metal missile on wheels that they had brought from Puget Sound. Taking one look at the missile's hot metal and the Toppenish girls' short skirts, Karen spread her handsome fringed shawl over the missile and all perched there in comfort.

Bud and I were grateful for the Yakama sense of humor, or perhaps their patience, at the 1970 Fourth of July celebration at the Toppenish Creek encampment grounds near White Swan. After watching the stick game and eating huckleberry-jam-topped fry bread, we went in to watch the dancing. This was enjoyable until Bud and I found ourselves alone in the center of the longhouse as judges for the Ladies' Dance Contest. Still new at these celebrations, we didn't know the criteria for judging nor could we recognize any of these women in their celebratory dress. Each time we asked for another short dance, then another, and another, a kind of low murmur went through the audience.

Finally, we whispered descriptions of our choices to the announcer. Picking up the microphone, he called out three names. The audience burst into laughter and applause, and we relaxed. Somehow we had passed the test. By chance our choices were the wife of a tribal leader, the daughter of a well-recognized traditionalist, and a much-loved visitor from Warm Springs.

During a tribal member's wedding in White Swan's diminutive Catholic church, I discovered a strange irony, but no humor, in the words of the hymn that followed the mass. It was "America the Beautiful"—appropriate, I thought, as I looked out the open windows to the hills toward Mt. Adams. When we sang Katharine Lee Bates's familiar words, I choked up. "O beautiful for spacious skies, for amber waves of grain, for purple mountain majesties. . . ." I knew the words by heart, but found myself actually reading them for the first time.

We moved on to the second verse. "O beautiful for pilgrim feet, whose stern, impassioned stress a thoroughfare for freedom beat across the wilderness." I stopped singing. *A thoroughfare for freedom across the wilderness? Freedom for whom?* There I sat, among families whose ancestors had heard the stern, impassioned stress of cavalry horses and settlers' wagons beating a thoroughfare across their homeland.

There were other discoveries that enriched our understanding of the people we lived among. At Warm Springs, Terry Courtney had shown Bud what he called an Indian wishing well out on the reservation. Impressing the children with the arcane nature of such places, Bud took us for a Sunday ride to find it. After careful search-ing, we came upon a hole in the ground about the width of a fence post. Peering in, we could see beads and coins and other talismans left by unknown visitors. I felt a strong urge to connect. Searching my pocket, I found a penny I'd picked up on a street, dropped it in, and made a wish.

For a long time I wondered if my coin had been an intrusion. Later, on the Yaka-ma Reservation, I told a Yakama friend about another such spot that Bud, Joe, and I had stumbled upon in the hills. "That's a spirit place," she said, when I told her where we'd been. "Did you take anything?"

Shocked, I assured her that we had not. "I dropped in one of the stones I'd picked up on the way in. I did ask for something."

"Good," she said. "You're catching on."

A New Career

By October 1969, the year we arrived in Toppenish, I was enjoying my new role as pie-maker, housecleaner, errand-runner, and all those other domestic jobs I'd skimped on during my five years working in Washington, D.C. By this eleventh move of our marriage, I was skilled at settling in. On Halloween, my forty-fourth birthday, I had a phone call from Gail Flint, the publisher of the *Toppenish Review.*

"I hear you're a journalist," he said.

"Uh, yes?" I stammered. "Who told you?"

"Your Joe. He was in with some photos for the sports page," he said. "He does a great job." We had built a darkroom in this house for Joe—the hobby now a serious interest—and with the new Pentax, he'd taken on the job as one of the photographers at Toppenish High School.

"We're losing our society editor this week," Gail Flint said, "and I'd like to talk to you."

My maternal grandfather had published newspapers in Idaho, Illinois, and Iowa; my sister had worked for the *Chicago Daily News* and, later, the *Tribune*; and I had loved my jobs on the *Iowa State Daily*. Our oldest was off at college, and it was my birthday. Why not? Almost giddy with the prospect and without talking it over with Bud, I made my way to the newspaper office for the interview and accepted the job—half time, to start the next morning.

My trainer was departing editor Sharon Laddrout, who took me across the Ya-kima River to nearby Zillah, then to Granger, another farming community fifteen minutes to the southeast. At each small town she introduced me to my major news sources: the city clerk, the postmaster, and the superintendent of schools. At each place, I was invited to the next meeting of the local chamber of commerce. These would let me meet the local movers and shakers, they told me. I was expected to attend the meetings every week.

Sharon stopped at what I later referred to as "spy drops" in Zillah, Punkin' Center and the Granger Library, where we picked up the news from the local correspondents. My job was to edit their reports into coherent columns that were true to the facts while retaining the writers' styles, she explained.

Before she dropped me at the paper, Sharon handed me the Rolleiflex camera I'd be using and ran through some quick instructions. I hadn't taken so much as a snapshot since the children were old enough to have cameras, but I was up for it.

"OK," she said. "That's what you do for the *Yakima Valley Mirror*. You're the new editor. Go on in and ask Jim about the society page. Have fun!" And she drove off.

I found Jim Flint, the publisher's son and *Toppenish Review* editor. "I thought I was hired as society editor," I said.

"Oh, didn't Gail mention the *Mirror?*" He didn't look surprised. "It's their first paper and his baby, so do it right." Then, about the main job, he said, "Just keep your eyes open and fill the page every week. Hand it in by Monday noon." How could he be so casual?

By the second week of November, I was well into the routine. When I came in Monday morning, I told Jim of the Veterans Day dinner that noon at the tribe's Toppenish Community Center. I had learned of it at the annual Veterans Day Ceremonial that finished there the night before. It had been a colorful celebration, with Indians coming from all over the Northwest. For us, it was another absorbing evening watching the dancers and meeting new tribal members.

Jim sent me over to the community center to see what was going on. "Get us something," he said, "but have it in by noon." Built on tribal land at the far southeast corner of town, the building functioned as longhouse, meeting hall, and sports center for the Yakamas who lived in and around Toppenish. The main door, where we had entered for the celebration, was locked. Finding a smaller entry around the corner, I took a big breath and stepped into the institution-sized kitchen. It was alive with women peeling potatoes and cutting salmon; giant pots steamed on the big range. They stopped briefly to look, then returned to their work.

I introduced myself to an older woman sitting at a nearby table, "I'm from the paper," I said. "Is it all right if I take a few pictures?" She nodded as she pared the skin from a potato. Taking that for a yes, I moved around the kitchen trying to stay out of the way, recording names as I went. When I closed up the Rollei, I realized I didn't want to leave. It was my first chance to sit down informally with some Yakama women.

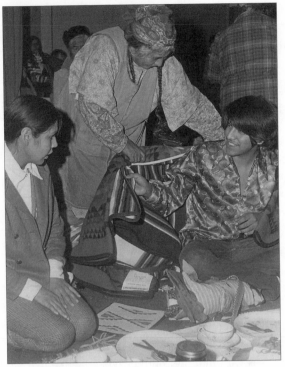

Mr. and Mrs. Arnold Barney serve as stand-ins for the bride and groom at the wedding trade feast (courtesy of the Toppenish Review.)

"Can I help for a while?" I asked the elder, whose name I now knew was Ellen Saluskin. She nodded at a stool nearby and handed me a knife. I began to peel with a deep sense of contentment. Up to this time, my contacts with the Yakama people had been as the superintendent's wife. Now I was on my own. Sitting in the center's kitchen peeling potatoes in the company of women, I felt at home for the first time in that new place.

Writing this, I'm struck by the circularity of what I sat down to do—peel a potato. The potato had nourished the peoples of South America for centuries before it migrated to Europe with the conquistadors. My mother's grandparents had fled to North America over a hundred years before to escape the potato famine in Ireland. The potato itself had migrated to North America in time to save the lives of my father's British forebears three hundred years before. I had eaten few childhood meals without this sturdy vegetable, and within two years I became the namesake of the blossom of the potato's wild cousin, *anipásh.**

Jim Flint continued to cover the hard news—the tribe's official activities, political actions, and major celebrations. My job was to offer a closer look at the everyday happenings in Toppenish and the nearby communities. The Yakama Indian families, the longtime farm and ranch families, and the Hispanic families coming into the valley for agricultural work offered a rich resource for stories and photos.

---

*Anipásh means Indian potato (*Claytonia lanceolata*). See Hunn and Selam, *Nch'i-Wána "The Big River,"* 345, and Beavert, *Yakima Language Practical Dictionary*. One of my photos that day made the front page of the *Toppenish Review*. The caption credited six women, including Ellen Saluskin, with peeling five bags of potatoes for the expected dinner crowd of twelve hundred. A family member sent the photo to a young granddaughter of Ellen Saluskin's. When the child came for her first visit, she was shy with the relatives until she recognized Ellen from the picture. Shouting "Grandma," she ran into her arms.

From my coworkers at the newspaper office I learned about a common misconception in the Yakima Valley—that the Indians received regular checks from the U.S. government. When we arrived in 1969 it was true that checks for timber sales, agricultural leases on Indian-owned allotments, and periodic per-capita dividends from tribal enterprises were drawn on the U.S. Treasury because all tribal assets were deposited there in the tribes' or individual Indians' accounts. During our years on the Yakama, the tribes began issuing checks under their own names, hoping to dispel the belief that Indians were supported by the U.S. government.

On the final day of 1970, my picture story of a traditional Yakama wedding trade—taken with the new Pentax Spotmatic that Bud had given me for Christmas—filled two pages of the *Toppenish Review.* Joe, now darkroom technician for the paper, had developed and printed the photos.* I learned that day that the "trade" was not to bring gifts to the new couple but a time for exchanges between members of the two extended families—a way of sealing the new relationship the marriage represented. The trading partners from the man's family would bring items made or purchased by men to exchange with relatives of the bride for items made or gathered by the women and agreed upon as of equal value.

The most interesting item I have seen offered for trade was a stick that a man placed on the floor at Wapato Longhouse. "What does that mean?" I whispered to the woman next to me. She tipped her chin toward the window, "That horse, outside." That day I did not see what was offered in return, but Marie Slockish told me later that as a child she had seen her mother give a three-gallon Klikitat basket for a mare.

At the end of our first year on the Yakama Reservation, we cancelled our subscription to the Sunday edition of the *Washington Post*—a great relief. The national and world news had remained grim and seemed increasingly far away. Yakama, like Warm Springs, was a restful oasis.

Through our years on the Yakama Reservation, we attended weddings and wedding trades, funerals, memorials, and name-givings at the big community center in Toppenish and at the longhouses. Among the memorable occasions at the Toppenish center were honor dinners for Washington's governor Dan Evans and Senator Henry "Scoop" Jackson. Once the ceremonies began—in the large gymnasium or the intimate setting of the smaller longhouses—the dignified manner and eloquence of the tribal leaders and the songs of greeting or prayer made such gatherings extraordinary experiences. Any trepidation Bud felt when summoned to say a few words was quickly

---

*I thank Virginia Beavert for alerting me to this story and to many more that offered readers a closer look at the living culture of the Yakama people.

dispelled by the courtesy of the tribal leaders. Such appearances looked difficult to me. But when I heard, "Miss-us Schlick, bring your camera," I considered it another photo opportunity and enjoyed it as part of my job.

On November 20, 1969, Alex Saluskin, chairman of the Veterans Day Ceremonial, wrote the editor of the *Review*, thanking the local business people who contributed to the recent celebration. He expressed hopes for better cooperation in the community and stated the tribe's willingness to work with any group "who will show equality and not show stupidity or ignorance." I realized that at our best the newspaper offered a forum for all residents. I had seen Alex Saluskin at the ceremonial and looked forward to meeting him.

Just before Christmas, the tribal and BIA employees put on a party. The affair was smaller than the tribal celebrations, where hundreds came from across the region, but it was festive. Accustomed to sitting on the sidelines mesmerized by the drumming and the color and motion of the passing dancers, I was surprised when an elegant older dancer stopped in front of me and gestured for me to join him. Believing that my sole responsibility was as a spectator, the invitation completely flustered me. "Oh, no," I said. "I cannot! No—but thank you!"

"It's not hard to do." the man urged, holding out his hand. "I'll show you."

"I'm honored to be asked," I said, completely embarrassed at my own timidity. "But I just can't do it." His face was serious as he said, "You owe me a favor!" He turned and joined the other dancers. Bud, sitting beside me, asked if I had recognized the dancer. "That's Alex Saluskin." I had not. He looked very different in his dance outfit from the man I had seen at the celebration in full regalia with feathered headdress.

My new role as reporter brought me into frequent contact with tribal members, and I hoped to find someone to ask about the favor business. Not long after the agency party, I was invited to speak in neighboring Sunnyside about my work on women's occupations in Washington, D.C. The other speaker was Mrs. Antoine Miller, a Yakama woman deeply involved in the passing along of traditional wisdom.

For me, her talk was a short course in current tribal issues—protecting reservation lands, retaining languages and culture, and enhancing education. It was good material for an article and another chance to learn more about the Yakama people. Work in the Washington, D.C., neighborhoods had convinced me that change has to come from within the group seeking it. Hazel Miller was an articulate advocate for her people's views. She also offered me the opportunity to ask what Alex Saluskin meant by saying I owed him a favor. I told the story to the Millers. "Oh, yes," Hazel said, as Tony nodded. "Anytime you refuse an invitation to dance you need to pay."

"How do I know what favor is expected?" I asked. "He'll let you know," she said.

I had forgotten about my debt until mid December of the following year when a nurse called me from the Toppenish hospital. "Alex Saluskin has asked me to call," she said. "He tells me you owe him a favor."

"Ye-s," I said. "I do."

"He wants you at the hospital immediately." That worried me. I'd heard something about a pacemaker for the tribal leader. "His grandchildren are here, and he wants his picture taken with them."

"Oh, good," I said, relieved. "I can do that." Camera in hand, I was ushered into Alex Saluskin's room, a bit anxious to find out if there were hard feelings about my refusal. He greeted me cordially and introduced the children of his son Joseph and their spouses. The photo in the December 10, 1970, *Review* shows the family reunion, Alex seated in a wheelchair, a plaid Pendleton bathrobe over his pajamas, and seven young, handsome adults nearby. The obligation was discharged. The pacemaker enabled this vital leader to continue his active life for another three years.

I learned many things about Yakama culture from Hazel Miller, and one related in a way to obligation or, as I later began to think of such exchanges, reciprocity. When I told Bud that I had met the Millers, he said he knew them. "In fact," he said, "she owes me fifty dollars." That surprised me, for I knew his firm policy against lending money. When he first arrived, he explained, she had come to him for advice, and the loan seemed the only way to be of real assistance. "I'll never see the money," he said.

Sometime after that, I was in Hazel's office gathering information for a story I was working on. As I started to leave, she took something from the shelf behind her. "Here," she said, "take this," thrusting a Ken doll into my hand. She had dressed him as a war dancer. Matching pale blue, red, and white beadwork decorated the breechcloth, vest, moccasins, wristlets, and tie; a tiny deer-hair roach was tied on his head. I drew in my breath and stared at the beautiful outfit on the pale body.*

"People come in," she said. "They call him 'Roger Swaps.' " That seemed to embarrass her. Roger Swaps was the name given to a local non-Indian trader and collector who danced at tribal celebrations wearing elaborate heirloom regalia. I realized she was proud of the outfit but had not thought how strange it looked on Barbie's Ken until her visitors identified him. "Oh, Hazel," I said. "I owe you something for this."

"No, it's yours." I thanked her, took Roger Swaps home and showed him to Bud. "OK, honey," I said. "You two are square."

Before snowfall that first winter, I finally had a beautiful coiled cedar root huckleberry basket for my own, another result of that invitation to speak in Sunnyside. Geoffrey

---

*"War dance outfit" was the term used to describe this regalia at the time.

Hilton, a well-known businessman in Zillah, introduced himself to me after the program. Bud had mentioned him as a friend of the tribes who served on the housing committee.

"I hear you collect Indian handcraft," he said, sitting down near me with pie and coffee. "I have a few things I'd like to find homes for." He spoke quietly. "If you are interested, give me a call."

I couldn't believe my good fortune. I had just received a check from my mother for $225, my one-fourth share of the royalties she occasionally received from a land-surveying book my father had published years before. I called Geoff and set up an appointment. Always interested in unusual arts, Joe came with me.

As we entered the sunny house at the west end of Zillah's main street, Geoff said: "Let me know what interests you."

"That berry basket?" I said, pointing to a beautiful Klikitat he was using for waste paper beside his desk. "I guess that can go," he said, and told me a price. I deducted it from my total. I pointed to a very large oval coiled basket with straighter sides and no loops at the rim. "How about that?"

"That can go." He gave a price. I was still within my limit. In the end, I also acquired a twined handbag with five eight-pointed stars on one side, a large twined storage bag (I wanted it for the woman who had advised Bud at the Relander funeral), and a brimless hat like the one worn by Minnie Yellow Wolf at that first parade we had attended on the Colville Reservation. Our only argument was over the price of the hat.

"Twelve fifty," Geoff said. "Twelve dollars and fifty cents?" I hoped it wasn't twelve hundred. He nodded. I was incredulous. I had seen one of these rare hats in a Yakima antique shop just a few weeks before priced at ninety-nine dollars. I knew then that I would never own one. "Twenty-five," I said. "It's worth more than that, but that's what I have left."

"OK," he said. "I'll sell it to you for eighteen!" With the remaining seven dollars, I chose a child-sized round root-digging bag made with cotton string. Joe bought a lovely small twined handbag as a gift for an artist friend. As we gave our thanks and began to leave, Geoff handed me a doll-sized beaded handbag, about three inches square. "I think it was a child's first project," he said. Geoff later told me that his son was upset at how little he had charged for the baskets. "But," he said, "I knew they would be appreciated."

Neither of us knew then that this close association with such fine objects and, subsequently, their makers would take me into a new field of study. Sometime later I realized that research into these basketry arts of the Columbia Plateau peoples had been a natural step for me. My college degree in the esoteric field known as "household equipment" and a minor in applied art had offered perfect preparation. What is basketry but art applied to the creation of household equipment?

At home with a berry basket that was mine to study at last, I marveled at the complexity of the weaving method the unknown basket maker had used to build the sharp-peaked mountain design.* I saw that the decoration was a layer on the outside of the strong coiled basket, not visible on the inside.

In time, I watched a Klikitat weaver fold shiny leaves of beargrass and darker strips of the cedar root's bark back and forward over the coil and secure the fold with a smooth strand of finely split cedar root. Examining this basket, I thought about our life—of folding back and forward through new experiences and repeating old. I felt strengthened, as the basket was, by this layering.

Widening the Circle

By the spring of 1970, I was settled into the newspaper job and writing about everyday activities of the reservation people as well as those of the town and farm community. I wanted readers to know that more was going on than tribal rodeos and powwows.

A big event in March was the annual Indian Trade Fair. By chance, my weekend visit to the reservation the previous spring had coincided with the annual event.** Bud had taken me around to meet tribal members and to see the variety of their arts. In addition to the work of contemporary artists, there were family displays of keepsakes—cornhusk bags and huckleberry baskets, basket hats, beaded clothing and bags, buckskin dresses, and men's outfits—in greater variety and quality than on view in the museum exhibits I had seen. There were ribbons and prizes—even awards for the best-dressed babies and toddlers.

Covering the event for the newspaper in 1970, I met the artists, including those who had established the showcase.‡ In 1971, I was better known and was commandeered as a judge for the baby contest. Judges did not walk around incognito; we made our decision and awarded the ribbons in front of parents and relatives. I figured we'd end up with one friend and a number of enemies, but I was wrong. Like volleyball at Warm Springs or bowling on the tribal team in Virginia, the participants simply enjoyed the contest.

---

*I learned later to recognize the design on that basket as the work of Klikitat weaver Lucy Cayuse Thomas and her daughters of Husum, Washington.

**The fair was later named Spilyay-Mi (Coyote's) Arts and Crafts Fair.

‡One was Will Sampson, a quiet but impressive Oklahoma Native who would play the part of Chief Bromden in *One Flew Over the Cuckoo's Nest*.

Although there were many beautiful baskets in the family displays over those years, I remember seeing only one woman weaving—Carrie Sampson from the Umatilla Reservation. She was twining a small round *wapaas*, a root-digging bag, at a fair held in the Toppenish Armory. When I asked if I could photograph her while weaving, she turned to Ellen Saluskin, who was keeping her company at the table, and pushed a half-made bag into her hands. "We'll both weave," Carrie said.

The photo shows Ellen puzzling over the loose warps. I thought at the time that she wasn't sure what to do next, but later, after mastering that technique myself, I realized she was figuring out where to start. Like most women brought up on the Columbia Plateau in her generation, Ellen would have learned this traditional off-loom weaving technique as a child.

When I began serious research into Plateau basketry in 1975, I could find only a few practicing weavers and almost no young people carrying on the art. Fortunately, by 1994, when my basketry book was published, there was growing interest in learning the unique weaving techniques so important to their Plateau ancestors. Today, many fine weavers are working again to "bring out" the old skills. Klikitat basket weaver Nettie Jackson, who began to weave in her mid thirties at the urging of her dying mother, told me the skill "was always in" her. Many other weavers feel the same.

It was May 1970 when the Yakama tribal council established a newspaper, the *Yakima Nation Review*. Although my *Toppenish Review* editor wasn't sure about having two *Reviews* in the same town, I considered it the greatest flattery. Ross Sockzehigh, the tribe's news editor, asked me to work with the new staff members. The young women were an apt crew and needed little tutelage. Most continued in the work, one serving for eighteen years on both the news and business sides of the newspaper and also as acting editor. Another went on to make journalism her career and has been honored for educating the public about tribal treaty rights and fisheries.[1]

Editor Jim Flint did a good job of covering the tribal celebrations held in Toppenish, but when I learned of smaller events of interest to the public, I tried to do some kind of story. Johnson Meninick told Bud of working since the fall of 1969 with a group of eight- to fourteen-year-old boys at Satus Longhouse to teach them the traditional war dance and social dance songs of the Yakama and other tribes. The boys' initiation was set for the spring of 1970 at the Satus Intertribal Dance Competition. Johnson invited Eagle Seelatsee and Bud to speak and asked if I would take pictures for the newspaper—my first opportunity to cover a longhouse happening.

We drove to Satus Longhouse, about ten miles southeast of Toppenish, and found a one-story rectangular frame building with the door on the east end. Entering an open hall with bleachers along the north wall and benches on the south, we saw men seated on a low stage at the far end. Tribal councilman and longhouse leader Watson Totus beckoned to Bud to join them there.

I turned toward the south side, where women sat along the wall. One appeared to be watching with special interest. I sat down beside her. Eyeing my beaded handbag, she said, "I made that bag."

Her expression was unreadable. What is expected of me here, I thought. Should I give it to her? "It was a gift from Mary Ann Arthur when we left Warm Springs," I blurted out. "I'm Mary Schlick."

"I know," she said. I had wondered who had made it and asked her name. "Mary Billy." She smiled.

I relaxed and held up the handbag. "I've puzzled over the orange sky."

She looked at me with a curious frown. "The deer is running from a fire," as if I should know.

"Oh, good," I said. "I hoped so." Satisfied, we settled into a companionable silence and waited for the event to begin.

Thirty-four years later, Mary Ann Arthur Meanus stopped at my small house in the woods above the orchards of the Hood River Valley. She had come over from Warm Springs to look for huckleberries. Commercial pickers from the west side had been using rakes in the traditional places, and the elders feared overuse was destroying the berrying grounds on Mt. Hood.

With three young helpers—Aaron, Austin, and Anthony Arthur, grandsons of her daughter Vivian—Mary Ann hoped to find a new place to pick their winter's supply. Vivian Arthur had been my daughter's age and one of my cherished 4-Hers. We had mourned her early death, and meeting these boys had special significance for me. I brought out the beaded bag with the jumping deer and told the boys how much their great-grandmother's gift had meant to me for forty years. Mary Ann said it had been a gift to her in the first place. "I wanted you to have something special," she said.

As they prepared to go, I looked for my map of the national forest showing places to pick. Not finding it, I slipped a bill into her hand to purchase another map at the ranger station. "I can buy it," she smiled up at me. "But I won't deny you this blessing."

As she drove away with these fine great-grandchildren, I thought, "Yes, it is a blessing to be allowed to give a gift."

The Satus Longhouse initiation of the young drummers was impressive, beginning with an honor dinner complete with a huge decorated cake. Johnson awarded each boy an "Indian diploma," a green-tipped and feather-trimmed drumstick. Then Eagle

Seelatsee recalled the history of the war dances, commending the singers for keeping the tradition alive. Bud told them that pride in their customs would help them achieve leadership in the tribe and nationally. "I hope one of you someday will have my job."[2]

Following the speakers, the boys' families presented gifts to those who had helped with the project. Johnson Meninick was master of ceremonies.* I had been told about give-aways, but this was the first I witnessed. I watched with fascination as blankets, beadwork, dress lengths, bright-colored yarn, and scarves were handed out. Suddenly, I heard, "Ma-ry Schlick." I didn't move. The woman next to me touched my arm. "You're being called."

"Why?" I asked, truly puzzled. "Ma-ry Schlick," again. "Come to the front."

This was a new experience for me. I looked at Bud on the stage. He was pointing at Johnson Meninick at the microphone. Then I heard a woman's voice, louder and strident, somewhere to my left. "Mary Schlick. Get on up here to the front!" As I walked forward, I saw Elsie WakWak sitting at the end of the benches on a chair. She gestured with her hand toward Johnson. "You're wanted up here."

As I stood by the master of ceremonies, he pulled a small round basket out of his pocket. Made of red and green yarn, it was trimmed around the top with Indian-tanned buckskin. He held it out to me. I must have looked puzzled, for Elsie cupped her hands around her mouth and shouted again, "Tell her what it's for."

"Well," Johnson said into the microphone, his voice solemn. "My mother told me if you have a small bag you're a slo-ow digger." The room erupted in laughter and applause. I caught on—that's what it was, a very small version of the round twined bags that I'd been told Plateau women tie on their waists to put roots into as they are digging. Johnson's wife had made it. I returned to my seat to study the bag, thrilled with the gift and warmed by the sense of inclusion Johnson's remarks had given me. Yes, indeed, I thought, I probably would be a very slow digger.

In 1974, I had the opportunity to find out. Bud had located a much-used *kápin* (digging tool), something I had requested for Christmas. Violet Tomaskin took me up on Ahtanum Ridge in April and pointed out the amazing variety of edible roots whose greenery was springing from the rocky soil. "People say these hills are barren," she told me, "but we know they are full of food." I watched her dig. It looked simple.

---

*Over the years at Yakama, we had many opportunities to hear Johnson Meninick's comments. In response to an anthropologist's remarks about Indians arriving in North America over a land bridge, he said in his rich and deliberate voice, "If we came from Siberia, we came with an Evinrude motor." Much later, I learned that an earlier Yakama Chief Meninock had expressed similar sentiments in 1915, saying: "I was not brought here from a foreign country and did not come here. I was put here by the Creator."

I placed the point of the curved iron shaft of my *kápin* in back of the sprout, lifted my foot to force it in, and nearly fell when there was nothing for my foot to push against. The *kápin* is not a shovel. Finally successful, I twisted off the green top of the small globe she told me was *mummin*, brushed away the dirt, and dropped it into the *wapaas* tied to my waist. It would be a hungry winter, I thought, if it were up to me to dig enough for a family.

As I walked along, eyes on the ground, I spotted a chipped stone and picked it up, a broken piece of an arrowhead. A shiver went thought me. I knew this land and these people. This chipping was a word on a page of their history. To carry it away would be to erase it. I set it back where it had lain.

We returned to Satus Longhouse for the war dance finals on Sunday after the drummers' initiation and were seated on the stage next to the announcer. Behind us were two of the five big drums, about eight men surrounding each drum. It was a new experience to be close enough to see the contests unfold. When the announcer called for entrants, he named the drum to accompany them. From this vantage, I could pick out dancers we had known at Warm Springs.

Between contests came the drawing for door prizes. "But first," the announcer said, "we have a gift-giving." I perked up. This might be a story. He held up a necklace with a red and yellow medallion. "This necklace is being given to Mrs. Schlick by Watson Totus." Again, I was astonished. I looked at Watson and his wife. Both were beaming. Tilda Totus, known as Tillie, had said very little to me the many times we had met, but her smile was reassuring. Perhaps her reserve was from shyness or not being comfortable with English rather than because she disapproved of me.

When Tillie made a pair of moccasins for me at Christmastime, she asked Flora Onepennee, her sister-in-law, to make the presentation. We sat together on a bench at the front corner of the longhouse, and I ran my fingers over the velvety buckskin decorated with a beaded tepee superimposed over a circle. When I thanked Tillie, Flora insisted that I try them on there in the busy longhouse. Seeing that the moccasins were too long, they laughed.

"She wanted them big enough," Flora explained, and marked where my toes ended. Without a word, Tillie disappeared with the moccasins. "She went home to fix them," Flora pointed with her chin toward the houses beside the longhouse. In a few minutes, Tillie returned and I eased on the moccasins. They fit like kid gloves. I assumed she'd used a sewing machine, but checking now I discover her fine rolled stitches that hold firm today. Within a few months, again at Satus, the Josh Umtuch family surprised Bud with moccasins made especially for him. We were well on our way to being properly dressed for a longhouse.

Each of these experiences expanded Bud's understanding of the Yakama people. A visit to the 1970 Celilo Salmon Festival offered a chance for him to begin to understand the deep hurt carried by the people of the river over the loss of the fishery at Celilo Falls. On Memorial Day weekend in 1970, Marcella Jim, 1970 Salmon Festival Queen, invited Kitty to attend the festival as Toppenish "royalty." Also being honored were Miss Yakima Nation, Karen Jim, and Linda Blankenship, visiting from Alaska, where she was Salmon Bake Queen. What might seem a frivolous activity for Bud as super-intendent, he looked at another way—a chance to learn more about a place of critical importance in Yakama history.

Celilo is a small settlement on the Oregon side of the Columbia about ten miles east of The Dalles. We had passed there once in the fall of 1955 on the way to Portland from Colville Agency. Indians must have been fishing at the famous Celilo Falls when we drove past, but my mind holds no image of that spectacular place other than from photographs. The photos are stunning of the ancient fishing grounds, where high wa-ter and channeled basalt turned the river into a great raging horseshoe. For ten thou-sand years or more, fishermen with huge dip nets had stood on rocks in the river and atop every crevice to lift a rich livelihood from those churning waters.

By the time we came to the Celilo Salmon Festival in 1970, The Dalles Dam had replaced all that with a docile lake that carried great barges of grain and frozen Idaho potatoes toward Japan. Completed in 1957 to control unpredictable floods and bring electricity to every corner of the west, the huge concrete structure drowned the fishery that twice each year was an economic, social, and cultural gathering place for thou-sands of Native people.

A poignant photo taken that March day in 1957 by Seattle photographer J.W. Thompson shows Celilo resident Maggie Jim and two of her daughters standing on the high hill above the village.* They are watching the waters surge backward behind the new dam to cover the magnificent Celilo Falls forever and silence the roar of its waters. The rich, exciting life that had sustained the Native people of the region for centuries was at an end.

Our visit to the Celilo Salmon Festival offered a chance for Bud to begin to un-derstand the deep hurt carried by the people of the river over the loss of this life and livelihood. Having joined the BIA in the 1950s, he knew of the government's efforts to end the trust relationship with Indian tribes—breaking a promise guaranteed by the treaties "as long the mountains stand and the rivers flow."[3] But the affected tribes—

---

*Over three thousand color slides of the Indians of Eastern Washington in the 1950s are in the collection of Maryhill Museum of Art near Goldendale, Washington, a gift from Lucile Thompson Munz, the photographer's daughter.

Klamath, Menominee, and others—were not those he worked with. The Colvilles, Warm Springs, and Yakama had been able to resist termination, but the stilling of Celilo Falls in 1957 was an example of policy that caused extreme hardship for many Columbia River families.

As I wrote the newspaper item about the Salmon Festival, I began to see the value beyond the pleasure of the time we spent at social and ceremonial affairs. These unusual opportunities helped us learn new customs and expectations.

At the 1970 Veteran's Day Powwow at the Toppenish, I sat with Marge Pease, a friend since our years together on the Colville. The Pease family were frequent visitors at Yakama celebrations—the boys award-winning dancers, as was Ben, Bud's old Nespelem basketball teammate, and their daughters. We had known Janine, their oldest, since she was two.*

During the evening, a beaded handbag, a gift from artist Nathan Olney Jr., was passed up to me where we sat in the bleachers. Astonished, I was wondering what I should do next, when an older woman nearby gestured for me to put the bag on my arm and join the dancers. Marge

Maggie Jim (right) and her daughters stand above their village to watch as the waters of the Columbia flood Celilo Falls on March 10, 1957 (courtesy of Maryhill Museum of Art).

Pease nodded, slipped her shawl over her shoulders, and stood up. "Come on," she said. "You need to acknowledge this gift by dancing with it."

We stepped out on the floor together, joining the women dancers. I tried not to watch my feet, but the stately hesitation step that gives the women such smooth movement was eluding me. I thought, too late, that I should have worked on this step at home. I also should have remembered to bring a shawl. "It's our fur coat," I'd been told. "It makes street clothes okay on the dance floor." I had not dressed to be a participant.

---

*An enrolled member of the Crow tribe, Janine Pease was founding president of Little Big Horn College on the Crow Reservation. In 2003, she was named vice president for American Indian Affairs at Rocky Mountain College in Billings.

As we circled the floor, I thought of our first celebration at White Swan when Ben Pease invited me for the Owl Dance and Marge invited Bud. Ben told me then that it was the custom for women to do the asking for that particular dance. Nervous as I had been, at least I'd not refused the invitation as I had Alex Saluskin's. I began to realize that I'd grown out of the role of onlooker in this life and needed to think of myself, as Bud did, as a participant.

7. TO EVERYTHING A SEASON, 1970-1973

We are measured not so much by how we
change, but rather what we mend.

— Tim Whitsell*

We Are Not Strangers

In late March and early April, before any family goes out to dig, selected women from the longhouses watch for the first green fingers of bitterroot poking through the rocky soil of the hills surrounding the Yakima Valley. This welcome sight signals the time for one of the feasts of the first foods, the time to thank the Creator for the return of the roots. Each ceremonial digger ties a round twined *wapaas* at her waist.** With the sharp point of her *kápin* she loosens the edible root from the rocky soil, brushes off the dirt, removes the greenery, and drops it in the bag. The *kápin* is today a slightly curved iron tool about two and a half feet long with a wooden or iron handle. Before European contact, they were made of fire-hardened wood with a handle of bone or antler.

Traditionally, the roots—bitterroot, wild carrot, camas, several varieties of lomatium, wild potato, and others—provided over half the calories that sustained the Native people of the Columbia Plateau and held a position of high importance in their culture. Men from the longhouse still provide the deer and salmon and eels. Chokecherries on the stems and huckleberries come out of cupboards and freezers for the spring feasts.

We attended our first such feast at the end of March 1970 when Delores Buck sent word that the Wanapum would be holding their feast on the coming Sunday. Delores had relatives at Warm Springs and had offered us her friendship when we first arrived on the Yakama. Her husband was Rex Buck, Wanapum tribal leader, and son of Puck Hyah Toot, nephew and successor to Smohalla. We arrived at Priest Rapids that day just before noon to find many cars and pickups but no people in sight. The sound of drums and soaring men's voices from the longhouse told us something had

---

*Tim Whitsell, "Daddy's Grace," *Fishtrap Anthology*, 1995, 9.

**Wapaas* is the Sahaptin word for a round twined bag to hold roots and other plants.

Violet Tomaskin gently lifts the bitterroot from the loosened soil. "These hills are full of food," she said.

begun, and, unsure of the protocol, we followed a blonde woman in dark glasses and her companion to the closed longhouse door. Rich odors of roasting salmon and deer meat sifted toward us from the kitchen window.

"Let's wait until the song ends," Bud suggested, but the blonde woman gave the door a firm rap. It opened a crack and we could see the stern face of an older man in gray braids just inside the door. Seeing the woman, he gave a sharp gesture toward her with the back of his hand and closed the door. We stepped back. The blonde turned and made a little grimace. "Oh," she said. "That's Frank Sohappy. He doesn't approve of me."

From his name, I knew Frank Sohappy was the husband of Julia Sohappy, the woman who had given Bud advice at the Relander funeral and a close relative of the Wanapum people.* I wasn't sure if he was being particular about who entered the service or about the time we could enter. In a few minutes, the song ended, and we heard the closing "Aiii" swelling up from the people inside. The door opened, and Delores came out to usher us in. She told us later that the blonde had been coming for years and had photographed and taped the Wáashat service when she knew both were forbidden.

"Was she punished for that?" I said. "Not by us." Delores looked over at the woman and lowered her voice. "Did you notice she's almost blind? She was fine before she did that."

Bud found a seat in front with the singers and the older men, who included stately Frank Sohappy, more relaxed without the doorkeeper responsibility. We met his wife Julia and discovered that she was the woman instructing Bud at the Relander funeral. I sat along the north wall with the women, recognizing that the sides were

---

*Sohappy is the English version of the Sahaptin name *Suxapi*. Amelia Sohappy, personal communication, July 2005.

reversed from those at Satus longhouse, and watched the swift set-up for the feast.

First, a line of young women came in with bundles of tule mats, which they rolled out in front of the benches and across the front. Girls, colorful in bright wing dresses, brought bowls of roots and berries from the kitchen. The hunters and fishers carried platters of deer meat and salmon. Small dishes of barbecued eels were placed with the other dishes at intervals along the tables. "No one will need to reach very far," I thought. Two youngsters carried a basket of cups while a third placed one at each place. A larger boy followed, carrying a big graniteware coffeepot, and poured a sip of water in each cup.

Within minutes we were ready to begin, and the women slipped off the bench to sit on the floor beside the mat that was our table. Always a challenge for me to find a place to fold my legs, I looked over at Bud and saw that, with the men near him, he would simply lean over from the bench to reach his food.

When all were silent, Rex Buck said, "*Nusux.*" The woman next to me whispered, "Take some salmon." The people took their forks, picked a bit of salmon from a nearby platter, and ate it. Then "*yáamash*" (deer). He named each sacred food in order, each root, huckleberries (*wíwnu*), and chokecherries (*tmísh*) dried on the branches. Each food was honored as it was named. Then Rex said "*chúush*," a strong, long drawn-out word. We lifted our cups and drank water, the greatest gift of all—the source of life. Setting down our cups, we were free to begin to serve ourselves from the heaped platters and bowls near us. Later in the meal, when all were finished, a spill of water again was poured into each cup.

Ringing the bell, Rex said again "*chúush.*" All drank the water and then stood while the drummers sang a closing prayer. We filed outside, the men followed by the women, circling the longhouse counterclockwise. We stood for the final prayer in a great arc facing the longhouse. Beyond, the six-pointed star on Smohalla's flag waved from the flagpole under the carved image of Wowshuxkluh, the sacred bird. I thought of Relander's words in *Drummers and Dreamers*: "Wowshuxkluh sleeps until the first faint signs of spring, then he talks to everything that lives and grows: 'Now is the time to come, now is the time to start growing.' "[1] With right hands raised toward the Creator, we all released a long "Aiiii."

In late November 1970, the reservation lost a respected elder when Frank Sohappy died. Attending a solemn wake for the Wapato Longhouse leader, I was struck again by the interrelatedness of the community we had become a part of. My good friend from Warm Springs, Mary Ann Arthur, sat nearby, and I recognized Anne George and Lucy RedThunder, women I had know on the Colville.

Through the years, I've taken part in many feasts of thanksgiving—at Rock Creek for the wild celery, at Celilo for the arrival of the salmon, at Wapato and Satus and Toppenish Creek for the roots, and at Warm Springs and in a Yakama family huckleberry camp near Mt. Adams for the berries.* These dinners always arouse in me memories of festive meals in my childhood at the home of my father's favorite cousins, the Howlands. Sophia Simpson Dodds, my paternal grandmother, was born into a large extended family that left Massachusetts in the 1830s to come to Illinois and then to Minnesota. I can name twelve generations back to Francis Cooke, who arrived in North America with his son John on the *Mayflower* in 1620. His wife and daughters followed the next year.

For much of my life, especially at Thanksgiving, I thought about the frightening Atlantic voyage in the small ship and the Pilgrim's struggle to survive in a new land in order to be free to practice their beliefs. I also thought about the generosity of the Native people who made that survival possible. I did not think about the dire consequences of that generosity on the future of the people who were already here—consequences that, ironically, were disastrous for the religious freedom of the indigenous people as well as for life itself.

Isaac Ingalls Stevens, Washington's first territorial governor, was responsible for negotiating the June 9, 1855, Yakama treaty with the United States of America. In the treaty, the Yakama people reserved 1,372,000 acres for their exclusive use and benefit, while relinquishing most of their rights on nearly eight times that area—10.8 million acres of ancestral homeland. In meetings with the general public, when Yakama Tribal Chairman Robert Jim referred to "your Governor Stevens" and the change in the peoples' lives brought by the 1855 treaties, I would think to myself, "He was not my Governor Stevens!" As an Iowan, I claimed no responsibility for this stranger from "Back East" in Massachusetts.

During our years on the Yakama, however—and much too slowly—the history of the settlement of this country began to come into focus for Bud and for me. His New Jersey progenitors, the Condits, had arrived from England only a few years after mine landed at Plymouth. We had known that the New World of our ancestors was not "new" but the ancestral home of those already here. I learned that in 1621 the people of Plymouth settlement and the Wampanoag Indians drew up a treaty that brought fifty years of local peace, an act unique in early Indian-European relations.[2]

On reflection, Bud and I came to realize that, like it or not, our ancestors' actions changed life for Native people. Helpless to alter history, we felt deep gratitude to the Indian people for welcoming us into their world. Our ardent desire was that our own

---

*When seeking out Warner Jim, maker of folded cedar-bark baskets, in 1978.

actions, if nothing else, would do no harm.

Working on this book, I discussed these thoughts with Ronnie Washines, managing editor of the *Yakama Nation Review*. I described my discovery that I bear even more of the burden of history because my ancestors came so long ago. The thought made me grateful for the opportunity to live among his people, to begin, at least, to see the world in a different way.

I began to wonder what Bud and I had learned from this life, how we were changed by it. I remembered Ron's brother Tony telling me it was not so much forgiveness that people offered us, but patience. Yes, I thought. Patience is a virtue neither Bud nor I had brought to our life together. Our new neighbors had honored us with the expectation that we would learn their ways. Slowly through the years of softer voices, a gentler pace, we had begun to learn to take life as it came. Once we discovered that life has its own

The Ceremony of Chiefs, an old tradition for welcoming visitors, was remembered and revived by Cecelia and Bert Totus at Satus Longhouse in March 1971. Following the young leader are Genevieve Hooper, W.T. Schlick, Eagle Seelatsee, Louis Mitchell, and Andrew David.

tempo, that "Indian time" is whenever things happen, we became better parents, better partners. It wasn't that the outside world was going on without us on the reservation; we simply realized that we didn't have to take on every problem it offered.

At a later time, another Washines brother put this nonjudgmental attitude in terms of acceptance. Clifford Washines, speaking to non-Indian state and federal resource managers, assured them: "We are all equal here—there are no dumb questions."[3] From the beginning of our life among Indian people, they met us with generosity, patience, and acceptance. We learned very early that we were not strangers.

For Bud, an unforgettable experience with Yakama generosity took place in March 1971 when Cecelia Totus, the wife of Watson's brother Bert Totus, invited him to attend a Ceremony of Chiefs. She and her husband were hosting the event on the final afternoon of the young people's dance contest at Satus Longhouse. Cecelia was the daugh-

Drummers Levi and Victor George, Robert Jim, Martin Hannigan, Louis Spino, and Lige Williams sing as they wait for dinner following the Frank Sohappy memorial service at Wapato Longhouse.

ter of a well-known Yakama leader, Yumtobe Kamiakin. Like many of the older Yakama women we came to know, she was well-versed in Plateau traditions and committed to seeing them continue. She told Bud that it had been a custom to perform this ceremony when Yakamas gathered—giving special recognition to tribal leaders and distinguished visitors. Alex Pinkham announced during the ceremony that the last time he had taken part in such an event was on his return from World War I more than fifty years before.

The ceremony began as Watson Totus announced the entry of the honorees: "Andrew David, Genevieve Hooper, Bill Johnson, Louis McFarland, Louis Mitchell, Alex Pinkham, William Schlick, Eagle Seelatsee, Louis Spino, Grant Waheneka." Led by a young Yakama man in full regalia and carrying an eagle feather staff, ten guests walked in solemn procession around the longhouse to the slow beat of a drum. Ten women followed, each carrying a Pendleton blanket, which she placed on a guest's shoulder. "Long ago," Watson Totus explained, "these gifts were horses, buckskins, and furs." Honorees faced inward and moved around the floor wearing their blankets as in a circle dance, the drum beating the familiar rhythm. After introducing themselves, each spoke a few words. The ceremony closed with a Wáashat song.

It had been a memorable day, but with a sad footnote. Just a week later, all were mourning Bert Totus, Cecelia's husband and the brother of Watson Totus. He died on March 27, 1971, at the age of sixty-nine.

In early June 1971, I was invited to write about the reopening of Wapato Longhouse for the newspaper. The article, "Wáashat drums return to Wapato Long House," marked the beginning of a long relationship with the Sohappy family.[4] By now I was comfortable in these settings and carried the camera in the car in case I was allowed an informal shot after the ceremony. Sometimes it was hard to know when a photograph would be allowed. The first time I covered the opening parade at the Toppenish Creek Encampment, I raised my camera to capture the riderless horse that honored a deceased leader. Fortunately, Robert Jim, riding the horse that followed, saw me and gestured a firm "No."

After the Wáashat service that reopened Wapato Longhouse, the men sat in a line, gently tapping the drums and singing quietly as they waited for the meal to be served. I asked Julia if it would be all right to take their picture. "Ask the leader." She pointed to Levi George of Rock Creek, who nodded.

We ran the photo with my story, which told of the eight large hand drums Frank Sohappy had made for the longhouse many years before. They had been given to Levi George on Sohappy's death, and the Rock Creek leader brought them back to Wapato for this memorial weekend. When Julia Sohappy next met Bud, she told him—he hoped in jest—that he needed to make drums to replace those that had gone to Rock Creek. She told him to go to Oregon, somewhere near Tygh Valley, to find the proper wood to steam and bend into the frames. "Tse-lee," she said, "by willows." By the time they opened Wapato Longhouse for the Christmas celebration, Bud had found a man recommended to him who made such drums and presented one to the longhouse. It was a beginning.

Along the Crest

In late May 1972, national newspapers were full of President Richard Nixon's journey to Russia to urge a new détente between superpowers. The editorial policy at the *Toppenish Review-Mirror*, however, was to stick to local news. "If an atomic bomb lands on Toppenish, then we'll carry the story," publisher Gail Flint told us. Within a month of the Russian trip, however, Nixon made the front page of our newspaper with the banner headline: "President orders Yakima land return."[5]

For over a century the Yakama people had fought for restoration of an important piece of the reservation lost because of a misfiled map. The land, known as Tract D, was part of the area originally reserved by the fourteen tribes and bands of the Yakama Nation when they signed the 1855 treaty with the United States. A sketch map, dated June 12, 1855, clearly showed that the western boundary of the reservation was as described to the Yakama before their headmen put their marks on the treaty, located "slightly west of the Cascades and enclosing all of Mt. Adams."[6] The map had disappeared after arriving in Washington, D.C. The Yakama leaders and their successors, however, accustomed to committing detailed information to memory, had no trouble recalling the specific terms agreed upon. A long and expensive succession of legal battles began, and the treaty promises remained an item on the tribal council agenda.

In 1930, the 1855 sketch map appeared among some unrelated records in a Bureau of Indian Affairs file. Of the 118,000 acres lost in the erroneous surveys, 82 percent had gone into private ownership. The remaining 21,000 acres, which included the eastern half of Mt. Adams, became the Gifford Pinchot National Forest. The discovery of that map began a renewed struggle by the tribes for the return of title.

The Indian Claims Commission ruled in favor of the Yakama in 1968. The United States paid the tribes fifty cents an acre, the value of the land in 1855, for the portion now in private ownership and impossible to return. The commission set June 30, 1972, as the final date for the tribe to settle on a price to be paid for the Forest Service land. "We do not want money for the land," Council Chairman Robert Jim told President Nixon in an appeal. "This land is not for sale." The tribes based their plea for restoration on the religious significance of Mt. Adams, known to the Yakama as Pátu. "The mountain is the source of life and the place where the spirit returns when life is over," Jim said.

By the late 1960s, the termination policy that had threatened Indian tribes since the early 1950s had changed to tribal self-determination. It may have been this that enabled the tribes to insist on partial restoration of the land rather than the payment they did not want.[7] The Yakama Nation pledged to allow public access during specified months to the portion of the Mt. Adams Wilderness Area, formerly under Forest Service supervision, and to retain the area as a wilderness. This reassured conservationists who originally had opposed the restoration of title to the tribes.

By August 1971, the tribe's plea caught the interest of actor Marlon Brando, who flew in on a chartered plane to help with the land issue. The actor had made it clear to the Yakama that he only wanted to speak with tribal members and was entertained at an Indians-only dinner at the agency. He continued his vocal support nationally for Native issues and even rejected an Oscar in 1972 in protest of Hollywood's failure to portray accurately the U.S. government's relations with Native Americans.

Robert Jim appeared on the NBC Today Show in October to talk about the tribes' efforts to obtain a presidential order for the land restoration. CBS newsman Richard Threlkeld arrived soon after with a television crew to film a report for Walter Cronkite's news program. Reservation viewers saw it at last on January 2, 1972—Threlkeld, Bob Jim, and Indians dancing at Wapato Longhouse. Even Bud and I had three seconds of fame.

At last, on May 20, 1972, President Nixon issued an executive order returning the lands in question to the Yakama Reservation.[8] The reservation buzzed with activity preparing the Toppenish Encampment Grounds near White Swan for the land return ceremony on July 8. According to the president's order, "the Secretary of Interior is directed to assume jurisdiction over the tract of land . . . and to administer it for the use and benefit of the Yakima Tribes of Indians as a portion of the reservation created by the Treaty of 1855." As the secretary's agent in place, Bud and BIA employees, many of them tribal members, joined in the preparations. The most startling feature of the huge new dance pavilion where the ceremony would be held was a one-hundred-foot-wide mural of Mt. Adams by Yakama artist Calvin Charley. Covering the west wall above the stage, the painting of the sacred mountain was prominent in every photograph of the ceremony. There were rumors that President Nixon himself would attend, but when the time came he sent Kim Agnew, daughter of Vice President Spiro Agnew, as his personal representative. She filled her role with quiet grace.

On the day before the public ceremony, I was invited by Chairman Jim to cover the presidential party's tour of the restored area. I considered it a great honor and, armed with camera and film, hitched a ride with Bud to the gathering place. It was a flower-filled meadow somewhere near Mt. Adams Lake, a blue-green jewel deep in the closed area of the reservation. The mammoth mass of snowy Mt. Adams dominated the view to the west.

Kim Agnew wanted to see some of the reservation on horseback, and part of the group—her Secret Service agent, a presidential assistant, a Marine colonel (Spiro Agnew's military aide), an official photographer, three tribal council members, and the superintendent—accompanied her. I wondered how Bud would fare on this first ride since his week's tour closing lookouts with the district packer in Montana twenty years earlier. He returned looking relaxed and comfortable as usual, and Kim Agnew had loved it.

A helicopter trip over the newly restored land, including a close look at the mountain itself, followed the horseback ride. I walked into the meadow to meet the party on their return and heard Kim Agnew ask tribal council member Genevieve Hooper for the names of the wildflowers. "Oh," Genevieve said, reaching down to touch a bloom, "we just call them 'flowers' and we love them." I thought of this comment recently when looking up a native plant in Eugene Hunn's fine book, *Nch'i-Wána, "The Big River."* The ethnobiologist writes that, when asking the same question, he frequently was told that it was "just a flower." Many flowers, however, do have names, Hunn writes, especially if they have dramatic roles in the myths.

The next day was the Fourth of July, the day of the ceremony and a complete contrast to that quiet time in the mountains. Bud had worked with the White House, the Department of the Interior, and BIA representatives over the years, and we invited them to our home for an early luncheon. Amiable co-hosts and servers were Kitty, on a break from running a day camp for children in Oregon, and Joe, who was loading potato sacks at a Wapato warehouse after his first year at the University of Washington. Bill was at Tieton Ranger Station in his third summer with the Forest Service and on call for the holiday weekend. I hoped he was working on the project whose completion had prevented his graduation in June. He needed to clear that up if he expected to go to Germany in the fall, as proposed.

When we arrived for the ceremony, Ernestine Jim, Bob's wife, was waiting in the parking area holding a red Chief Joseph blanket. "This is for you." She placed the fringed wool robe in my arms. "With my thanks." I was never certain what prompted this gift, but the beautiful blanket reminds me still of that time and of her friendship.

Joe captured the historic scene on film for the *Toppenish Review-Mirror,* and I wrote: "A massive mountain and a slight shy girl were the stars of last weekend's events on the Yakima Indian Reservation."[9] Over five hundred tribal leaders from across the continent joined the two thousand Yakama people, federal and state officials, and friends for the long ceremony.

"'As long as the mountain stands' up to now were only words on paper," Robert Jim said.* "The president in his highest capacity as trustee has acted to restore our faith in a system we had come to mistrust."

Simon Fraser, an early nineteenth-century fur trader and explorer, wrote of the Yakama's "extremely handsome manner of delivery."[10] Through our years on Plateau reservations, we continued to marvel at the eloquence of those who spoke—in less formal settings as well as times such as this. The three-and-a-half-hour program closed as it had begun, with a reverent Wáashat song, the first by Watson Totus, Satus Longhouse leader, and the closing by Rock Creek leader Levi George.

Since the time Bud came into the Bureau in 1950, he had supported the idea of tribal self-government. It made sense to him that the able people he worked with should be in charge of their own land and lives instead of working in subordinate positions with federally selected "experts." As he watched the progress in the early 1970s toward this goal, he began to think about his own future—when he could no longer be useful in the BIA. He realized there would never be another job in public management that would give the challenge or the satisfaction he had found in this superintendency. But he could not stay at Yakama forever.

Never interested in political connections, Bud realized that it would help to have someone with influence know of his capabilities. It was 1972, an election year. Richard Nixon had a good chance at reelection in the fall, and both Brad Patterson and Assistant Secretary Loesch were Nixon appointees. Bud was happy for the chance to work with them on the land return issue. As a non-Indian, he knew the time would come soon when he would need to find opportunities outside the Bureau of Indian Affairs.

---

*The Yakama cite this phrase as part of the promise made by Territorial Governor Isaac Stevens in reference to the treaty's tenure.

Soon after the Tract D festivities, Bud and I took off on an overnight backpacking trip into the high Cascades. It was hot in the valley, and we figured that enough snow would be gone for us to explore a new section of the Pacific Crest Trail south of Walupt Lake. With a map and a current tribal permit, we accessed the trailhead by way of the Potato Hill road. Packs on backs, we headed north just after noon. The snow was gone where the sun had melted it, but it was difficult to slog through in shady areas. Mosquitoes swarmed from every moist edge between snowbank and sun-warmed trail, and we gave up.

Bill, the late afternoon sun in his eyes, at home where goats walked noisily at night, on September 3, 1972.

Retreating to the pickup, we followed the Cispus drainage west into the Cowlitz Valley and called Bill at Tieton Ranger Station from Randle's Big Bottom Tavern. We had seen little of him since ferrying his gear up there early in June. In 1949, we had to use the longer route from Yakima over Chinook Pass, but it was now an easy trip from Packwood and Randle to the Yakima Valley. Tieton tunnel was open, and the highway went right past his ranger station. Bill met us at a cafe along there for supper.

The summer had been good for Bill, filled with the excitement and exhaustion of smoke chasing, following thunderstorms and fighting fires in the scrubby uplands above Lake Chelan and in the draws of the North Cascades. He also had studied the basics of mountain climbing with the wilderness guard in the Goat Rocks.

When the lookout stationed on Timberwolf Peak returned to college at the beginning of September, Bill welcomed the chance to replace him. Instead of fighting fires, he could have a turn now as spotter. Inviting us up on Labor Day weekend, he wrote, "I eat my meals with Adams, Rainier and many miscellaneous peaks. The goats are highly visible in mornings and evenings—I hear them walking slowly and noisily through the talus below me at night." Who could resist such an invitation? Kitty was home from her summer job, and we were eager to see the place. Not wanting to be on the road on Labor Day, we chose the day before. Joe was baling hops for a grower at

Moxee, near Yakima—hard but lucrative work—and could not go. He arranged with Bill to come up later in the week.

When Sunday came, we loaded Bill's grocery order, a picnic supper, and the dog into the back of the yellow pickup and made our way west on Highway 12. At the Tieton Ranger Station, we stopped for a short visit with our friends Shirley and Walt Tokarczyk. Walt, Bill's supervisor for the last three summers, told us how much he had enjoyed working with him. We went on, turning just beyond the ranger station on a well-marked road and climbed thirteen miles through the forest to the 6,391-foot summit of Timberwolf Peak. As we pulled up the last rise, we could see the lookout himself standing by the solid cabin, slim and smiling, with hair trimmed neatly above his ears for the first time since we had left Virginia three years before.

The little building at the top of the world had no need for stilts and stairway, but sat on solid ground with the 360-degree view shining in. Shutters that could be dropped in storms shaded the multi-paned windows. While the dog raced through the scrubby brush below the cabin to check for four-footed neighbors, Bill took us inside.

With a grin of relief, he told us he had sent off his registration for an eight-week session at Goethe Language Institute in Grafting, Germany. "It begins at the end of October—Joe will go with me." He watched for our reaction. "We'll spend the rest of the school year traveling." There was more certainty and anticipation in his voice than we had heard for months. We both nodded. "Sounds great," Bud said.

I found a cluster of white fur or hair of some kind on a windowsill. I held it up. "Goats," Bill said. "Take it, Mom. I find it caught on the brush around the cabin." He pointed across to a steep slope west of the lookout, and we saw mountain goats dusting themselves. They were "munching on grass, resting, and in general offering a rare spectacle to us flatlanders," I wrote in a description of the memorable visit in the "Musings" column that appeared the following Wednesday.

After supper it was time to take off for home—before sunset. Bill followed the pickup partway down the mountain on his motorcycle, then gave a wave and pulled off to turn around. As we descended through the trees, I watched until he was out of sight, then startled: "Oh Bud! I didn't pick up the goat hair."

"That's okay." He smiled—it had been a great day. "He'll bring it down next time he comes."

Give Sorrow Words

But there was no next time. About 7:30 on the Thursday morning after Labor Day, I heard a quiet knock. Opening the front door, I found Julia Sohappy and her daughter

Laritta Yallup standing there, eyes lowered. Laritta held a huge salmon in her arms, and her mother carried a blue Pendleton blanket.

Pulling the door wide, I beckoned them in. "How did you know to come?" The women had surprised me. I had finished picking up the kitchen after our sketchy breakfast. Joe was on his way to Moxee to bale hops. He'd asked for the day off to visit Bill at the lookout but had signed back on the night before when Bill had called to say he needed to drive a friend to Seattle.

"We heard the radio," Laritta said. They knew I needed them and followed me into the house. I took the salmon from Laritta, slipping it into the kitchen sink. We walked through and into the family room, and they sat side-by-side on the sofa. I pulled up close in a chair facing them clutching the blanket Julia had handed me. She held a small eagle fluff in her hand.

"The police came early, about four," I said. Somehow, I poured out the story. Kitty had taken Bud to Seattle to catch a plane to Washington, D.C., for a meeting the day before. She had driven on down to Oregon to visit friends. Joe and I were alone. The doorbell rang—it was still dark. Joe went to see who it was. I could hear low voices in the front hall when he opened it, then his urgent voice calling me. "Mom!" In my panic I couldn't find my bathrobe. Joe knocked on the bedroom door. "Mom, come!"

There in the dark hallway stood my younger son with a Toppenish policeman and a state patrolman, hats in hands. It had happened in the Tieton tunnel on White Pass, they said, just before midnight. "It looks like your son fell asleep."

Numb, all I could do was tell the officers how sorry I was that they'd had to deliver such terrible news. When they left, I found the number for the Mayflower Hotel where Bud stayed in Washington. He told me later that I had caught him just as he was leaving for the Interior Building. When I heard his voice, all I could squeak out was an agonized "Bud!"

Joe took the phone. "Dad," his voice rough, "Bill's dead. An accident in the Tieton tunnel." He put his hand to his eyes and pushed the phone at me. "On the motorcycle?" I could hear Bud ask as I took it. "No, honey." I was able to talk now. "In the VW bus."

I stopped my story, and Laritta reached across for my hand, saying, "When is the service?" Service? I thought. Of course. What will we do?

"Bud's on his way home," I told her. "I have to talk to him." I had reached Kitty by phone. She would pick her father up at the Portland airport, and they would be here by evening. I realized then what the blanket was for and knew, too, that I had to tell them it would not be used in the casket. "There will only be ashes." I looked into Julia's eyes. I wanted her understanding; this was not their custom. I explained that we, as they did, believed the body should return to the earth. This was our way to be certain.

One face smooth and young, the other creased with the beauty marks of a long life, their expressions of concern and acceptance did not change. Julia put the small eagle fluff in my hand. It would carry the loved one's spirit to the Creator, I had been told. Much later, I read that the eagle is the messenger to carry our thoughts to the heavenly land and bring help when we are in sorrow.[11]

"Will you sing at the service?" I asked Laritta. She nodded. "Just tell us when." I remembered a song I had heard many times at Warm Springs and at Yakama, a sad song of farewell. I could not understand the words but was told that the story of loss is much like that of *Madame Butterfly*. I didn't know it was not a prayer song. I only knew that we needed their presence and their singing.

On Saturday, after the Methodist congregation sang "Amazing Grace" and our minister's last prayer, Julia's daughters Amelia, Lena, Laritta, and LaRena rose from their seats in the front pew.* They turned to face us all and began the plaintive farewell song that had become so familiar to our family. As the song died away, the sisters sat down, but Lena remained standing in place.

"This song was given to me by my father." She began to sing, her voice rising and falling and rising again in the scale and cadence of the sacred songs we had heard so many times during Sunday services in the longhouse. But we had never heard this song—a prayer for healing, Lena's gift to us.

We wanted the service to be as simple as possible and, because the committal would be at a later time, had asked that there be no flowers other than the baskets we had arranged for and no visitors' register. The latter was a mistake, for even though Bud and I shook the hand of everyone who wanted to greet us, I have no record and little recollection about who was there that day. When we turned around to walk up the aisle at the end of the service, I was surprised to find the pews full.

My mother, eighty-three and slowed by painful arthritis, had flown out from Iowa and my brother and his son Pat from California. Fred and Donna Mae Rickard and Jack and Jeanne Condon made the long trip from Nespelem. It was Donna Mae's mother who had given me respite from our stair-step children so many years before, and Bill's name, William Condit, was the same as Jack's famous grandfather, Wild Goose Bill Condit. The Galbraiths, who also knew Bill from birth, and the Hadleys, longtime close friends, were there from Portland.

Shirley and Walt Tokarczyk came from Tieton Ranger Station with the ranger and Bill's coworkers and close friends, Kris Allen and Emily Guilland. Those new and old friends, among many others there, continued to be important in our lives over

---

*Viola, Julia Sohappy's fifth daughter, was living in the Southwest at the time.

the years that followed. Ruth Dunn, the wife of Bud's assistant superintendent, Barney Dunn, had baked Laritta's salmon during the service, and some of the travelers stayed to share supper with us before heading for home. Our good neighbors Maxine Maupin and Shirley Barnes had straightened up the house and pitched in as needed.

The lookout in front of Bill's favorite view—Mt. Ranier centered on the western horizon.

Before Laritta left the church that afternoon, she asked us to join her family the next day for Sunday dinner. "And your mother and your brother and his boy. We'll do it at the longhouse." The future looked dark at that moment, and I was grateful to have something ahead of us—if only one day.

Thus began our life as a changed family. I knew from my mother's five years of deep mourning when my father died that I could not indulge myself in that way, and I was grateful to the close friend who reminded me not to let the loss destroy my marriage. Probably the best advice came from Joe. When he had closed the door behind the departing policemen early that Thursday morning, he turned to me with an anxious look. "Mom," he said, "I am not Bill. I cannot be Bill. Don't make me be Bill."

I yearned to talk with someone who had gone through this. I called a woman in our church whose son had died in an automobile accident just before we came to Toppenish. "Oh, no," she said. "I can't. Just hearing your voice brings back the pain."

Sitting at my desk soon after, I caught a glimpse through the window of someone approaching the front door. My mother answered the knock. I could hear a frantic voice, then the door closing. "That was Violet Rau." Mother came back into the room. "She says you don't know her and she's too sad to talk, but she sends love and this." She handed me a worn paperback. "You're to read it!" I looked at the title: *From Prison to Praise.*[12] If she cares enough about me to bring a book, I thought, I'll read it. I found the message puzzling but, later, effective. The author's advice: "For all things, give praise."

This warm gesture from a stranger began a close friendship that lasted until Violet's death twenty years later. I had met her briefly when working on a story about tribal preschoolers and knew her father, tribal councilman Baptist Lumley, through Bud. Violet and I later collaborated on many culture-based projects for the tribe and elsewhere, including writing a regional Head Start training module for teachers.

Preoccupied with my own grief, I was startled when Joe told us soon after the memorial service that he wanted to leave for South America when the hop harvest was over. A friend was planning a trip. "I need you to go back to college," I told him.

Cruel as my request seems to me in retrospect, he did not object and went to Seattle with Kitty within the week. Transferring to the University of Washington, she began her junior year. I suspect that both were glad to leave the sadness behind. I learned later from Kitty that Joe would make his way across the city to St. Mark's Cathedral late at night to play Bill's flute—a heartbreaking image. When he told me much later that he'd gone with a friend who also played, I felt much better.

Tribal leader Stanley Smartlowit's funeral was held just two weeks after Bill's death. I knew Bud had to attend, and I accompanied him with great reluctance. It was at that place, when we circled the longhouse shaking every hand, that Josephine George had spoken the words that gave me such comfort. From that moment on, I was glad to be there. Looking around, I realized that most of us here had experienced loss, some people many times.

When the drums stopped, I could hear a woman of the leader's family sobbing. My own tears began to rise. I searched in my bag for a handkerchief. The song, whose words I did not understand, released tears I had not been able to shed. Later I was told that the words could be translated as "My child is gone, my child is gone, only the birds know where he's gone." Others near me were crying, too. Calmed by the sense of camaraderie, I looked across the longhouse to find Bud and saw his face among the men, stern, stoic. I wished they felt free to express their feelings. We had assembled to acknowledge this death, each of us knowing that it would not be the last such gathering. I began to understand the importance of this ritual.

On the day of Bill's memorial service, Joe had asked, "We're going to be all right aren't we?"

"Yes," I thought, sitting there against the longhouse wall. "I think we will."

My Heart in Hiding

The day was clear and sunny, with a clean bite to the air; the crest of the Cascades shone scarlet and yellow and deep green ahead of us. Raisin-sweet huckleberries that had escaped the bears clung to bushes near the place where we parked.

We followed the dusty trail up the sidehill. The scree slope was brown with duff and remnants of summer's growth; it had been a dry summer. The air held a faint hint of smoke. We stopped to take in the view. From the minute we left the pickup at the end of the road above Howard Lake, we knew this was the day we needed.

We moved on, snaking our way up the long slope toward the trees on Nanny Ridge. Across to the south, the raw face of Lakeview Mountain loomed, behind it Mt. Adams, dark patches edging the high glaciers. Bud waited for me to catch up, and, pausing in the rich silence, we could hear a faint rasping sound that ended in a sort of wail. A black spot moved into the sky from the shadow of Lakeview Mountain. The bird soared, catching the wind, then slipped off with wings spread. Suddenly, tucking in its wings, it plummeted earthward. It was then, during the freefall, that we heard the sound again. Such joy, I thought. I let out my breath. It seemed as if I had been holding it for a long time.

Strangely, on this steep slope, I felt we were on firm ground again. These mountains had been our first home. There to the west, hidden beyond the next ridge above Short Trail Camp, lay Walupt Lake—the place, in a tiny Forest Service guard station, where Bud and I began the long process of rubbing the raw edges off each other's egos. Over the years we had hiked the Crest Trail and camped on Lakeview Mountain and Nanny Butte. Only two months ago, Bud had met Bill on this trail for their trek to Cispus Pass. We were here this day to decide if it was the place for his ashes. I sat down beside Bud. The bird still soared, as if performing for us—hurling itself into the wind, hovering, then peeling off and gliding back. We watched a long time.

I broke the silence. "Bill's already here in these mountains." I scuffed a boot at the trail. "I need a place—someplace to go, to take flowers, to put his Little League trophy . . . to bring stones." Bud put his arm around me. "Okay." His eyes were on the sky. "I feel the same way."

We picked up our daypacks, turned back toward the reservation, down the trail to our pickup parked above Howard Lake. We drove through the woods of the Yakama closed area, dropping into the canyon to cross the Klickitat, and climbed again past Signal Peak to the checkpoint where the guard gave us a smile and waved us through. Without a word we crossed the hills where a decade later I would dig roots with Amelia Sohappy and moved on past the rodeo grounds at White Swan and the 1910 Shaker church turnoff and over LookBack Hill. The hop yards were empty, their green papery blossoms long gone to the kiln and into Joe's bales and off to the breweries. We drove on past McKinley Mission into Toppenish and home.

"I'll talk to Watson," Bud said as we climbed out of the pickup. "Maybe he can be at Smohalla."*

"That'd be good."

---

*The cemetery at Satus Point is named for the famous Wanapum holy man who died on a visit to the Satus and was buried there in a warm March of 1895.

On many days that fall when I was feeling especially bereft, I would go into Bill's room, take a book off the shelf, and look through it for underlinings or notes or simply to feel some contact with him. We had come at last to a friendship where we shared ideas. His own bent was toward literature and philosophy, and having missed that in my technological education, I loved to talk with him.

On one of those days, I came upon a dog-eared copy of *The Poems of Gerard Manley Hopkins.* Bill had written his senior thesis on the nineteenth-century poet, who was a Jesuit priest. But I had not read Hopkins' works, thinking there would be time for that later, when we would talk about it.

I opened the book to a page Bill had marked and read the poem. Then I came to the words:

> . . . *the hurl and gliding*
> *Rebuffed the big wind.*
> *My heart in hiding*
> *Stirred for a bird. . . .*[13]

I caught my breath. It described a falcon, so like the bird that stirred our hearts on the sidehill in the mountains.

On another respite in his room, I came upon copies of *Fore and Aft,* the high school literary magazine Bill had edited his senior year. Leafing through them, I found an article about Jeane Dixon, the syndicated newspaper columnist known for her crystal ball. Remembering that Bill had met her, I decided to read the article again.

It told of an early spring 1968 visit by Bill and two other student writers to the "famous clairvoyant who predicted President Kennedy's death." The small, warmly intense woman met them in her husband's realty office in downtown Washington, D.C. Dixon told them of her early life when she first was aware of a sixth sense and described the gypsy woman who gave her the crystal ball that she used for her predictions. She told them that Lyndon Johnson would not be reelected, that the Republicans would enter the White House, and that there would be "further trouble in the Middle East." Before the young people left, she looked in the crystal ball for the writers' futures. With Bill she said, "The ball is cloudy." She tried again. "No," she said, "I'm sorry. I can't get a reading."[14]

I had attached no significance to the Jeane Dixon comment until I sat in his room that day in September. Earlier, we had found a tightly folded piece of lined notebook paper in Bill's wallet. Written in fine calligraphy, it said: *"For now we see through a glass darkly; but then face to face; now I know in part; but then shall I know even as also I am known. Corinthians 13, 12."** I thought about the crystal ball and the quotation he carried and

---

*The verse continues: "So faith hope and love abide, these three; but the greatest of these is love."

felt strangely comforted. Perhaps he had not been destined for a long life. A "three inch scar under chin" notation on his draft card reminded me of the St. Bernard attack when he was four. I thought of a frightening tumble among rolling logs at the Oregon coast with Joe at twelve and of his fall on rocks during a picnic at thirteen—both at Warm Springs. And, finally, the terrifying ulcer surgery at fifteen.

Not long after we returned from the mountains the day we watched the falcon, Bud visited Watson in his office at the agency and told him of our dilemma. The Satus leader nodded. "He can go over there beside that white man."

He referred to Nipo (Nee-hah-pouw) Strongheart, a Hollywood actor who had portrayed many Native Americans over a long career. Born at White Swan in 1891, Strongheart was eleven years old when he joined Buffalo Bill's Wild West show as a trick rider with his father, George Mitchell, the grandson of a Hudson's Bay Company factor. He appeared in his first motion picture in 1905 and was an actor and technical advisor for Indian

View to the east from Smohalla Cemetery, across the Yakima River to the Rattlesnake Hills in the far distance.

and Western movies for more than forty years. An early version of the film *Brave Heart* reportedly was based on his life and his role in the fight for passage of the Indian Citizenship Act in 1924. Strongheart died in California in 1966 and at his request was buried at the Satus Point cemetery near Kate Williams, the tribal member who was his foster mother. Upon settlement of the estate, the tribe learned that the actor had left a large collection of books, baskets, and other valuable artifacts to the Yakama people.*

We followed Watson's directions to Satus Point, a knob at the end of Toppenish Ridge that faces the sunrise. A sign on the gate said Smohalla Cemetery. We found Strongheart's monument in the southeast corner of the graveyard. Next to it was the

---

*At the time when Bud talked to Watson Totus about a place for our son, the council was beginning to plan what now is known as the Yakama Nation Cultural Center, with a museum and library to hold Strongheart's gift.

stone for young Karen Tomaskin, daughter of the chairman of the Yakama general council, Leonard Tomaskin, and his wife, Violet. We read the dates, December 31, 1958—June 17, 1971. Born on New Year's Eve, her death was just over a year before. Strongheart considered Tomaskin a nephew. The family knew him well, having lived in Los Angeles in the late 1950s while "on relocation," the federal program to train Native people for jobs off the reservations during the termination era.

Although we had been in many tribal cemeteries, this was our first visit to Satus Point. The dry ground, the mounds of earth that marked the graves, each plaster horse, each personal memento were reminders of those buried there. No perpetual care, no flat lawn for mowing across the graves, this was earth and sky—a place cared for by families, a place where spirits could dwell. Yes, this was what we wanted. We set the last day of the year for the committal.

The Thanksgiving holiday was easier than we had anticipated. We spent the holiday in Portland with friends; Kitty and Joe came from Seattle. On our way, we attended the Warm Springs McQuinn Strip restoration ceremony. That valuable property, more than sixty thousand acres of forestland, was part of the original reservation by treaty and was lost through a faulty survey in 1871. With the McQuinn Strip, the Yakamas' Tract D, and the people of Taos Pueblo holding title to their sacred Blue Lake, 1972 was a good year for land restoration.

On the last day of the year, we picked up our minister and drove out to the cemetery where Donnie Sampson waited, shovel in hand, beside an opening the size of a child's grave. He explained that he had dug the grave longer than needed because he did not want it to look strange among the full-length mounds nearby. Cremation was not common for the Yakama and, we knew, possibly would offend some tribal members. We hoped for the same understanding that Julia Sohappy had offered.

Several pickups were parked nearby. As we talked with Don, a small clutch of Satus people came over to shake our hands and stand with us. I have only a vague memory—Tillie Totus with Lena Meninick, Johnson Meninick, Mose Dick, and Watson and Don. There may have been others. All I know is that their presence filled me with a sense of the rightness of the day.

Holding the small box, Wes Arms stepped into the grave and gave a prayer, laid the box on the dry soil of Satus Ridge, and stepped out. The men from Satus began to sing. The song was familiar and spread over us on the still air. *"Our child is gone, our child is gone, only the birds know where he's gone."*

When the song ended, the men filed past the grave, each taking a handful of dirt from Don's shovel and tossing it into the grave in three gestures. We women did the same. Then Don began to fill the grave. Joe stepped forward and picked up the other shovel. When they finished, Don smoothed the dirt into a mound on top. As I placed a spray of greenery on the grave, a noisy chattering drew our eyes to the sky. We watched as a fluid wedge of wild geese swept across above us.

Late that evening, we drove to White Swan and on to Toppenish Creek Long-house to greet the New Year. We stood with the crowd near the door of the packed room waiting for the arrival of mysterious creatures the announcer reported "passing through Chicago," then "Boise," and soon "at Lewiston." It reminded me of imagining Santa coming down from the North Pole through Minneapolis to Iowa on Christmas Eve.

Promptly at midnight, the door behind us opened and a howling parade of wildly garbed adult-sized creatures pushed their way in, war dancing through the crowd. "These are the Old Years," someone whispered. Then tiny masked figures, "1973," followed, marching to the center of the floor, beating hand drums. The judges moved among them and finally awarded first prize for the old-timers to a wizened old Father Time with bent, hobbling gait. When the winner pulled off hat and mustache, beard and nose, there stood Mrs. Wilson LaMere, the police chief's wife. Oliver Meninick, in a blonde wig, was awarded second; and Martin Hannigan and Louis Sohappy, wearing strange fur- and yarn-trimmed headdresses, took third and fourth. First prize for the '73ers was young Wilhelmina Howard in an Indian mask. Terry Jo Meninick was second, and third place went to a bundled-up figure with a stocking cap pulled over its face who told the judge she was "Sylvia." Little Linnea George was fourth. The New Year offered hope.[15]

We were ready to leave when Violet Tomaskin found me by the door. She said quietly, "You buried your boy." A statement. "Oh, Violet." I'd thought that we should have let her know. "I should have called—but it seemed so hard to do." I shook my head. She was looking at me intently, but, as was the custom, waited for me to finish. "How did you know?" I said.

"The Old Man had a dream."

"A dream?" I leaned down. It was hard to hear above the revelers.

"He saw your boy." Her face was serious, but gentle. I held my breath. I couldn't imagine where this was going.

"My daughter was helping him dress. . . ." She looked closely at me. "In a dance outfit . . . for the New Years."

I remembered the date on the gravestone. My heart jumped. "For here? This would be her birthday." She nodded. And who was the Old Man?

I thought about the cemetery and a name came into my mind. We passed his house on our way up there. Through the years that house had held a strong presence for me. "Henry Beavert?"

She nodded again. She seemed to be searching my face for something. "Do you understand what I'm telling you?"

Suddenly my anxiety dropped away. I felt she was giving me a blessing. "I think you are telling me that he's all right."

Violet reached up and put her arms around me. "Yes," she said. "They both are all right."

8. WE WEAVE WITH COLORS ALL OUR OWN, 1973-1975

*Twining off: The weaver loops the warp
ends into the final row of weaving to make
a smooth finish on her flat bag.**

All Things that Speak

Nineteen seventy-three began with Patricia Umtuch's selection as Miss Yakima Nation, the revival of medicine dancing on the reservation, and Richard Nixon's naming of Tribal Chairman Robert Jim to the National Council on Indian Opportunity.[1] Washington was in disarray. The tiny item in the news about a break-in at the Watergate Hotel in Washington, D.C., eight months earlier had ballooned into guilty pleas by the "Watergate" defendants. Michigan Congressman Gerald R. Ford was the first appointed vice president in U.S. history. Spiro Agnew had resigned in disgrace the month before, convicted of tax evasion on payments from Maryland contractors. We had no way of knowing that these events were the beginning of two years of unprecedented upheaval in the nation's capital that would affect our own future.

The New Year's dance at the Toppenish Creek Longhouse had been good for me. The arrival of the young 1973ers helped me realize that Bud and I, too, could begin to move ahead. When Joe proposed dropping out of college for a trip to Mexico with friends, we were glad for him to have the break. Kitty, too, stretched out by moving into a Seattle apartment off-campus with one of her dormitory roommates.

Most important to me, 1973 marked the beginning of what became a passionate interest in the extraordinary basketry arts of the people we had lived among for nearly twenty-five years. Those arts had declined through years of cultural suppression of American Indians. As we began to be welcomed into ceremonial life on the Yakama, however, we discovered that many rich traditions still survived among the Plateau people.

My growing awareness that basket making was not a long-lost art on the Yakama Reservation had begun the previous September when Laritta Yallup had brought

---

"We weave with colors all our own" is from John Greenleaf Whittier's *Raphael.*

*Paraphrased from Schlick, *Columbia River Basketry,* p. 219.

her mother for a visit. As Laritta and her mother left our house that day, Julia noticed an oak-splint basket in the front hall. It was full of colorful ears of Indian corn that I had grown in the small patch behind the house in Toppenish. She pointed. "What's that for?"

"Uh . . . the basket? The Cherokees made it." It passed through my mind that she was admiring it and maybe I should give it to her. "No, this." She reached down and picked up an ear with the dried husks fanning out above it. "Oh, I grew it," I said. "I thought it was pretty—would look nice in that basket." I could tell she liked it. "I'm growing more this summer. Do you want some?"

"Just this part," she said, and twisted off the husks, dropping the red ear back into the basket. "It's stronger than what they grow around here." I was puzzled, but we all set about removing husks and stuffed the lot into a paper sack. "I can make a hat with this," she said as they left.

That exchange gave me my first real glimpse into the world of basket making. By Christmas 1972, I had harvested my third summer's crop of Indian corn and filled a plastic garbage bag with the husks. Tying Julia's name to it, we slipped the big black bag under the tree on the Wapato Longhouse stage, where family gifts waited for Santa's delivery to those gathered there.

My circuitous route through the study of the rich world of Plateau basketry had begun a couple of years before on a visit with son Bill in Seattle. Browsing on the rear shelves in an antique store in the University District, I came upon a pair of small, round bags connected by a short strand of pale blue-and-white trade beads. The light was so dim that it was hard to make out the design, but what appeared to be horizontal skeletal figures circled the basket. I had seen something like them on a handbag at Maryhill Museum and recognized that they were from the Columbia River region. Haunted by the unusual bags, I asked Bill to find out what they cost. "Seven hundred dollars," he told me later. I crossed them off my wish list. But the designs intrigued me, and I began to watch for that image in the Native American art books that were just coming on the market.

After Bill's death, my sister, knowing I could use some diversion, sent me a small needlepoint project, an Aleut basket design stamped on canvas and complete with tapestry yarns and instructions. I sat down to learn the new handwork. When I finished the panel, I realized it could be one side of a handbag and charted out the face from the skeletal figure on the Seattle bags for the second side.

From books, I now knew this motif was a design from the Wasco or Wishxam people of the Columbia River. I sewed the completed pieces together, lined it, and added buckskin strips for handles. Carrying the handbag, I wondered if anyone on the reservation thought it tacky of me to make this copy. I had my answer when a friend from Satus Longhouse asked if she could buy it. Thrilled to know she admired it but unwilling to part with this first project, I made another for her as a gift a few months later. True to custom, she reciprocated with a silky blue-fringed shawl.*

Not long after I finished the first needlework project, I was drawn to a handsome twined handbag in an exhibit of Plateau arts from the University of Washington's Burke Museum in the Seattle-Tacoma airport. I sketched out the star design on a scrap of paper. Noting the colors, I found all of them in tapestry yarns, but made one change. In the center of the Burke bag was a bright pink square. Pink looked wrong to me, and I chose a medium blue instead. I worked the design in needlepoint on canvas and made the finished piece into a handbag. One of the first Yakama women to see my completed bag looked at it a long time. "You know," she touched the design, "it's just like a real old bag." I felt proud about that. "But," pointing at it, "that center part needs to be pink."

This handbag, too, has a history. After we moved to the nation's capital in 1975, I returned to Toppenish on a Head Start consulting visit. Coming into El Paso Cafe, I saw Flora and Gilbert Onepennee smiling at me from a table. Gilbert shook my hand, saying, "How's William T. Bud Schlick?" Flora nodded.

"He's fine. Tired of Washington already." I thanked them for their care of Bill's grave. On our infrequent trips back to the valley, we had found the weeds raked away and remnants of flowers or some new memento on the small mound. This was a mystery until the Onepennees' Christmas card had explained it. We had written, but this was the first opportunity to thank them in person.

Flora commented on my handbag. Thanking her, I said I would teach her to do needlepoint when I could and settled into the booth across from them. I noticed Gilbert looking over at us.

"She sure likes your bag." He nodded toward Flora.

Realizing the perfection of the moment, I walked back to the kitchen, asked for a paper bag, and dumped the contents of the purse into it. Presenting the handbag to Flora, I said, "I'd be honored if you'd accept this."

There was one last needlepoint event before I tackled the much more complex work of basket weaving. It happened as a result of a challenge from a class I was teaching for the tribal Head Start staff. I had pushed the students to come up with ideas for using specific Yakama cultural material in teaching basic skills such as numbers

---

*In March 1985, after we had returned to the Northwest for good, I gave the original needlepoint handbag to Josephine Umtuch, my guide at Click Relander's funeral in 1969. The occasion was the memorial for her daughter, our dear friend Delores Umtuch Buck. It seemed the right time for the bag to move on. I would love to know where that handbag is today.

and letters. They suggested using traditional designs from the handsome root-digging and storage bags and berry-picking baskets. The children saw this art at home and at longhouse functions and would soon see the traditional basketry in the new Yakama Nation Museum.

The next day I found a handful of necklace beads, a piece of abalone shell, and a bear claw at my place at the table. "Okay, teacher," the ringleader said, "you've been pushing us. Let's see what you can do with these by tomorrow." Combining my new needlepoint skill with an awakened consciousness of Plateau design, I worked a motif from our Warm Springs cornhusk bag onto a small piece of canvas in yarn. Backing it with a circle of deer hide, I hung the treasures at the bottom and attached a hide string. I wore it to class as a necklace. The teachers asked to learn to do the needlepoint, which we did. But the exercise led to a better plan.

By this time, I had begun to realize that I was learning nothing about Plateau basketry from copying the designs in needlepoint. We began to talk about the twining itself as the heart of the tradition—how design grew from the constraints of the technique. A few brought in family baskets, including one amazing round twined bag, a *wapaas* or Sally bag, with an American flag on it.* Although only a few weavers were carrying on the weaving tradition, many of the women in the class told of memories of grandmothers doing the work in winters, with children around them to watch and learn. The image put a new face on the art for me.

I had enjoyed the large display of basketry in the Native American gallery on frequent stops at Maryhill Museum, but hearing these stories and seeing the baskets in use by people I knew made all the difference. My father, a civil engineer widely recognized for his knowledge of the history and practice of land surveying, had advised me long ago to choose a narrow field and learn everything I could about it. As my fascination with Plateau basketry grew, I realized it had chosen me. I soon discovered that I had no need to own every basket I saw. I simply wanted to be able to understand how and of what each was made, for what purpose, and, if possible, by whom. If I wanted to know more about the basketry, I needed to learn to twine. I remembered the cornhusks from my garden that I had given to Julia Sohappy. It was time to learn to weave.

Early in the spring of 1973, I sat by Julia at a community meeting as she worked on a basket hat for the root feast. Mustering up my courage, I asked if she would

---

*There are several intriguing possibilities for the source of the term Sally bag. Wasco weaver Pat Courtney Gold suggests the most logical: *schkully*, a Wasco word for basket. Another possibility is *saulée*, the French word for a row of willows, or *sallow*, the British word for willow. Both French and English were early visitors to the Columbia River, where the Indian hemp used for making these bags grew among the willows. Julia Sohappy described the place where willows grow as "Tse-lee."

teach me to weave, explaining that I wanted to do a small story on it. Joe, now safely back from Mexico, could take the photos while I concentrated on learning. To my surprise, she agreed, with one stipulation: "Don't write that I was the wife of a chief."

Joe and I drove to Julia's house west of Wapato and had just started to knock when we heard her high soft voice: "Come." We found her in a room near the door, perched on the bed with one moccasined foot across her knee, the long strings of

Using cotton twine and cornhusk, Julia Sohappy weaves a hat to be worn for the root feast at the Wapato Longhouse in April 1973.

buckskin tied around the high top like a ballerina's slipper. A cup of water nestled in the covers beside her, dried cornhusks and balls of yarn nearby. She held a half-finished hat in her small, plump hands. The white strings that I later learned were the wefts showed up against the dark rose-sprigged print of her wing dress.

I pulled up a chair, and Joe brought out the camera. She set her work aside and picked up two bundles of what I recognized as warps, the basic skeleton of a basket. Each string with a knot tied in each end. She was ready with a lesson for me.

"To start," she said, crossing one bundle over the other at right angles. She eyed me gravely as I sketched and made a few notes. "Okay. What happens next?" I asked, my pencil ready.

She gave me a long look, her face unreadable, the deep wrinkles forbidding. I looked for the little smile she often had in her eyes. But this day, all was business. Without a word, she picked up a long piece of string and looped it over one of the bundles. "Ahh," I said, realizing she was showing me how to begin. At the sound, she gave me the look again. I was quiet as she continued to twist the two wefts over each bundle in turn, then divide the bundles and divide again, until I could see the flat base of a basket or the top of a hat begin to form.

When she knew I had figured out how to start, she put the bundles down and picked up the hat she had been working on and began to twine. But now it was more complicated. She dipped her fingers in the cup, ran a strip of cornhusk through them and wound the narrow strip around the outside weft before taking another twining stitch—at least, that's what I thought I saw.

"But . . ." I said, as she flipped the cornhusk over the string. Her look stopped me. I knew I was supposed to watch to learn, as she had as a child. But I didn't have a child's time. I was in a hurry. Sitting back, I tried to sketch what I saw while she wove, and Joe snapped his pictures. Today's lesson is patience, I thought.

I looked at the kerchief tightly drawn over Julia's graying hair. It concealed all but the tiny ends of her braids that were tied across the top of the scarf as if to hold it in place. They made me think of my mother and the long braids that she wrapped around her head when I was a child—and how their ends as she aged had grown gray and thin.

After a bit, Julia told me about *taxús*, which grows in damp areas and makes strong string.* Although she used cotton string and yarn for this project, she explained that *taxús* was used for everything in the early days—making fish nets; weaving hats, root digging bags, and root storage bags; and sewing tule mats together.

It was several years later when I first saw this strong string made—when I watched Julia's daughter Amelia and other women spinning this plant's fiber on upper leg and knee into a tightly spun two-ply string. The string was used in making the tule mats to cover the display of a winter lodge in the new Yakama Tribal Museum.

When writing *Columbia River Basketry* in the early 1990s, I learned from an entomologist that dogbane (*taxús*) is an insect repellent, a fine attribute for bags that hold and store food. Knowing also that cedar used for berry baskets was preservative by nature, I marveled at those First People who discovered such useful materials. In 1997, I heard an explanation that satisfied me. Yakama elder Clifford Washines said "All things that spoke in the right manner, the Creator allowed to thrive."

The hat Julia was making that day came into focus for me as an item of ceremonial clothing at the root feast at Wapato Longhouse in April 1973, several weeks after my twining lesson. I had seen the basketry hats, *patl'aapá*, worn by the women of the Plateau; but until I saw Julia twining one, I had never wondered how they were made.

After the feast, Laritta Yallup gathered the young girls together outside the longhouse for Joe to photograph. They had been busy since early morning helping the cooks, taking part in the Wáashat service, setting the tables and bringing in the foods provided by the women. All wore moccasins and new wing dresses, as col-

---

*Its name, *taxús* was not easy for me to pronounce. Much later, soon after we returned to the Northwest in 1978, I brought an old *wapaas*, root-digging bag, to a Yakama senior citizens' dinner. Generally, people had been forgiving about my attempts at the language, but when I asked if the material in the bag was "taxos," a woman laughed. "Not tacos," she said. "Not what you get at El Paso Cafe. Taxús!" I finally heard the sound, made back in her mouth like a gargled Greek letter *chi*. No, it is not "tacos."

**Apocynum cannabinum*; common names are Indian hemp or giant dogbane.

orful as the wildflowers in bloom on the hills. Laritta and four of the girls wore a *patl'aapá,* or basket hat. As I look at that photograph now, I realize that three of the hats were heirlooms, and Julia, using corn-husks from my garden, had made two that spring.

That root feast in early April 1973 also brought an occasion of such generosity and kindness that it stands as a milestone for me in a long life of memorable happenings. Julia Sohappy and her daughters, who had brought us such comfort at the time of Bill's death, opened their hearts to Bud and me again by giv-ing us Indian names. I've attended many name-givings over the years, for children and for young and old-er adults. Except for situations like ours, the honoring of friends, the names are those from the family's

Bud and Mary with Delores Buck at the Rock Creek Longhouse celery feast. The needlepoint bag Mary holds was later given to Delores's mother, Josephine Umtuch. Delores carries a beaded handbag.

past—sometimes from very long ago. Often the name belonged to someone whose qualities the family hopes or sees signs that the child will emulate. My first such expe-rience had been the year before as a reporter. I found all the benches full at the Top-penish Community Center that day, all eyes on the center, where the young grand-son of a Yakama leader stood. Small and serious, he waited as his grandmother piled gifts on his slight frame. Blankets and shawls, articles of clothing and ceremonial regalia soon covered the child; a high-crowned hat lay on the floor beside him.

The grandmother talked quietly with the elder who served as echo at the micro-phone. He turned from her and called out the ancestor's name in the arresting voice of a crier. "From today," the elder said, "this boy will be known by this name."

At the grandmother's prompts, the announcer called the names of friends or relatives. Each came forward to take an article from the child's shoulders. All, in turn, talked of the one whose name the boy would now carry. I was witnessing an ancient ceremony—the validation of this child's lineage by the giving and receiving of gifts.

Rock Creek leader Levi George conducted our naming ceremony. To Bud's great surprise, he received the name Náutahluk, conferred on Click Relander long before by Frank Sohappy. Levi, holding his arms out to the sides, told Bud the name represented "a great bird that flies high in the sky and descends only to help those below."* When I asked Amelia Sohappy later about the name, she translated it as "overseer."

The name given to me was Anipashn'mi Latiit, blossom of the wild potato. Appropriate, I thought, for a descendant of those who came to America to escape Ireland's potato famine. The reason for the gift of a name was compelling: "So we will know you later." I realize that meant when we meet in the next world, and I wait to hear it then. Nothing makes me happier today than being addressed as Anipashn'mi Latiit or simply as Latiit. Following our naming ceremony, Delores Buck offered another of the gentle instructions that through those years helped Bud learn what was expected of him. "Click Relander brought coffee and candy to the longhouse," she said. "It's your job now."

Bud and I received clothing for our new roles. Julia had made a fringed vest for him of soft deer hide decorated with the sun outlined in beaded rays, the raised hand of a Wáashat prayer, and two tiny hanging beaded baskets. A traditional breechcloth in plaid wool completed the outfit. Mine was a ribbon-trimmed wing dress with matching leggings. Except for the breech cloth (Bud was more comfortable in trousers), we wore the clothing at the longhouse at later times. I cherish it all today. On our part, I netted the silk fringes on woolen shawls for the sisters and bought Pendleton blankets for the men.

I had purchased a classic cornhusk storage bag from Geoff Hilton to give to Julia at an appropriate time and realized this was that time. I knew by now that for gift or trading purposes, the bags should be full of dried food roots. I puzzled over a suitable substitute. The logical choice—carrots, potatoes, or other root vegetables—eluded me; all I could think of were gladiola corms that resembled some of the native roots to me. I hope no one tried to cook them.

Much later, when I realized how strange the contents of that bag must have seemed to Julia, I recognized a new dimension to Plateau basketry—a kind of harmonic integration among them. I was first attracted by the baskets' distinctive beauty and long history. Then my interest grew as I learned of their important uses in the culture and the unusual technology of their weaving. Seeing how bizarre the inedible

---

*Frank Sohappy is credited with the naming in the 34th Anniversary Washington Birthday Celebration Program. In *Drummers and Dreamers* (p. 58), Click Relander wrote that the name came from Puck Hyah Toot, who said, "This I do so that all may know about Smohalla and his songs, and so that his deeds may not be forgotten for the day that is sure to come."

gladiola corms were in a food storage container helped me recognize the complexity of the baskets' relationships.

The ceremonial food-gatherers wear basketry hats when harvesting for the first foods feasts. They place their root harvest in round twined bags, the huckleberries and chokecherries in coiled cedar root baskets or quickly made folded cedar-bark baskets. When dried, the roots and berries are safe from insects and dust in the large cornhusk storage bags. Women carry twined handbags during celebrations where hats are worn. Not until Plateau baskets became collectors' items did they function independently.

A Time to Pluck Up That Which Is Planted[2]

While life was peaceful at Yakama in early 1973, the actions of the American Indian Movement (AIM) soon changed this for us. Speaking out in opposition to unjust tribal governments and the operation of the Bureau of Indian Affairs, AIM caught the attention of the Interior Department, and some federal action did result. Bud hoped that a new consciousness of federal responsibility to Indians would help bring national Indian policies, set by Congress, into agreement with regulations established by treaty.[3] Although the BIA was the major target for the activists' dissatisfaction, real decision-making went on at higher levels of the Interior Department. Native interests often were at odds with mining leases, gas pipelines, water and irrigation rights, and other concerns of congressional constituents.

AIM did not come to the Yakama Reservation that winter, as had been rumored, but about fifty AIM members and a large number of supporters invited by traditional Lakota elders arrived on the Pine Ridge Reservation in South Dakota on February 17, 1973. The elders were discouraged by repeated efforts to impeach their tribally elected governing council president, Richard Wilson, for corruption. They hoped AIM could help with this and the long-standing issue of the United States' government's failure to meet Lakota treaty obligations.

The elders chose as the symbolic place of protest the village of Wounded Knee, located northeast of the agency headquarters at Pine Ridge. It was on Wounded Knee Creek in 1890 where the U.S. 7th Cavalry had left the bodies of 146 Lakota women, children, and old men on a cold December day—the same cavalry defeated by the Lakota at the Battle of the Little Big Horn four years before.

AIM took over Wounded Knee village and erected bunkers around the Sacred Heart Church. It was a complicated story, and we followed the bare bones of it in the news—reports of hostages and standoff but nothing about the tribal people caught in

Bud briefs visiting Secretary of the Interior Rogers Morton about the situation at Wounded Knee.

the middle. All of it seemed far away from our busy life on the reservation—until May 12, 1973.

Knowing that this first Mother's Day after Bill's death could be a hard time for me, Bud suggested that we drive north through Wenatchee to check out the recently completed highway through the North Cascades Mountains and visit Kitty in Seattle. A long drive, we had planned to spend the night there; but after a brief visit with Kitty and roommates, I asked Bud if we could head for home. This city, so closely associated with Bill's last years, filled me with a deep sadness. We headed over Chinook Pass and arrived home in the twilight. Joe was out the door as we drove into the driveway. "Dad," he said. "Call Washington."

The call was from the Interior Department. The White House had promised a meeting over the Wounded Knee issues, and the militants had agreed to lay down their arms. That ended the siege, and the exhausted BIA superintendent was sent on leave. Bud was to report May 15 to Pine Ridge Agency. As "senior Interior official responsible for all federal operations at Pine Ridge," his jurisdiction would be over the Interior and other departmental employees, including the federal marshals from the Justice Department.[4] With the charge of restoring normal operations on the reservation, Bud flew out the next day.

His quick calls home during the weeks that followed made me realize he had no simple job. On reviewing the detailed notes he kept during that period, I now see what a mammoth undertaking it was. He was to organize the cleanup and rehabilitation of Wounded Knee village and roads, provide temporary housing for more than two hundred returning residents, see that utilities and services were restored, deal with other results of the siege, and see that order was maintained. There were frequent contacts with White House and Interior officials and notes on disaster relief, mediation for racially related conflict, postal service problems, rumors of clandestine meetings, and confrontations at road blocks. Every situation was affected by the tense political atmosphere of the pending impeachment by tribal members of the Oglala tribal president, issues of ranchers versus landowners, and long-standing efforts to go back to the treaties and do away with the BIA.

Out of concern for him as well as curiosity about a critical episode in our time, I wanted to see the place. Bud finally agreed that I could visit over Memorial Day. The weekend turned out to be one of those pieces of time set apart from the rest of life.

Bud and the federal marshals responsible for maintaining law and order on the reservation stayed in a motel in Gordon, Nebraska. The FBI, there to deal with any criminal activity, also were housed in Gordon but kept to themselves. The boundary of the Oglala Lakota Reservation was the South Dakota state line, the agency at Pine Ridge about thirty-five miles away. I arrived in Gordon late at night by way of Yakima, Seattle, Denver, Scotts Bluff, and Chadron, where my plane landed.

It was a holiday of sorts. We set out the next morning to visit two tourist places Bud had heard about in that part of Nebraska, the Museum of the Fur Trade near Chadron and a small museum in Rushville. The former interested both of us, but we were shocked to find a human skull on display in the latter. I protested to the volunteer, who thought it was a strange complaint. I thought of the bones that were stored in the attic of the Smithsonian's National Museum of Natural History. Some of them, I knew, had been taken for research by archaeologists from ancient graves on an island in the Columbia River.* I thought of a Yakama friend's question: "How would you like it if your grandmother might be among them?"

After the Nebraska tour, we drove to the reservation and to the village of Wounded Knee. Three weeks after the end of the occupation, residents were beginning to return. Small white parachutes hung like tiny crashed kites in the trees and fluttered on wires on the perimeter of the village. Bud said they were remnants of the flares, "thousands of them at eight dollars apiece," sent up by the marshals for illumination to prevent the smuggling of food and ammunition to the occupiers. I could see where flares had started fires in the pines. But with the spring rains, the place was a fresh green.

Construction had started again on the housing project that had been underway when AIM took over. The protestors had used the contractor's heavy equipment to build fortifications around Sacred Heart Church on top of the hill in the center of the village. The church had served as a sanctuary for Lakota elders. Entering the church, we could see bullet holes in the windows and the altar, signs of gunfire from the outside. A saint's figure had lost a hand. It was a sobering scene. An opening cut into the wall indicated returning fire from the church. Priests had removed AIM slogans and

---

*The Columbia River tribes reinterred these remains near the river on December 20, 1994.

names and addresses from the walls, Bud said, and bags of refuse waited for pickup. They had told him they hoped to hold mass again soon.

We went outside, and I looked at the freshening of the landscape that surrounded us. There were signs of life. Raked and decorated graves brightened the Sacred Heart cemetery, and flowers also lined the mass grave from the 1890 massacre nearby. I thought about Bill's grave. Would Joe take flowers?

Looking down at the ground in front of the church, I found two metal casings, one from long ago and one from very recently. Hoping that it was not federal land where we stood, I dropped them both into my pocket. One casing, slightly larger than the other and dark brown with age, represented, at least to me, the guns of the cavalry in 1880. The other, newer in nickel-colored metal and marked "38 special," represented the siege just ended. Both were marks of the Oglala's unsettled disputes with the federal government, as well as within the tribe. That none of these disputes had been truly addressed was as disturbing to me as the skull in the museum.

When we drove back to Pine Ridge, Bud stopped at the red-brick agency building to check in—he never knew when he might be needed, he said. I had spotted a pottery shop nearby with an "open" sign in the window and told him I would check it out.

"Keep your eyes open," he warned, giving me a steady look. "And watch what you say. This isn't Yakama."

Walking over to the small shop, I felt unusually exposed. It was a bleak place. An older Lakota woman looked up from a table as I walked in. I assumed she was Ella Irving, the name on the sign. She nodded at my greeting and went back to reading. Her work was lovely. I picked up a handsome globular pot and turned it over to see the mark. The contrast of the rich blue of the pot's glaze with the red Dakota clay on its unglazed bottom startled me. In the base, the potter had scratched "Pine Ridge Sioux, E. Irving." Beside this she had scribed the sweeping lines of mountains and a tall pine tree. The Black Hills, I thought, the sacred homeland of the Lakota.

I told the woman my name as I paid for the blue pot and, feeling I had to explain why I was there, said I was visiting my husband from the Yakama Reservation, where we lived. She had a friend there, she said, a public health nurse named Marsh at the Health Center. I had met her.

As we talked, she relaxed a bit, telling me she had opened the shop with a tribal loan and hadn't been able to work at her pottery since the beginning of the siege. Discouraged, she feared for the land, for the business, and that "they might take over the reservation." I thought she was referring to AIM activists.

When I described going into Sacred Heart Church and seeing the damage to the statues, she brightened. She had once repaired a hand on a religious statue by using her own hand as a mold. "I can fix them." She gave me a small smile. "That will be my contribution."

The Rushville skull was not the only shock of that trip. The major one came on Memorial Day. Although it was a holiday, Richard Wilson, president of the Oglala Lakota tribal council, had summoned Bud to his office to discuss some pressing issues. Bud was well aware of the dissatisfaction among many Lakota people with their tribal president. During his first year in office, Wilson had been the subject of four impeachment efforts, the most recent on hold because of the general turmoil at Pine Ridge. As the federal government's representative, however, Bud was obliged by law to listen to and support the elected leader. Reading Bud's notes written at the time, I realize now what a tightrope he had been asked to walk. He was ordered "not to undermine the tribal government" but to "help convince them of the need for proper checks and balances."[5]

The summons by Wilson meant delaying our drive through the Black Hills to Rapid City, where I would catch a plane for Yakima the next morning. We would leave as soon as the meeting was over.

We entered a side door of the closely guarded agency building. Admitted by a federal marshal, who examined my driver's license, we moved on to sign the register at a kind of barricade—time in and out, purpose, contact. Serious, the marshal's demeanor was very different from the night before when I had met them at dinner. Bud led me down a corridor to the superintendent's office and told me to sit at the desk. "I'll be in with the president next door." He pointed out a button on the floor under the desk. "Step on that if you see anything strange. It calls a marshal." That gave me pause, but I took out my twining and began to work on a small bag I had started on the plane from Yakima. Still very awkward, my weaving would make Julia laugh. I welcomed the time for practice, and it was a sunny place to work—the window facing south across some plantings beside the building, a sort of garden with a flagpole.

As I looked out, a couple of cars and a pickup pulled along the curb and stopped. Several men stepped out, one man reaching back to pull out a rifle. I drew a quick breath, then saw another do the same. Heart thumping, eyes on the men with guns, I searched with my foot for the button on the floor. Just as I felt it, I saw the first man reach into the back pocket of his khaki pants, pull out a folded khaki "overseas" cap, and put it on his head.

Oh my God, I thought, a veteran. I recognized the cap from Warm Springs parades where Veterans of Foreign Wars formed the honor guard. I realized that the men in the garden were from the local VFW post, here to honor their fallen comrades from World War II—I could see that there were names on a memorial stone in that small garden.

Two women and some children joined them and stood at attention as the honor guard ran the American flag up the pole. Three men raised rifles to their shoulders, and three guns blazed three times. Although it had begun to rain, one happy dog played with the children on the lawn. I was moved by respect for the scene and thought of all the demonstrations of patriotism I had witnessed among Indian people over the years.

When Bud brought the president into the office for me to meet, Wilson said, gesturing toward the window, "I hope you watched that. You know, Indians are very patriotic."

I waited until we were alone, to tell Bud of my scare. "Well, that was a close one," he said. "If you'd stepped on that button, all hell would've broken loose." He told me of a call that came in a few days before reporting a caravan of armed AIM supporters headed for Pine Ridge. The marshals, FBI, and tribal police went screaming up the road to head off the armed caravan, guns ready. When they saw the lighted head-lights, they realized it was a funeral procession.

Bud let out a long breath as we drove out of Pine Ridge toward the dark forms on the horizon. Not long after we left the reservation, we turned north toward Rapid City, choosing the road through the Black Hills. We were tourists again retracing a route taken on our first anniversary twenty-three years before on our way to the For-est Service job in Thompson Falls.

Traveling through the dark wooded hills, we caught glimpses of those huge faces of American presidents staring out from Mt. Rushmore. We talked about the startling contrast between this man-carved mountain and the natural beauty around it—and about the Black Hills, a forested oasis in the open central plains of North America. It is a sacred place of ceremony for the Lakota people, where they come for vision quests and to camp, fish, and hunt as their ancestors had before them. It is their homeland, just as the Columbia River is the homeland of the people of the Plateau.

All I could feel was gratitude that the Colville, Warm Springs, and Yakama tribes had not lost their forested lands. The resource that had brought us into their country also has been the source of income that has allowed them to thrive. I was grateful, too, for their rich and inclusive social and ceremonial life, which connected them with each other and with their past.

Six weeks after my visit to Pine Ridge, I read in the *Oglala Nation News* a story that made me sad. The Sacred Heart Catholic Church at Wounded Knee, described as the "land-mark on the site of the mass grave of the victims of the 1890 massacre," had burned to the ground in early July. By then, the priests had reopened the church, and tourists were coming to see the now-famous place. I wondered if Ella Irving had been able to make her own contribution to sanity and grace by repairing the statues before it had happened.

Finally relieved of his duty at Pine Ridge, Bud returned to the Yakama Agency sometime in late July. He brought a beautiful star quilt—the kind Lakota women are known for—that he had won in a raffle and a great sense of relief that the difficult job was behind him. When Interior Secretary Rogers Morton had jetted into Pine Ridge to check on the status of the Oglala a week or so before, he had commended Bud for bringing physical order out of the chaos at Wounded Knee. Both of them knew it would take much longer to change the atmosphere of distrust that lingered among the tribal factions. They recognized that changes were needed in BIA leadership at all levels if that were to happen. Still, Richard Wilson retained control over the Oglala Lakota tribal council until 1976.

Secretary Morton assured Bud that there would be a place for him somewhere in the Interior Department when the time came to leave Yakama. Although once considered for the BIA deputy commissioner's job, such leadership positions were no longer possible under the Indian self-determination legislation that he had supported. Bud knew he needed to find a new challenge that would be as satisfying and as interesting as this life had been for twenty-five years. It would take some thought and a few breaks. He wasn't certain he wanted to stay in federal service.

Chicago Tribune columnist Bob Wiedrich wrote on July 17, 1973: "The Sioux did not deserve the destruction visited upon them. They are a kind generous people to whom children are a resource and tribal elders a cherished fount of knowledge." Bud had spent his career among the Columbia Plateau Indians, who could be described in the same way. He knew that Washington needed to turn the same attention and resources that they provided for the cleanup at Wounded Knee toward solving the serious human and political problems at Pine Ridge. But the shadow cast on the Nixon administration by the Watergate investigation in the summer of 1973 appeared to leave little energy for such hard work.

On Bud's first day back from Wounded Knee, Watson Totus walked into his office with a beaded and fringed pipe bag. "Peace for you now," Watson said, as he placed it on Bud's desk. Reaching into the bag, Bud found a long ceremonial pipe, the bowl carved from beautiful red Minnesota pipestone.

A Time for Peace

Waking on the anniversary of Bill's death, I knew the day needed to be acknowledged. "If we were a Yakama family," I told Bud, "we could have a memorial and give-away and bring out his name again." Those ceremonies had seemed healing to me. "Right," he said, putting on his helmet. He had begun to ride Bill's motorcycle to work, taking the shortcut from our backyard past Garfield School. "We can talk about it at noon."

But I couldn't wait. After cleaning up the kitchen, I made the beds, picked up the Pendleton car robe I had bought some weeks earlier, drove out Progressive Road west of Wapato, and turned in at the gate of Julia Sohappy's house. I rolled up the windows as the dust overtook the car and sat for a minute eyeing what Julia called her watchgoose grazing at the side of the house. I'd been warned about this bird, and when she moved toward the back I picked up the new blanket and hurried across the yard.

As I climbed the wooden steps, Julia's daughter Amelia came out on the small porch. "Latiit," she said. We were about the same age, but like her mother she stood no taller than my chest. She wore a jacket over a print dress, a kerchief tied over her black hair. Mine had begun to gray this year.

"Is your mother home?" I held up the small blanket. "It's a year today." With those words, I felt again the ache of that morning when Julia and Laritta had brought the salmon and blanket and eagle fluff.

"She's gone to town." Sensing my distress, Amelia stood back, holding the door open. "Come in." I wasn't sure of the protocol, but I stepped in. "I had to mark this day in some way." My voice felt thick. She realized why I was here.

"It's been a year since we sang for your boy." She reached up and drew me down for a hug. I bent to receive her comfort. A soft loosening moved through me and, with it, the tears. This is what I had come for.

"Thank you, sister." I stood, wiped my eyes with my fingers, and put the blanket in her hands. "This is for your mother. It's all I know to do." I turned to go, stepping out on the little porch. I could see the dark hills above Medicine Valley to the west and Mt. Adams looming on the skyline. The mountain's snowy summit was intact, but the summer sun had revealed great spots of black rock that formed the gaunt image of a starving horse against the white glacier. I drove home.

When Bud came in for lunch, he looked at me closely. "How was your morning?"

"It was just right," I said, and told him where I'd been.

Within two months, we began another year of mourning, this time for Robert Jim, chairman of the Yakama tribal council. Well-known nationally, he had gone out of his way to help Bud understand the history, customs, and concerns of the Yakama people. He died in Tulsa, Oklahoma, on October 30, 1973, while attending meetings of President Nixon's National Council on Indian Opportunity, which had coincided with the National Council of American Indians. He was only forty-four years old. Of all the news events I covered during my years with the *Toppenish Review-Mirror*, his funeral may have been the most difficult.

From the time we arrived on the Yakama Reservation in 1969, Bob Jim had recognized Bud's desire to serve the Yakama people well. He encouraged Bud to study Yakama history, answered questions about customs, and discussed hopes for the tribe. Bob helped Bud do his best to fulfill the duties of the superintendent, the modern "Indian agent." Bob also gave me, as a reporter, access to tribal news sources and steered me toward stories I might otherwise not have found. His wife Ernestine was a good friend, and we enjoyed their growing family.

When Bud came by our house that day to tell me of Bob's death, he asked me to go with him and the tribal attorney to bring the news to Ernestine. As she seated us in her living room, the men remained silent, their eyes on me. I realized that I had learned from Bill's death that we should not keep her in suspense. Hard as it was, I had to tell her why we came and to do it with directness. It gave me courage that she knew that Bud and I, too, had been through this brutal process—but it was a task I will never forget.

Tribal representatives and political dignitaries from across the nation stood on the wind-scoured hillside at Toppenish Creek cemetery south of White Swan for Robert Jim's burial. The place reminded me of his stories of early years rounding up wild horses with his father, Kiutus Jim, who also had served as tribal chairman. Bob had told us of living in the mountains and of hunting and fishing with relatives at Celilo. As I planned the story for the newspaper, I thought about the pride in the chairman's voice as he had talked of those earlier times and of their contrast with the public life he had given such energy to. And so I began: "The man who chased wild horses has returned to his hills."[6]

By the autumn of 1973, my work had increased as a consultant helping Head Start centers in the Northwest develop programs based on the cultures of the children they served. I was also volunteering with the tribal preschool programs and teaching at Yakima Valley College and had cut back to writing features and an occasional news story for the *Toppenish Review-Mirror*.

Bob Jim's death and that of seventy-six-year-old Alex Saluskin in July that year were important losses in a time of change that had begun for us with Wounded Knee. But there also were reminders of the continuity we experienced through our years on the reservations. By chance, I interviewed a former Redskins player, Louis (Rabbit) Weller of Albuquerque, who was visiting his son, a new member of Bud's agency staff. A football fan from childhood, Bud had suggested the interview. Weller had an illustrious record—two years on the collegiate all-American honorable mention teams and player for the Redskins on their first team in 1932. What Bud didn't know, however, was that Weller had a tie to Alec Arcasa, Bud's first mentor on the Colville Reservation. Weller and Arcasa were named charter members of the American Indian Athletic Hall of Fame, along with Jim Thorpe and eleven others. It was just one more connection on the giant web we had stumbled into.

The year ended with the peaceful change of leadership for the tribe and, in an unrelated incident, we learned another way to look at a common experience.

First, the experience. Invited to Satus Longhouse in mid December for birthday cake for Donnie Sampson and Levi George, we armed ourselves with a couple of dollar bills, the usual gift when birthdays are announced. We carried a few extra in case others were celebrating. Word leaked out that Bud, too, was born in December. To his surprise and consternation, he found himself included in a shower of greenbacks. One of the women, seeing his discomfiture, reminded us that life is precarious and precious—birthdays celebrate the gift of another year of life for our loved ones.

Then, at the end of December, Watson Totus was chosen to fill Robert Jim's vacant position. The fourteen council members, elected by a vote of all Yakama over eighteen years old, represent the leaders of the tribes and bands that became the Yakama Indian Nation at Walla Walla, Washington Territory, on June 9, 1855. They, their predecessors, and their successors represent the people who have lived peaceably near one another "since time immemorial." It is a good record for any nation to emulate and was particularly reassuring to Bud to see the traditional process work.

On a Sunday in the middle of January 1974, a gorgeous enfolding warmth engulfed the Yakama Reservation, now deep in snow. The thermometer had been hovering around 18 degrees Fahrenheit earlier in the day, but before we knew it the temperature was at 40 and going higher. We stepped out on the patio to feel the welcome spring-like breath and realized this was a classic Chinook wind from the coast sweeping across Mt. Adams' glaciers. Bud, worried about the possibility of flooding, began to marshal the agency's forces—road department, social services, forestry. He called the Red Cross.

As snow melted on the slopes of Mt. Adams and the hills surrounding the valley, the waters began to flush across the flat and fertile farmlands of the central Yakima Valley. Before nightfall, flooding had begun. Those who could get out evacuated to shelters in Toppenish and White Swan. Road and bridge washouts marooned others. Helicopters were called to rescue and to drop food. By the end of the week, the waters began to subside, draining off into the Yakima River through the network of irrigation canals. A helicopter pilot was dead, and many residents of the rural areas were without shelter or food.

The massive cleanup began. One old-timer reported it as "the worst flood in 74 years."[7] Strangely, the *Yakima Herald Republic* ran a photo of me peeling potatoes for the refugees' dinner with Betty Moses and seven-year-old Sonya Watlamet "learning to peel potatoes."[8] We are in the kitchen of the Toppenish Community Center, the same place and activity shown in my first published newspaper photo five years earlier. Only the names of the peelers are different.

Soon after the flood, Bud and I drove out to visit Bill's grave. From that gravelly shoulder of Toppenish Ridge, we could see the Yakima River, now tamed and back in its banks. Here and there a puddle reflected the sky. We noticed a car turning onto the road to the cemetery. Full of people, it crossed the World War II Bailey bridge over the canal and wound its way up and through the cemetery gate we had left open. Nervous now, we watched as the car came around to the corner where we stood.

"Oh," I said to Bud, much relieved. "It's Rosita Wesley." Karen Jim's sister, daughter of Maggie and Howard Jim of Celilo, she lived just off the highway from Toppenish on the road to Granger. "We could see the pickup turn in," she said. "We didn't recognize it, so came on over." She introduced her children, then said to me: "He'll be all right up here. We keep a watch on this place." She drove off.

Twenty-six years later, in 2000, we were cleaning and decorating the gravesite again on a Memorial Day weekend. After arranging flowers at her family graves, Rosita stopped by on her way out of the cemetery and rolled down the car window to talk. She had heard I was working on another book. "When are you going to write about us?" she said.

"Well, I did—in a way."

"No, not our baskets—about us, as people." She turned her head toward the children in the backseat. "The things people don't understand about us." She stepped out of the car. I realized this was a serious matter. "I want you to write about how the schools mark our kids down for going to funerals or make us cut our boys' braids." She had been thinking about this. "And other things, like it's our business how we punish our kids." She shrugged. "I'm in trouble if I lay a hand on them, but social services isn't much help." What she wanted seemed beyond me.

"I wish you'd write it, Rosita."

"Well, then," she asked, "when can I tell you the stories for you to write down?" As I think about this, I realize that during those years writing for the *Toppenish Review-Mirror*, I was telling her stories—but only those that were easy to tell. I did not think I had the words for the complexity of what I knew she wanted. Yes, when can she tell me those stories to write down?

Patricia Ann Umtuch and Fred Ike Jr., followed by their attendants, approach the drummers for their marriage ceremony at Rock Creek Longhouse,March 16, 1974.

Wedding stories were among the easy ones, and I was delighted when Patricia Umtuch's parents invited us to the marriage of their daughter to Fred Ike Jr. at Rock Creek in March 1974. Rock Creek Longhouse was a small frame building nestled in a sheltered valley about ninety miles south of Toppenish near the Columbia River. Sunny, the valley was already in bloom with balsamroot and lupine when we arrived. With windows open to the spring air, the greening sagebrush and salmon roasting next to the longhouse gave the place a wonderful odor.

I had permission from the families to take pictures and sat with Bud along the wall near the front. When the seven singers raised their drums, a soft light from the windows behind diffused through the rawhide surface. Hearing the slow steady drumbeat, we all stood. Two tiny girls entered the longhouse door in pastel wing dresses sifting petals from baskets onto the earthen floor, one wearing moccasins, the other saddle shoes. A small boy was with them, perhaps the ringbearer. The father of the bride was next, then the solemn young couple dressed traditionally and in white, the bride's long braids wrapped in strips of otter fur that fell to her knees.

Astonished to see the bride wearing a traditional Plateau-style head covering, I lifted my camera. Made with dentalium shells, beads, and Chinese coins, it was an adornment rarely seen since the nineteenth century. Often described as "wedding veils," they were explained to me as a sign of maidenhood worn by girls old enough for marriage. Pat's sister and the best man came next, followed by three young women in pastel wing dresses. Two of them also wore the heirloom head coverings. The bride's mother followed, giving a dignified closing to the procession led by her husband.

Nearly thirty years later, I called Toppenish to ask Pat and Fred Ike for permission to use one of the wedding photos in an exhibition of Plateau arts at the Oregon Historical Society. Pat loved the idea and agreed, adding, "We're still married!" And still handsome. The couple came to Portland for the opening of the show and posed in front of their life-sized photo. The only difference was that this time they were smiling.

President Richard Nixon looked as serious as that young couple at the wedding, but grimmer, when I saw him two months later at the opening of Expo '74 in Spokane. Bud was attending a BIA superintendents' conference there. On the May 4, I stood in a claustrophobic press of onlookers hoping to catch sight of the president as he entered the central plaza for the opening ceremony. When he arrived at last, I was grateful to my tall ancestors for the clear view of his taut mask-like face. He passed only a few feet in front of me—preceded, flanked, and followed by grim-faced Secret Service agents.

Every day is a moment in history, I know, but seeing the president's frozen demeanor lent a solemn weight to this one. Impeachment hearings were about to begin in Washington for Nixon's role in the Watergate coverup. On August 9, 1974, three months after he opened the Spokane World's Fair, Richard Nixon resigned.

Bud came away from the superintendents' conference knowing it was time for him to move on. The proposed Indian Self-Determination and Educational Assistance Act, Public Law 93-638, further expanded the tribes' rights and the role of superintendent would change. Also, under Indian preference, only tribal members could be selected for leadership positions.

Looking for a 1974 Thanksgiving food feature for the *Review-Mirror*, I called Virginia Beavert, who suggested that her mother, Ellen Saluskin, could make *lakamíin,* a kind of salmon gravy that can be eaten as a soup or served over baked potatoes or rice.[9] I had tried this popular food at longhouse dinners and, finding it bland at first, had developed a taste for it.

Ellen was ready for me when I arrived. For this late twentieth-century version, she brought a quart of water to boil in a saucepan and stirred in a can of salmon. Pouring some cold water into a cup of flour—her present-day substitute for the dried and pulverized root known locally as *seekowya,* she said—she worked the mixture deftly with her hands to form small clumps of dough. She stirred the salmon broth while flaking the dough into the liquid, letting it bubble a few minutes until thickened.

As she worked, she talked about this dish from her childhood—made with fresh or dried salmon, deer meat, bear, grouse, whitetail rabbit, or duck. Topping sliced elephant ear mushrooms and onions with the *lakamíin* was a favorite. To prepare the powdered salmon formerly used for this dish, the fresh fish was cooked slightly on a stick facing the fire. The women laid the salmon, skins removed, out on racks to

Yakama Head Start children try on a basket hat, one of the distinctive basketry forms of the Plateau peoples, during a presentation on traditional arts by Mary.

dry, then pounded the dried salmon with a stone pestle in a deep wooden mortar. This made a fine powder "like flour," known as *ch'láy*, which they packed tightly into round woven bags lined with fishskin and stored in a warm place. "The *ch'láy* would spoil if it got cold," she said.

Writing this in 2005, I realize that Ellen Saluskin had described a commodity more valuable than gold. Explorer William Clark mentioned the powdered salmon repeatedly in journal entries written on the Columbia in October 1805. Only in the dry climate of the Plateau could such a product be produced. The prime trading commodity for the Native people of the Columbia River for generations, this high protein, portable, and storable food was traded by Indians from all directions who congregated at Celilo and The Dalles. Rarely made today, it is one more treasured memory of the days when the salmon did not have to climb ladders to return to home waters to spawn.

No More *Lakamíin*

In January 1975, *The Way it Was (Anaku Iwacha)*, a book of Yakama Indian legends, made its public debut. Concerned that teaching through storytelling was disappearing, Yakama parents had asked the Johnson O'Malley (Indian Education) Committee to sponsor the publication.

At first, the elders had been hesitant about being taped; but realizing that their children and grandchildren would have the opportunity to hear the old stories, many agreed to participate. In the end, it fell to Virginia Beavert, the project director, to translate the tapes from twelve storytellers speaking in six different Plateau dialects. She had been well trained for this job—growing up speaking the language and later working with accomplished native speaker Alex Saluskin and linguists from the University of Washington. The book is an amazing product of local talent, from traditional storytellers to the illustrators—seven Yakama artists, whose ages ranged from the teens to over seventy. For those of us looking for appropriate materials to use with Yakama children, it was a gift.

By the time the book was launched, I was deeply involved in working with teachers in multi-cultural classrooms. In mid February 1974, my name dropped off the masthead of the Toppenish paper. I had enjoyed five years in this favorite job, but it was time to concentrate on a new, growing interest.

Under the leadership of Martha Yallup and Violet Rau and with assistance from Head Start staff development funds, the tribal education department brought college classes to the reservation. Both teachers and aides were enrolled for credit, the goal to provide quality culture-based preschool programs in the valley. A group of us—Indian, white, and Hispanic women with undergraduate degrees—had been working together in the programs for some time and had vowed to continue our own education as well. I, for one, needed a master's degree if I was to continue to teach adults.

It was the beginning of a heady time for education in the Yakima Valley. To describe the results, I have to move forward in time. By 1978, when Bud and I returned to the Northwest, all of my colleagues in the Yakima Valley had earned advanced degrees—mine at Washington's Dulles Airport, where Virginia Polytechnic and State University flew our professors from Blacksburg, 250 miles away, and Martha Yallup with a doctorate from Seattle University.

Fort Wright College in Spokane had been one of the schools that brought classes to Toppenish. Sister Kathleen Ross, the Fort Wright vice president for student affairs, agreed with Martha Yallup and Violet Rau that many of the people with jobs and families needed the opportunity for a college education to come to them—as Virginia Tech had come to me. By 1982, the three women had established Heritage College near Toppenish "to provide higher education to the culturally diverse population."[10]

By 2000, more than 3,200 graduates from the Yakama Reservation, the rural Hispanic community, and others from the region had entered the workforce as environmental scientists, social workers, business and computer science specialists, administrators, and educators. Of these, 96 percent were employed, and more than 90 percent at jobs in the Yakima Valley. By 2005, the fully accredited Heritage University offered advanced degrees. Having served on the first Heritage board of directors, I have maintained contact with and interest in that amazing institution.

Late in 1974, Bud was invited to apply for a two-year Federal Executive Development Program in Washington, D.C., to begin in May 1975. When we learned that he had been selected, we were not eager to leave this place we had come to know as home. But Bud knew it was time for the Yakama to have an Indian superintendent, and he saw the move as an opportunity to prepare for and find his next challenge. I could enter a master's program in the East. When time came for us to leave, Katherine would stay to teach high school in nearby Zillah, and Joe would finish the hop season and, possibly, return to The Evergreen State University in College. We would be back before long, we knew, at least to somewhere in the mid-Columbia region.

By chance, another development in the spring of 1975 led to a turning point for me. It was connected to the reservation-born Hollywood actor whose grave lay next to our son's. A bequest in the will of Nipo Strongheart brought his extensive collection of Native American arts and over ten thousand books to the Yakama Indian Nation. As a result of the gift, tribal leaders were making plans for a cultural heritage center that would include a museum and library to house the Strongheart collection as well as a theater, restaurant, and meeting place.

I told Gary Young, the program director for the new project, that I hoped to begin my research on Plateau basketry in Washington. Although I wasn't sure where to go—the Library of Congress, maybe—I planned to look for early writings about the Plateau and search for references to basketry. The other task would be to examine early photos of Plateau Indians for evidence of basket use. Gary suggested the Smithsonian Institution's National Anthropological Archives (SINAA) as a place to start. It was the first I had heard of that collection of twenty thousand photographs of Indians. And, perhaps, Gary said, I could save the tribes some time later by developing a list of the Yakama references and related photographs that were available there.

"It's a deal," I said, and carried an official letter of introduction from the Yakama Nation to SINAA archivist James Glenn at the National Museum of Natural History. That opened many doors for me during the next three years.

Bud's new assignment began at the end of April 1975, with two months at the Civil Service Commission's Federal Executive Institute at the University of Virginia in Charlottesville. I would remain in Toppenish to finish up some projects and help Kitty and Joe get settled. Before Bud left, the Yakama Indian Agency planned a gala send-off for him at the Chinook Hotel in Yakima.

On the day of the party, I flew to Olympia with Martha Yallup to receive an award from Governor Dan Evans for "outstanding voluntary action" with the tribal preschools. Our return flight was supposed to bring us to Yakima in time for the party, but thunderstorms over the Cascades grounded our plane. Scrambling, we caught the flight to Wenatchee—anything to get over the mountains—and found a pilot there to take us to Yakima. As the small plane circled slowly upward to gain enough altitude to cross the mountains, I realized that ego had put me in this predicament. Desire to accept the award had kept me from supporting Bud on this important night.

Walking into the Chinook Hotel ballroom just as the program ended, we were met with a standing ovation—enough to satisfy anyone's ego—and relieved laughter.

Neither my family nor Martha's was laughing. We had given them a real scare.

As I write this, I have a prized relic before me—an enrollment card for the Confederated Tribes and Bands of the Yakama Nation with Bud's name, photo, and his signature. Vital statistics were enrollment number, 99,999 (total enrollment at the time was about 6,000); place of birth, Wounded Knee, South Dakota; degree of Indian blood, 1/5 Old Crow, 4/5 Push-tan (white man). What gives me pause is the final sentence of the certification: "The Act of June 2, 1924, provides that all Indians born within the limits of the United States are citizens of the United States." This was 1975, the year before the much-celebrated bicentennial year of the United States of America. Those whose ancestry predated all other residents had been recognized as citizens for only fifty of the nation's two hundred years.

The weekend following the agency party, we were invited to Wapato Longhouse for supper with families of several of the women who had embraced me as a friend and sister. The photos that Joe took that night reflect the warmth of their friendship. In one, Ernestine Jim and I pose with dishtowels in our hands, Irene Pinkham Cloud holds a clean bowl, Edith Sampson and Violet Tomaskin stand at the sink working, and Laritta Yallup just stands there. I tower over all of them. We are laughing.

April 27 was our final hurrah—during the Fourth Annual Individual Satus Longhouse Pow-Wow.[11] There were speeches with gifts, including a gorgeous white buckskin vest made for Bud by Elsie Dick with the Yakama arrowhead complete with Mt. Adams and "Treaty of 1855" worked in beadwork on the back. As I followed my family out of the longhouse, eyes down to keep from stepping on the toes of seated onlookers, I felt a woman jump up from a seat beside me. Startled, I looked up and saw that it was Ellen Saluskin. Her face impassive but with a twinkle in her black eyes, she slipped a long necklace of glass and shell beads over my head and said, "No more *lakamíin!*" The memory of that nimble gesture and the reference to the salmon gravy she had made for my story gives me a chuckle today.

9. A GIFT OF FISH, 1975–1992

Wherever there is ritual, celebration,
grieving, there is salmon.

—Cynthia Stowell*

Bud's session in Charlottesville over, he returned to Toppenish in early June 1975 in a full leg cast and on crutches. He could get around well enough, but he hated to admit that he had torn his Achilles tendon in a tennis game on the first weekend at the university. We thought he had gone to Virginia to improve his management skills, not his backhand. But we also knew that he approached the game as he had approached everything from changing diapers to running a large agency. The son of a loving but exacting father, he wanted to do it all well.

Delores Buck made the long drive over from Priest Rapids to tell us goodbye. She brought a frame filled with photos of Wanapum people and a note:

> To Now ta—luk and La—te—et, a good friend. Hope you have a good trip wherever you go and carry your Indian name with a memory of the day you received it (and what it means). Just a token of what the Wanapum are today . . . this gift of pictures of our sons and grandsons. All from Rex and Frank Buck. PS—Tell them in Washington D.C. when they all decide to move to moon, please leave this country clean for the Indians.

We carried her gift to Washington to begin the next phase of our lives—I to a summer of research at the Smithsonian, then night classes at Dulles Airport for a year, with daytime work as an editor, and Bud to an intense two years of rotations through federal agencies to see if anything felt like a fit. He settled into the Department of Interior as assistant to the deputy director of the U.S. Fish and Wildlife Service, a good place.

We made occasional trips west and especially enjoyed the visits with Yakamas who came to D.C. on tribal business. During that first summer, I spent most days at the National Anthropological Archives reviewing every reference to Plateau peoples I could find. I put together a scrapbook of photocopies showing twined cornhusk

---

*From *Spilyay Tymoo*, 1987.

storage bags, handbags, root-digging bags, hats, and coiled or folded cedar-root berry baskets.

When Johnson Meninick and Joe Jay Pinkham came to our house in Annandale for dinner one night, I pulled out the scrapbook. Johnson identified some of the people in the photos and recognized a handbag that had disappeared from his family long ago. The men's comments brought life to what had seemed a sterile project. I did not want to study the baskets as art objects; I could do that in a museum. I wanted to understand them as part of a complex and thriving world of cedars, grass, animals, people, berries, roots, and fish.

Joe Jay brought a jar of huckleberries in his camera case, sent to us by his wife Tallulah. It could not have been timelier, reminding me that the world of food-gathering and sociability that the old photos portrayed is real today. A later visit was with Tallulah herself, who was in D.C. for a meeting. When we picked her up at the motel, she handed me a little Tupperware container filled to the brim with dried and ground roots of some kind. "*Cous*," she said. "Now you can make *lakamíin*." But I did not use them to make that salmon dish I had written about; instead, I kept it in sight for a touch of home while we lived in Virginia. I have it today. The little round box represents to me all that is generous and reverent, patient, sociable, self-sufficient, and real.

In the summer of 1976, I visited Yakama friends who had come to take part in the Smithsonian's Bicentennial Folklife Festival on the Mall. Watching Mary Jim Chapman twine a round bag, I learned a helpful trick—to shorten my long twining wefts to keep them from tangling by making a series of slipknots. Although my twining skills were slowly improving, I never would have figured that out on my own.

I worked on small bags every day—on the commute into the city from Virginia and watching the evening news. By the end of the summer I had accumulated a box full of miniature root bags showing great variations in materials and skill. As I worked, I thought about Julia Sohappy and her kindnesses to us. We kept up on reservation news through the *Yakima Nation Review*, and I was pleased to see a photo of Julia celebrating her seventy-eighth birthday at a senior citizen's luncheon in the November 9, 1976, issue. She looked as I remembered her when we said goodbye, unsmiling and serious, as if sizing me up, but kindly. I wondered what she would think of my work.

Early on November 18, I found myself suddenly awake. I knew it was early by the steely Virginia sky, and a dull discomfort nagged at me. Something's wrong. I sat up, picked up the phone beside the bed, and dialed my mother. Her sleepy hello calmed me. Looking at the clock, I realized it was five a.m. in Iowa. "Mother, are you okay?" I asked, wondering how to express this odd feeling. "Something worried me."

"I'm fine, dear." She did sound like herself. I felt better. "I'm so sorry I woke you." "You've just had a bad dream," she said. "Go back to sleep." And she broke the connection.

I lay there trying to remember what had awakened me. The phone rang, startling me. Oh, dear, I thought. Now I've worried my mother. But the voice was not hers. "Latiit?" The sweet voice, tentative, took me into another world. "Latiit!" Now urgent.

"*Eee* (yes), I'm here." My response was automatic. It was Viola Sohappy. I would know her voice anywhere. "Viola," I said. "What's happened?"

"Mom's gone." Her voice thickened. What to say? All I could think of was to ask when. "Just now. You needed to know." I couldn't reply. "Latiit?" She was anxious.

"Somehow I knew it," I said. "I was awake." And all those images of Sunday services, dinners, memorials, funerals, wedding trades, name-givings, weaving lessons, and just plain visits flooded in. All I could say was, "It breaks my heart."

Bud had flown to the reservation that week to testify for the tribes in a lawsuit. When I reached him at the agency, he told me he was feeling ill but would try to make the funeral. Overtaken by flu, however, he spent the rest of the week in bed. We both were disappointed.

By that fall, my small weavings had begun to fill a larger box. I packed them up, beginners as well as later work, and sent them off to Wapato for Julia's memorial. At least I could participate in some way in honoring Na'ilas, my first teacher. I probably sent along an apology for my "primitive" handwork, but I hope not.* Sometime later, I gave a shrug when Lena Owens admired a small cornhusk bag I was weaving. She admonished me: "Be proud of your work. It is a gift."

In 1977, Bud and I began to feel that life was too short to be living so far from our children and the places we loved. The opportunities in Washington were less appealing to Bud than working directly with tribes in their move toward self-sufficiency. We knew what we wanted to do could best be done in the West. Bud also wanted time to study black-and-white photography, a long-held interest, and I could continue my basketry research and work with culture-based learning.

In June 1978, Bud completed thirty years of federal service, including time in the air corps in World War II. With that in mind, we had bought a piece of property in the woods above the orchards of Oregon's Hood River Valley, and Bud requested early retirement. He was fifty-three.

In early July, we drove into the Columbia River town of Hood River in our trusty 1975 Audi, followed by Joe in the U-Haul truck bursting with household goods. Kath-

---

Na'ilas means my mother.

erine, now in graduate school in Seattle, was there to meet us. Putting the furniture in storage, we lined up a contractor to begin building when we returned in the fall and set off for a newly acquired cabin on Rainy Lake's Canadian shore—detouring to New Mexico to return Joe to his home in Santa Fe.* The words of Henry David Thoreau resonated in our heads:

> *I went to the woods to live deliberately, to . . . see if I could not learn what it had to teach, and not, when I came to die, discover that I had not lived.*[1]

Yes, the woods—those that surrounded the island cabin on the Minnesota/Ontario border and those that sheltered the spot where our new house would be. For a couple who began their marriage in the woods, it was the place to discover what was next.

We returned to Oregon in September with a floor plan for the house. Twenty feet by forty, it was compact but luxurious by Thoreau's standards. We moved in the following June. As Bud helped me put dishes in the kitchen cupboards, I noticed a car in our driveway. A woman was pulling something out of a cooler in the trunk.

"Delores," I shouted, and ran down the half flight of stairs to open the front door. There was Delores Buck, from Priest Rapids, nearly four hours away, with daughters Lenora and Ramona and son Joseph—our first guests in the new house. In Delores's arms was our first housewarming gift, a huge salmon. When I saw Lenora a couple of years ago, she asked if I remembered that welcoming visit. "Of course," I said. "We knew we were home again when we saw all of you at our door with that fish!"

Another time when I saw Delores, I was surprised to hear of the death of one of the young men from Satus. "I thought you might have known about it," she said, gesturing toward Satus Point, "since your boy's up there." My mother had been frightened by her own prescience, and I wished I had inherited more of that gift. The Satus news reminded us that we had some catching up to do, and we drove up to Satus Longhouse on a Sunday. We sat near Watson for the dinner that followed the Wáashat service. He looked toward us as he stood to make his usual remarks before the song that ended the meal.

"We want to welcome home W.T. Bud Schlick and his wife Mary today." A soft "Aiii" went through the dining room. I could feel tears rising. Catching Bud's eye, Watson asked: "You *have* come home, haven't you?"

---

*To our surprise, we discovered when we arrived at Rainy Lake that first summer that the cabin we had purchased through a newspaper ad from a retired Norwegian builder was not on Crown land, leased to cottagers by the province of Ontario. It was on a reserve, the ancestral lands of the Stanjicoming First Nation, a small family group of Anishinabe people (known also as Ojibwa or Chippewa). Thus began another warm relationship that, like the others, continues today.

All Bud could do was murmur, "Yes." He looked around at the familiar faces. "We've come back to stay."

Bud's decision to take early retirement was a wise one. It gave him fifteen years to explore black-and-white photography and interests that had developed from his work with Indians. His independent status made closer relationships with the tribes possible. He served as a consultant on natural resources for the Warm Springs tribes, encouraging and enabling tribal members to take over those responsibilities. I continued con-

With Mt. Hood in the background, Mary and Bud look south toward Warm Springs from an outlook near their new home.

tact with the childhood programs there and on the Yakama and pursued my study of Plateau basketry. We were honored, with others, on the fiftieth anniversary of the Warm Springs tribes' constitution with a certificate of appreciation "for assistance in the development and progress" of the reservation.

In 1992, an aneurysm sent Bud to the hospital in a coma. My only comfort was knowing that the weakness in the blood vessel may have lurked in his brain from birth. During the painful month that followed, I called Mary Ann Arthur Meanus in Warm Springs. "Bud's dying," I said. She was silent, then began to sing. The cadence and pitch now familiar, I felt my anxiety disappear. In the quiet that followed the song, Mary Ann murmured, "Now go to sleep." Later, after Bud had slipped peacefully out of this life, the Sohappy family came from Wapato for the memorial service. Mary Ann joined them when they stood and sang for us once more.

I had hoped that Bud could be buried at Satus Point beside Bill. I had been puzzling over who or how to ask about it when the phone rang. "I hear you're looking for me." Startled, I recognized Johnson Meninick's strong, certain voice.

I explained my concern. "Yes, he can come here." Neither of us used the name. "The old man said you all can."

I realized he was speaking of Watson Totus, whose funeral services we had attended just four years before. How Johnson knew I needed him and when Watson gave the permission were not questions I needed to have answered.

Epilogue

We become who we are by being in a place a long time. We become part of a place so that never again do we arrive or leave. We stay. We stay always.

—Ray Hudson*

As I sit at my desk I can see Mt. Hood framed by dark sweeps of fir boughs, her glaciers gleaming and refreshed by recent snow. A screen of oaks and dogwood, hazel brush and alder fill the near view where the doe shepherds her fawns through the yarrow that greens my ragged yard. From the bridge where the road enters my woods, I can see Pátu gleaming fifty miles to the north, across the Columbia.

It is my twenty-seventh year in this small house above the orchards in the Hood River Valley. The Colville and Warm Springs and Yakama reservations, where much of this story has taken place, are not far. Bud left this life on the sixth of February in 1992. As we few stood again on that rocky ridge at Satus Point and heard the Washáat song fade into the wind, I knew for certain that we had come to stay forever.

The complex basket-making techniques of the Plateau weavers offer an elegant metaphor for our long life among the Columbia River people. The folding back and forth of beargrass on berry baskets, the twists that bring out the lively designs on root-digging bags, and the bright colors that cover the plain underlayer on the cornhusk bags all bring beauty to their strong foundations in different ways. Woven into our years of folding back and forth from coast to coast were twists of unexpected change; colorful ceremony brightened the sturdy progress of daily life, and, always, we were supported by the strength of the people.

Mary Dodds Schlick
Mount Hood, Oregon
June 2005

---

*Ray Hudson, *Moments Rightly Placed: An Aleutian Memoir*, 1998.

Those who had sturgeon spirits
were exceptionally brave:
no matter what wounds
they might have received,
they would not succumb.

At the time of Bud's illness and death, I was curating
the exhibit *Ancient Images of the Columbia Gorge* for
Maryhill Museum and used this quotation from *Wishram
Ethnography,* by Leslie Spier and Edward Sapir, to explain
the traditional fish graphic found on Wasco/Wishxam
baskets. Maryhill's Colleen Schafroth selected it to present
to me on the day of the opening. I've taken much courage
from it.

Endnotes

CHAPTER 1 (pp. 3–20)

1. The Mann Gulch fire happened in August 1949. It was later described by Norman Maclean in *Young Men & Fire* (Chicago: University of Chicago Press, 1992).

CHAPTER 2 (pp. 21–44)

1. The treaty reduced the area occupied by the Yakama, Nez Perce, Walla Walla, Cayuse, and Umatilla peoples to three reservations in what was then Oregon Territory. See *Treaty with the Yakama*, 1855; 12 Stat. 951, June 9, 1855.

2. Kinney, *Indian Forest and Range*, 167.

3. For a discussion of the Bluejay, see Verne F. Ray, "The Bluejay Character in the Plateau Spirit Dance," *American Anthropologist* 39:4 (October-December 1937): 593-601.

4. See Haruo Aoki, *Nez Perce Dictionary* (Berkeley: University of California Press, 1994). *Ee'ysin* is the Nez Perce word for celebration, meaning "with happiness." It is pronounced "eye-seen," with the accent on the second syllable.

5. Moses, *Wild West Shows*, 51.

CHAPTER 3 (pp. 45–52)

1. Heizer, *Handbook of North American Indians*, 122.

2. Wilkinson, *Blood Struggle*, 178.

3. See John Hartle, review of *Kruschev, the Man and his Era*, by William Taubman, in *Portland Oregonian*, March 30, 2003.

4. *Washington Evening Star*, March 19, 1959.

CHAPTER 4 (pp. 53–90)

1. McClure and Evans, *The Homesteader's Son*, 49.

2. Mary Dodds Schlick to Josephine Hungerford Dodds, September 20, 1960.

3. Oregon State University, *Nutritive Value of Native Foods of the Warm Springs Indians*, 15.

4. *Spilyay Tymoo*, September 19, 2002.

5. Aguilar, *When the River Ran Wild!*, 178.

6. A photo of Geraldine Jim instructing Tina Aguilar in a wing dress class sponsored by Warm Springs Extension Service appeared in *Spilyay Tymoo*, November 19, 1982, 3. "Wing Dresses with Loretta Alexander" appears in a listing of Crow's Shadow Institute classes on the Umatilla Reservation, summer 2000.

7. The hobo stove was known as the "Vagabond Tin Can Stove" in Oregon State Extension Services Bulletin 4-H93222, *Oregon 4-H Outdoor Cookery II*, reprinted July 1989.

8. Gary Moulton, ed., *The Journals of the Lewis & Clark Expedition* (Lincoln: University of Nebraska Press, 1988), 7:264.

9. Stowell, *Faces of the Reservation*, 125; see also Aguilar, *When the River Ran Wild!*, 208.

10. Minutes of Tribal Council of the Confederated Tribes of the Warm Springs Reservation of Oregon, October 10, 1963.

11. *Spilyay Tymoo*, March 7, 1983.

12. *Spilyay Tymoo*, November 6, 1987.

13. *Oregonian*, June 25, 1992.

14. *Spilyay Tymoo*, May 16, 2002.

15. Zucker et al., *Oregon Indians*, 98.

CHAPTER 5 (pp. 91–98)

1. ECW projects were funded along with the better-known Civilian Conservation Corps by the Emergency Conservation Act of 1933. The War Department ran the CCC programs but did not "desire to take any part in the administration of the act on Indian reservations." Kinney, *Indian Forest Range*, 276.

2. "Cigars and Wooden Indians, An Interview with Art Buchwald" in *Fore and Aft*, Winter, 1966, 11.

CHAPTER 6 (pp. 99–128)

1. Carol Craig, letter to the author, 2003

2. From unpublished article typeset for the *Toppenish Review* February 19, 1970, and omitted for lack of space.

3. Tribal leaders used these or similar words whenever speaking of the 1855 Treaty. For a discussion of the Indians' inherent right to harvest fish, see Dupris et al., *The Si'Lailo Way*.

CHAPTER 7 (pp. 129–150)

1. Relander, *Drummers and Dreamers*, 10.

2. *The Washington Spectator*, October 15, 2004.

3. Washington State Cultural Resource Training, The Dalles, Oregon, 1997.

4. *Toppenish Review-Mirror/Wapato Independent*, June 9, 1971.

5. May 24, 1972. The Flint family merged the *Yakima Valley Mirror* with the *Toppenish Review* in April 1971.

6. Fisher, "Not for Sale at Any Price," 11.

7. Ibid., 27.

8. Executive Order 11670, Vol. 8, No. 21, Washington, DC: Government Printing Office, 1972.

9. *Toppenish Review-Mirror*, July 12, 1972.

10. Saum, Lewis O. *The Fur Trader and the Indian*. University of Washington Press, 1965, 181.

11. Dubois, *The Feather Cult of the Middle Columbia*, 25.

12. Merlin R. Carothers, *From Prison to Praise* (Watchung, N.J.: Charisma Books, 1970).

13. Gardner and MacKenzie, *The Poems of Gerard Manley Hopkins*, 69.

14. Wulf, Virginia and John Hussey. "The Gypsy and the Crystal Ball," *Fore and Aft*, Spring 1968, 10.

15. *Toppenish Review-Mirror*, January 10, 1973.

CHAPTER 8 (pp. 151–176)

1. *Yakima Herald-Republic*, January 30; *Toppenish Review-Mirror*, January 3 and 17, 1973.

2. Ecclesiastes 3:1.

3. *Wapato Independent*, December 6, 1972.

4. Teletype, Marvin L. Franklin, assistant to the Secretary of the Interior to BIA Area Director, Portland, OR.

5. William Schlick papers, May 13, 1917, in author's possession.

6. *Toppenish Review-Mirror*, November 7, 1973.

7. *Toppenish Review-Mirror*, January 23, 1974.

8. *Yakima Herald Republic*, January 17, 1974.

9. "Lukameen, a Thanksgiving dish as American as pumpkin pie," *Toppenish Review-Mirror*, November 27, 1974. Thanks to University of Washington linguist Sharon Hargus for the correct spelling in this text. Phil Cash Cash ('ishtísh-pa) suggests that the word may have been borrowed outright from the French la commun, "the common pot." Nez Perce Language Discussion List, May 23, 2005.

10. Heritage College 2000 Annual Report.

11. Souvenir Program No.00149, April 25, 26, 27, 1975.

CHAPTER 9 (pp. 177–184)

1. Henry David Thoreau, *Walden; or, Life in the Woods* (New York: Crowell, 1966).

Bibliography

Ackerman, Lillian A. *A Necessary Balance, Gender and Power Among Indians of the Columbia Plateau*. Norman: University of Oklahoma Press 2003.

Aguilar, George W. *When the River Ran Wild! Indian Traditions on the Mid-Columbia and the Warm Springs Reservation*. Portland: Oregon Historical Society Press, 2005.

Akwesasne Notes. *Voices from Wounded Knee, 1973*. Rooseveltown, N.Y.: Akwesasne Notes, 1974.

Beavert, Virginia, project coordinator. *Yakima Language Practical Dictionary*. Consortium of Johnson-O'Malley Committees, Region 4, Toppenish, Wash., 1975.

—. *The Way it Was (Anaku Iwacha)*. Consortium of Johnson-O'Malley Committees, Region 4, Toppenish, Wash., 1974.

Deloria, Vine, Jr. *Behind the Trail of Broken Treaties. An Indian Declaration of Independence*. New York: Delacorte Press, 1974.

DuBois, Cora. *The Feather Cult of the Middle Columbia*. General Series in Anthropology, no.7. Menasha, Wis.: George Banta, 1938.

Dupris, Joseph C. et al. *The Si'lailo Way: Indians, Salmon and Law on the Columbia River*. Durham, N.C.: Carolina Academic Press, 2006.

Earling, Debra Magpie. *Perma Red*. New York: Penguin Putnam, 2002.

Fisher, Andrew H. "Not for Sale at Any Price: The Restoration of Mt. Adams to the Yakama Indian Nation." Seminar paper, Arizona State University, Tempe, May 1996.

—. "'This I Know from the Old People': Yakama Indian Treaty Rights as Oral Tradition," *Montana: The Magazine of Western History* (Spring 1999), 15.

Gardner, W.S., and N.H. MacKenzie, eds. *The Poems of Gerard Manley Hopkins*. New York: Oxford University Press, 1970.

Guillemin, Jeanne. "American Indian Resistance and Protest." In *Violence, Cooperation, Peace*. Edited by T.R. Gurr. Thousand Oaks, Calif.: Sage Publications, 1989, 153-72.

Heizer, Robert F. ed. *Handbook of North American Indians*. Vol. 8. *California*. Washington, D.C.: Smithsonian Institution, 1978.

Hunn, Eugene S., and James Selam and Family. *Nch'i-Wána "The Big River."* Seattle: University of Washington Press 1990.

Kinney, J.P. *Indian Forest and Range*. Washington, D.C. Forestry Enterprises, 1950.

Lurie, Nancy Ostreich. "The Contemporary American Indian Scene." In *North American Indians in Historical Perspective*. Edited by Eleanor B. Leacock and Nancy O. Lurie. New York: Random House, 1971, 418.

McClure, Don, with Jon Evans. *The Homesteader's Son: The Indians, The Cowboys, The Homesteaders & Me*. Nespelem, Wash., 2002.

McClure, Rick, and Cheryl Mack. *"For the Greatest Good." Early History of Gifford Pinchot National Forest*. Seattle, Wash.: Northwest Interpretive Association, 1999.

McKeown, Martha Ferguson. *Come to Our Salmon Feast*. Portland: Binfords & Mort, 1959.

Moses, L.G. *Wild West Shows and the Images of American Indians 1883-1933*. Lincoln: University of Nebraska Press, 1996.

Nisbet, Jack. *Sources of the River*. Seattle, Wash.: Sasquatch Books, 1994.

O'Brian, Patrick.*The Hundred Days*. Thorndike, Me.: Thorndike Press, 1999.

Oregon State University. *Nutritive Value of Native Foods of the Warm Springs Indians*. Extension Circular 809, July 1972.

Relander, Click (Now Tow Look). *Drummers and Dreamers*. Caldwell, Idaho: Caxton, 1956.

—. *Strangers on the Land*. Franklin Press, 1962.

—. *1855–1955 The Yakimas*. Toppenish, Wash.: Yakima Tribal Council, 1955.

Schlick, Mary Dodds. "Nearly 1,000 mourn loss of Robert Jim." *Toppenish Review* and *Wapato Independent*, November 7, 1973.

—. "Yakima Celebrations Offer Heirloom Fashion Shows." *American Indian Crafts and Culture 7* (December 1973): 10-13.

—. "Art Treasures of the Columbia Plateau Indians." *American Indian Basketry Magazine,* no.2 (1980), 12-20.

—. *Columbia River Basketry, Gift of the Ancestors, Gift of the Earth.* Seattle: University of Washington Press, 1994.

Shane, Ralph M., and Ruby D. Leno. *Historical Map Warm Springs Indian Reservation.* April 1949.

Smith, Paul Chaat, and Robert Allen Warrior. *Like a Hurricane: the Indian Movement from Alcatraz to Wounded Knee.* New York: The New Press, 1977.

Splawn, A.J. *Ka-Mi-Akin, The Last Hero of the Yakimas.* 3d ed. Caldwell, Idaho: Caxton, 1958.

Stowell, Cynthia D. *Faces of the Reservation.* Portland: Oregon Historical Society 1987.

Wilkinson, Charles. *Blood Struggle, The Rise of Modern Indian Nations.* New York: W.W. Norton, 2005.

Wright, Robin K., ed. *A Time of Gathering, Native Heritage in Washington State.* Seattle: University of Washington Press, 1991.

Zucker, Jeff, Kay Hummel, Bob Høgfoss. *Oregon Indians, Culture, History & Current Affairs.* Portland: Oregon Historical Society, 1983.

Index